M000195262

FAULKNER, WRITER OF DISABILITY

SOUTHERN LITERARY STUDIES

Scott Romine, Series Editor

FAULKNER, WRITER OF DIS-ABILITY

TAYLOR HAGOOD

Louisiana State University Press *Baton Rouge*

Published by Louisiana State University Press

Manufactured in the United States of America
First printing

Designer: Barbara Neely Bourgoyne
Typefaces: Whitman; Courier Prime; Arno Pro; Cinta; Calluna; Sentinel
Printer and binder: Maple Press

Portions of "The Body of the Text" first appeared in the "Secret Machinery of Textuality, Or, What Is Benjy Compson Really Thinking." *Faulkner and Formalism: Returns of the Text.* Edited by Annette Trezfer and Ann J. Abadie. Jackson: University of Mississippi Press, 2012; "Disability Studies and American Literature." By Taylor Hagood. *Literature Compass* 7.6. 2012; and "Disability, Reactionary Appropriation, and Strategies of Manipulation in Simm's *Woodcraft.*" By Taylor Hagood. *Southern Literary Journal.* Vol. 45, Issue 2. 2013.

Library of Congress Cataloging-in-Publication Data
Hagood, Taylor, 1975–
Faulkner, writer of disability / Taylor Hagood.
pages cm. — (Southern literary studies)
Includes bibliographical references and index.
ISBN 978-0-8071-5726-8 (cloth : alk. paper) — ISBN 978-0-8071-5727-5 (pdf) — ISBN 978-0-8071-5728-2 (epub) — ISBN 978-0-8071-5729-9 (mobi) 1. Faulkner, William, 1897–1962—Criticism and interpretation. 2. People with disabilities in literature. I. Title.
PS3511.A86Z78424 2014
813'.52—dc23

2014019174

The paper in this book meets the guidelines for permanence and durability of the Committee on Production Guidelines for Book Longevity of the Council on Library Resources. ♾

to

Joe Urgo

and

Noel Polk

CONTENTS

A BEFORE WORD ON THE (DE)FORM OF THE BOOK

Before delving into an examination of disability in William Faulkner's writing and biography, I would like to take a moment to speak on structure and style in this book and in scholarly writing generally in light of the field of disability studies. Discussing disability requires also exposing *a*bility as a construct against which disabled bodies and minds are juxtaposed and judged. Ability as a construct and ideal, however, affects more than just human minds and bodies; it permeates culture on many levels. This permeation arguably even reaches to and dictates scholarly-critical writing style in contradictory ways themselves potentially disabling. In discussing constructs of ability and normality I thus want also to acknowledge and address the constructedness of critical writing as a genre and the ways it is touched by the forces surrounding disability and ability. My way of doing so is to model a style that works to consider that constructedness in accordance with principles of disability studies.

Disability studies at its most expansive if not also at its best explores the most subtle and minute ways a powerful "ideology of ability," as theorist Tobin Siebers calls it, enforces a disablement that is the source of its hegemonic outrage. Siebers concisely defines this "ideology of ability" as the "preference for able-bodiedness" that "defines the baseline by which humanness is determined, setting the measure of body and mind that gives or denies human status to individual persons 'affecting' nearly all of our judgments, definitions, and values about human beings" (8). Despite its crude broadness, this definition hopefully serves to attach a tag to the dynamics of literary critical writing and publishing. Such an ideology enforces itself in writing as a human-act, if I may be allowed such a generalization in a pragmatic sense—the asserted act of humans struggling to confirm their humanity, which is a significant act in the context of disability. Even as literary critical writing so often works to desedimentize dominant ideology and structures of power, its style ironically often finds itself dominated by the ideology of ability. While standards of excellence in scholarship are so important, they can also be enlisted in invisible hegemonies of abledness and career pressures themselves driven by underlying structures of ability, including the abled ideal of the autonomous employed individual. Despite its best intentions, literary critical writing can, with its formulaic insistence on and fidelity to established guidelines of form, remain heavily policed by institutions that both promote and require these guidelines.

Disability scholars from Leslie Fiedler to Lennard J. Davis have implicitly and explicitly challenged and made visible scholarly writing's conventions of ableism and normality along with the largely silent policing forces surrounding them. Their relentless challenges of normality in all ways have made them especially sensitive to form and the processes of and attitudes toward structural and stylistic *de*forming. This sensitivity flows with particularly stunning power through David Wills's *Prosthesis,* a volume that blends sensitively rendered autobiography and creative nonfiction with Derridean theory and literary criticism. *Prosthesis* not only presents a powerful argument, it also offers an engrossing reading experience. It exemplifies the kinds of energies disability studies has to offer for both content and style. In this volume, I seek to draw on those same energies to forge a style that I hope engages as it both deforms and disables. I do this to foreground the fact of normality as incarnated in literary critical conventions. If the field of disability studies works to revise ideas about what "being human" means, then it can also work toward revising what humans writing literary criticism means. There is of course a Spivakian paradox of speech in such a formulation. In a sense my effort is a kind of Derridean desedimentization just as is Wills's creative-theoretical exploration of the ways a prosthesis "completes" a body, driving it into proximity to normality and registering the deferring of meaning in inscription. For me to write criticism experimentally in this book is to be true to the precepts of challenging invisible strictures and structures of normality produced by a sensitivity to disability's challenging of the normal generally.

In approaching form and content in these ways, I am also contributing to a growing body of criticism that blends literary critical style with creative-essayist approaches in order to explore William Faulkner's life and career as being characterized by lacks, failures, constricted points of view, and dependency. The ideology of ability traffics deeply in the conventional image of Faulkner the noncontingent uberachiever who fights through adversity to a fate silently assumed to have been predestined. But recently critics have worked to find a less impervious Faulkner, and their scholarly writings access wells of authority deeper, wider, or just different than typical literary critical-theoretical application as they seek to penetrate the thick enveloping shell of Faulkner's Nobel Laureate greatness to find a person who could be unsure and afraid even as he attained the highest levels of literary accomplishment. Although these works are typically not informed by disability theory and do not approach disability explicitly or systematically, they nevertheless exemplify the principles of disability studies.

There are a few major examples of such work. In *Faulkner and Welty and the Southern Literary Tradition,* Noel Polk achieved a riveting essayistic style in the strong voice of a critic who spent a lifetime promoting Faulkner and Faulkner studies, applying the wisdom of an aging man to his thinking about Faulkner. In the same vein, Houston A. Baker Jr.'s *I Don't Hate the South: Reflections on Faulkner, Family, and the South* considers the author's Louisville, Kentucky, childhood South in relation to and in the context of Faulkner's Oxford, Mississippi, South, and thereby glimpses the raveling skein of these related incarnations of southern society through the eyes of an African American man, attaining and accessing the power of a creativity deeply guided and informed by a lifetime of scholarly conditioning that provides a reading experience which scholarly writing often does not. Writing in a more explicitly biographical mode, Philip Weinstein in *Becoming Faulkner: The Art and Life of William Faulkner* paints a portrait not of Faulkner the great achiever but rather Faulkner the struggling person who only painfully succeeds in publishing and gaining a level of critical acclaim and who does not yet know how his life will turn out while he is still living it—a Faulkner sometimes a little and at other times a lot scared, unsure. Like Polk and Baker, Weinstein's own life remains always slightly visible in the volume's production, his "biography" being a scholarly-literary version of method acting in which he digs deeply into himself in order to explore the possibilities of another's being in time and history that amounts to an unsealing of a closedness that allows Faulkner's life processes a new life. Sally Wolff's *The Ledgers of History: William Faulkner, an Almost Forgotten Friendship, and an Antebellum Plantation Diary* reveals a Faulkner paradoxically bigger than ever by seeming smaller than ever: rather than a magician capable of a fabulous *creatio ex nihilo,* he emerges as a brilliant shaper of already existing material found in an authentic plantation record. Then there is Judith L. Sensibar's *Faulkner and Love: The Women Who Shaped His Art* in which Faulkner's life and writing are reopened by utterly fresh (and at times disturbingly problematic) insights offered through the eyes of the women who shaped him and whom he shaped, exposing Faulkner's dependencies, his cruelties and limitations.

Faulkner, Writer of Disability makes the topic of Faulkner's limitations, dependencies, and inabilities its primary focus as it continues the prodding of critical writing style's limitations, dependencies, and inabilities. Polk, Baker, Weinstein, Wolff, and Sensibar utilize the authority of their experience and historical and/or spatial propinquity to fashion their innovative styles. Although I draw on personal experiences and connections I have with Ripley, Mississippi, the ancestral home of the Fa(u)lkners and of my own family, there are few instances of autobiographical engagement in this book. Instead, I employ other genres as modes of alternative authority; specifically, I bring into play biography, digital communication, sensational horror, and various forms of filmic rhetoric. My goal is to allow the interplay of these genres with the genre of scholarly-critical writing to provide shifts in viewpoint and approach that can move toward something perhaps otherwise unseeable in a conventional literary critical treatment of Faulkner and his writing. Genres carry their own unique histories of authenticity, and it is in this juxtaposing and blending of genres that I hope meaningful things about both the conventions of literary critical style and about Faulkner's work can be illuminated. Just as I seek to probe Faulkner's own style according to principles set forth in disability studies, so I want the style of this book to work in subtle ways toward promoting variety in scholarly writing.

My efforts to de-form critical writing style are influenced not only by the Faulkner scholars and disability theorists mentioned above but also by my work in digital humanities, both in co-editing the H-Southern-Lit discussion network and in my work with the currently developing website *Digital Yoknapatawpha*. The latter project has been particularly enlightening for the ways a different platform—in this case one only enabled by digital means—brings a critic to questions not otherwise thinkable. For one thing, simply reorienting Faulkner's works into an innovative digital spatial form makes it look different, bringing previously less- or unnoticed things to light; so, I think, hybridizing critical form into a kind of creative nonfiction can at least show a way toward new and flexible ways of seeing primary texts. Furthermore, when attempting to present visual representations of stories which do not appear on any known map Faulkner himself drew, the editors in the project find themselves confronted with the real possibility that they must create where Faulkner has not created as they imagine the placement of events in Yoknapatawpha County and beyond. Such "writing" into Faulkner might seem sacrilege, and yet literary criticism does different versions of the same thing constantly—digital humanities merely offers new ways of doing so. My interest is to bring the same kind of shifting of viewpoint and creating rethinking digital humanities offers into the traditional form of the literary critical book. The time of considering online scholarship as being inferior to paper-published conventional scholarship in any simple way has passed as it has become clear that the two forms are the equivalent of tangerines and oranges, although if digital humanities scholarship is to be seen as a tangerine in this comparison it may be more accurately viewed as a tangelo. It seems appropriate to me to mix that hybridity back into conventional literary critical form.

In addition to my employment, incorporation, and allusion to genre, I also use a single comprehensive discursive "note" at the end of the book, which is to say I position it as the final part of the body of the text. To employ a single note is hardly original, but my purpose in using it is not just to facilitate the experience of reading the other parts of the body of the text. While such facilitation usually constitutes the purpose of providing a single such component instead of a series of notes in-line or at the end of each chapter or the text proper in books of literary criticism, I also see the single note as a disabling thing for the reader. By placing it at the end I attempt to evoke even the disablement that comes of putting notes in such a position. My purpose is to make evident that gains in facilitation can simultaneously create a kind of disabling. While the eschewing of footnotes can clean up the page of text, the reader must still thumb to the back of the book to read the endnote, and in a single note the reader must search for material.

I well realize that speaking of the single discursive note in such terms threatens to reduce it in the reader's mind to a sophomoric trick, and readers may well see other efforts I make to prod form in the same light. Again, I reiterate that my goal is to benefit from the authorities of genre, and the particular ways I do so invite such techniques. In order to be true to the precepts of disability studies and to try to approach the sartorial depth and felicity of the authority exemplified in the writing of Polk et al., I believe it important to make visible conventional form as being the arbitrary construct it is, however staid its enforcement may be. In addition to these matters of authority and constructedness, I would point to the fact that disability studies can likewise interrogate the experience of a disabled reader's encounter with a book as a physical object. Viewed from the standpoint of someone sensible of disability, the common practice of positioning notes at the end of a text can be a significant problem for a reader who cannot turn pages easily or at all. If such a book should appear in electronic form, the placement of the note might suffer from obstacles created by the reading device. These issues may seem small, but they are the bread and butter of disability-sensitive discourse.

I close by acknowledging that, even as it mixes in alternative genres, this book's form nevertheless deliberately follows the general arc of critical writing conventions. It proceeds as an unmistakably academic discourse, and it in certain ways roughly follows the convention of moving from a more general discussion to exploring specific thematic matters. While I am working to address the constructedness of critical style, I also understand, respect, and promote it and its distinctive purpose: there is a great need to preserve the genre of rigorous, insightful, theoretical writing. It is therefore hardly my goal to swamp the text in other genres to the point that it ceases to fulfill its designated functions altogether. Rather, I hope my incorporating dimensions of these genres into the genre of literary criticism can do the work of exposing the edges of its own limits. Such a practice of course becomes paradoxical, perhaps even self-disabling. But such unsettledness haunts the very topic and situation of disability. Indeed, my hope is that readers' desires will be at once satisfied and foiled. If I may be forgiven the hubris of such a statement: I hope this book fails in the grandest ways Faulkner believed any book should.

FAULKNER, WRITER OF DISABILITY

THE BODY *of the* TEXT

Citizen Faulkner

A Fable, Disability, and the Public/Private Nobel Laureate

EXT. OXFORD, MISSISSIPPI, YARD AND HOUSE BEHIND FENCE—CONTINUOUS

Faulkner

The very name has aberration in the sound of it, and an unglamorous fatality, like diseased death at sunset, or a murmur of insanity along the road to Jackson. It carries with it not a little of the bizarre, the unhealthy, the ugly unredeemed by even the most glorious prose rendering. It is scene one all to itself, enigmatic as the tiny snow globe and an untraceable spoken word. Through variegated chain-links appear the gables of a Rowan Oak that could be the Compson house, and between those links the fingers of a gelded brother, mouth spittle-strung, and eyes intelligible only as pale.

CUT TO:

1943

William Faulkner received a $1,000 advance from film producer William Bacher to work on a screen-play about the Unknown Soldier of World War I. The contract allowed him to turn the concept into "a play or novel, with the rights remaining entirely his" (Blotner 452). Faulkner conceived of the story as "a fable, an indictment of war perhaps" (*Selected Letters* 178). He began working on this project at home, away from Hollywood in the obscurity of Oxford. Thus began a nearly ten-year process during which Faulkner wrote and rewrote, published a section of what would be a novel along the way, scribbling different parts of it on the walls of his study, and became more known to the public than he had ever been before in his life. The finished product of this work was *A Fable*, and I am beginning this exploration of Faulkner, writer of disability, with this novel and its composition because the novel and the matters surrounding its composition distill the workings of disability in Faulkner's writing as he transformed from a relatively obscure literary writer to a highly visible cultural icon via his being awarded the 1949 Nobel Prize in Literature. Among the many things this Citizen Faulkner represented, one was the ability to write disability in powerful ways, not only in terms of fashioning disabled characters (something his other blindingly illustrious contemporary Ernest Hemingway too did) but also in presenting profoundly disability-inflected metaphorical and stylistic elements in his fiction. I like to believe it would have pleased Faulkner to see this novel positioned as a site in which can be identified the principles of disability that appear throughout his oeuvre since he saw the novel as his grand achievement. At the same time, from the standpoint of a scholar writing now, the novel seems his greatest failure—literally, not the "good" type of failure Faulkner championed, which is an attempt to create something so vast and true it must fail, and thereby perversely becomes a gestural success—for while Faulkner thought of *A Fable* as his magnum opus, readers and critics have often been less kind.

* * *

The latter fact takes on especial force, I believe, in light of the fact that disability so haunted the man Faulkner as he struggled to produce the novel, whether in the form of ill health, debilitating alcoholism, deeply troubled relationships, or the sense of an underappreciated writing career strained by the need to work in Hollywood for money. The novel produced in this time is so heavily freighted with weighty themes, symbols, and prose it can be a chore to read. There are those who appreciate it, but it often fails to make the cut as a major Faulkner novel because most scholars and readers see it as lacking the finesse of the great works in the middle of the author's career. At the same time, though, it represents an interesting aspect of the Nobel Laureate Faulkner because it exemplifies the shift in the focus of Faulkner's career from simply writer to writer-ambassador, both officially and unofficially, of United States culture. When Faulkner works some of the language from his Nobel Prize acceptance speech into the old French general's speech to the corporal, he laces into the text what can be seen as a strong inducement for the reader to recognize or imagine a connection between the author's exalted global image and the old general's lofty status. This apparent self-referentiality gestures in fact both to the image of Faulkner and to the author and man himself, inviting the reader and (presumably less explicitly, heartily, or welcomingly) the critic to consider Faulkner and his Nobel Laureate image in relation to the myths and realities of this powerful military figure which the novel exposes.

What exactly are we to read in this strong suggestion of self-referentiality? It can be tempting to think that Faulkner had fallen prey to his own apotheosis, understanding himself to be the holder of great wisdom the old general arguably sees himself as possessing and dispensing. It is more likely and consistent with his career to see Faulkner as making fun of the very idea of succumbing to such a role or image just as he had maintained an ironic understanding of himself in past fictional self-references. In *Mosquitoes,* the character Jenny Steinbauer talks about having encountered a Mr. Faulkner, whom she describes as a "little kind of black man" (371). The story "Afternoon of a Cow" clearly spoofs Faulkner as told through the eyes of the fictional Ernest Trueblood. It stands to reason that likewise in *A Fable* Faulkner gestures toward a determination not to let himself off the hook, and that the basic function of this move is to achieve the dualness of irony, a negotiation of an image of greatness with the reality of a human being's weaknesses.

The way I want to approach this self-referentiality is in the unsettled and unsettling binary of ability and disability because *A Fable*'s production and appearance coincide paradoxically with an increase in *both* of these conditions simultaneously in Faulkner's life and image. That Faulkner's abledness and disabledness could increase at the same time might seem paradoxical, but that paradox only extends the characteristics of the mutually constitutive relationship between ability and disability. It is with the constructedness of this binary that disability studies, at least in its humanities incarnation, is most obsessed, since the notions of the abled body and mind are so closely related to the broader construct of normality, which is so relentlessly enforced by dominant ideology in the many variations of culture loosely referred to as Western.

* * *

CUT TO:

(specificity and the ideology of ability)

I outline the basic counters of disability studies in the note at the end of the book for readers unfamiliar with the field; here and in the parts of the book that follow I want to focus on specific theoretical elements as they come into play in discussing Faulkner and his work—in understanding Faulkner, writer of disability. I mentioned in the previous part of the book what Tobin Siebers refers to as the "ideology of ability." The concept strives to comprehend the many ways disability exists, from the conditions of actual bodies and minds to more abstract notions about behavior. As Siebers conceives of it, the ideology of ability pervades powerful culturally constituted values of achievement which in turn require abled bodies and minds for such accomplishment. Seen this way, this ideology is insidious indeed, being deeply rooted in the drive toward success and autonomy that, as Rosemarie Garland-Thomson has noted, lies at the foundation of the ideal United States citizen's identity. Garland-Thomson argues in her seminal volume *Extraordinary Bodies* that the Emersonian individual requires an autonomous independent body and mind while a *de*pendent person ranges from a problem to an outrage of this national identity-bound conceptualization of individualism. Without reducing this individualism conception to a facile concept of the "American Dream," it takes little effort to trace the profound workings of such an individualistic, success-oriented ideology in U.S. culture as well as the fears and exclusions that appertain to the inability to conform to the values of that ideology. The ways this ideology of ability appears or shapes aspects of culture are manifold. The drives to succeed in school, work, relationships, health all can be tinged by this ideology. The concept of the fully functioning capitalistic body able to produce its role within a given division of labor stands stark in the ideology of ability. And the moral value attached to competence in practically any endeavor can be filled with the insistence of the ideology of ability.

When disabled bodies or minds fail to attain the prizes set forth by the larger machinery of abledness, they simultaneously outrage and confirm the system. Not that all disabled bodies and minds do so fail: while the construct of the disabled body by definition stands as an opposite of the abled bodily construct privileged by the ideology of ability, in many cases actual disabled bodies find ways to accomplish the tasks otherwise imagined left to the abled. Siebers and others have applied the term "complex embodiment" to account for the subtle mix of ways that both the construct and actual physical experiences of individuals come into play in discussing disability, allowing a way to understand both large cultural forces and individual experiences of disability. But the ideology of ability is relentless in its demands, directing the construction of physical spaces, legislation, art, a multitude of technics, and entire moral systems in accord with its principles and requiring a loose but strategically applied ideal abled body, understood pragmatically in various situations. If a given disabled person can perform within the strictures of the ideology of ability, she may be granted provisional or even full status within the fold of the abled, especially if she is passing as abled. As disability theorists insist, disability is a matter of degree not of kind, just as it can be a matter of environment—a blind person for example might well be able to negotiate total darkness better than a sighted one. Yet the ideology of ability can be pernicious, demanding that an abled body or mind *is* a kind and that only the environments approved by its own dictates be legitimate.

A problem with Siebers's theory of the ideology of ability though is ironically that of environment in a different sense, for as described by Siebers it does not necessarily so well apply to places and situations outside of Western culture or whose relationship to Western culture is atypical (itself a problematic designation). Siebers's conception of this ideology seems most relevant to a U.S. context and its values conceived largely in the ways I have myself been assuming them. But not even all U.S. spaces or situations necessarily conform in their social-cultural-political dynamics to this broadly conceived ideology. The southern states throw this matter into relief. As scholars from C. Vann Woodward to Leigh Anne Duck have shown, the South not only operates under different value systems but it is very often seen by people in the rest of the country, if not most of the world in the know, as grotesquely different. I use the term "grotesque" on purpose because of its long-standing association with southern writing's characters and settings and its undertones of abnormality, deformity, and disability. In an instance often referenced by disability studies scholars, Erving Goffman noted in the 1950s that there existed "only one complete unblushing male in America: a young, married, white, urban, *northern,* heterosexual, Protestant father of college education, fully employed, of good complexion, weight and height, and a recent record in sports" (128, emphasis mine). While "northern" might not necessarily imply "southern," this litany exemplifies the kinds of figures the ideology of ability champions within a definite spatial context, and it is not difficult to hear a silent association of stigma with some notion of southernness that serves to orient "grotesque" in a logic of abnormality in very literal physical and cognitive ways.

It is not my intention to think of or to discuss Faulkner as a southern writer only; nor do I mean in this book to box his characters into some overarching and difficult-to-define notion of southernness, in its many racially- and placially-inflected forms. It seems clear to me that there are many modes in which the ideology of ability is deployed in and policed by the specific forces of individual communities; these communities often borrow from some larger ideology, but their specificity can grow out of tightly defined life happenings. One of the things that can make reading Faulkner so disconcerting and mesmerizing is his refusal to allow alien ideological forces to colonize specific situations isolated from them. *As I Lay Dying* shows this dynamic powerfully because many of the Bundren family members insist on a worldview all their own and ply it in the face of characters they encounter who hold to more recognizable notions of normality. Plenty of readers might however well see the "normal" characters as themselves failing to conform to notions of normality; for example, they can be rural people who speak in colloquial idiom. It is tempting to imagine an alternative distinct southern poor white ideology of ability, but I want to be careful not to do violence to Siebers's grandly conceived notion of ideology of ability since its power depends on its deeply embedded broad force. Despite the seeming limitations of his description and application of the ideology of ability, I would not speak of ideolog*ies* of ability but rather would insist that it behooves a reader to see the specific ways this abstraction expresses itself in different situations and environments. Doing so, however, does seem to require a more specific focus on such environmental incarnations than Siebers offers.

A Fable presents a highly useful text for observing specific situations; it also reveals deep ways in which degrees of disabledness can flood the ethos of a novel through the curious simultaneous presence of Faulkner's authorial hand and of his public image. As with any approach sensitive to authorial positionality, disability studies can turn its eyes not only on disabled people written (such as Captain Ahab or Jake Barnes) but also disabled people writing (such as Flannery O'Connor or Eli Clare). But this binary, like any, is insufficient not least because disability theory imagines a universality of disabledness (a problematic matter taken up in the fifth part of this body of text) since no body or mind can conform to a construct always already both so ambiguous and so strategically employed, not to mention again that environment can transform ability into disability and that humans naturally evolve into a state of disability. Faulkner's "disability experience"—that is, his own disabilities, his encounters with disabled people, his conceptions of disability, his imaginations of disability experiences—thus are part of this book's discussion. And I want to inaugurate this strain by recalling *A Fable*'s gestation period because it is such a dramatic one for both Faulkner's visibility and invisibility, his attainment of vast public recognition while struggling to keep his private life, including its pain, hidden.

* * *

CUT TO:

WILLIAM FAULKNER

Our tragedy today is a general and universal physical fear so long sustained by now that we can even bear it.

In order to trace the thread of disability running umbilically from Faulkner the writing private and public person through the stages and styles of development into *A Fable,* I would focus on a key moment in the novel that manifests the convergence of Faulkner's life and writing with disability. The scene is the one in which the German general meets with the British, French, and American generals concerning the stoppage of the war in the trenches. In this encounter the German general blames civilians and politicians for the war and its perpetuation, his motivation not that he thinks war should end but that it should be reorganized according to a military instead of a political ethic and agendum. He explains in an impulsive manner oddly anticipating the rhetoric of General Jack D. Ripper in *Dr. Strangelove* that the civilians and politicians "would be the first to vanish under [the new alliance and order] which [he and these other generals] would establish" (948). "Think of it, if you have not already," he says, "the alliance which would dominate Europe. Europe? Bah. The world—Us, with you, France, and you, England—[. . .] An alliance, the alliance which will conquer the whole earth—Europe, Asia, Africa, the islands—to accomplish where Bonaparte failed, what Caesar dreamed of, what Hannibal didn't live long enough to do" (948). The old French general rejoins with the question, "Who will be emperor?" in a tone "so courteous and mild that for a moment it didn't seem to register" (948) and to which the German general offers no reply.

What is interesting is what happens next. When the British general echoes the question of who would be the emperor of this military alliance, the German general simply looks from the French to the British general respectively. Upon doing so, his monocle falls from his right eye, revealing an empty socket. "There was no movement of the face at all: the monocle simply descended from the eye, down the face and then the tunic, glinting once or twice as it turned in the air, into the palm lifted to receive it, the hand shutting on it then opening again, the monocle already in position between the thumb and the first finger, to be inserted again; and in fact there had been no eyeball behind it: no scar nor healed suture even: only the lidless and empty socket glaring down at the British general" (948).

It may be that Faulkner means the reader to understand the German general's missing eye to be a combat wound; at any rate, I will read it that way, seeing it not as disability endemic to the character himself but as a disability linked to his military involvement and status. To cast a disability in such a symbolic way has a long precedent in literature (for example, Shakespeare's Richard III), and it is one way of using disability as a tool in characterization, blindness being a particularly overworked symbolic and metaphorical disability. Given the arguably anti-German cant of the novel, the eyeless socket would seem to signify a half-blindness representing literally a metaphorical blindness caused by ruthless ambition linked to a specifically German imperial drive. I, at least, read the scene as situating the German general as the bad guy, and that character and the old French general both seem to think of warlike impulses as residing deep in Germanic "blood" and culture. Faulkner thus may be seen as relying on an established tradition of using a physical disability to embody a supposed internal trait, which is to say an "ethnic" trait in the context of at least certain major voices in the novel, be it philosophical, behavioral, attitudinal, or otherwise.

But there may be additional things at work in this wound too in ways other than the obvious symbolic one. This empty eye-socket and the pathetic fall of the monocle from it also undercut the otherwise overwhelming abledness of the German general. Faulkner sets him up as a monster who shoots his own pilot in the face once his airplane lands on enemy soil, and his status of and decoration as general establish his unassailable power. Yet Faulkner presents his killing of the pilot, remorseless as it may be, as an act circumscribed by a set of "Germanic" rules, and another—perhaps related—structure of rules supersedes his own authority, these being the policies and maneuverings of the civilian politicians. These matters alone do not necessarily posit the German general as sympathetic the way Faulkner means certain other war-wounded characters in his career to be, such as Donald Mahon and Linda Snopes Kohl. The German general's almost laughable rigidity of command—his impulsively flinging his empty brandy glass crashing against the wall and his exclamation of "As you were!" (947)—works to make him ridiculous in his practically unconscious commitment to his own so-called "ethnically"—or "nationalistically"—dictated behavior. At the same time, though, the German general's unbending conformity to an essentialized myth of Germanic personality coupled with his visible disability arguably signal a kind of submerged fear intimately connected with Faulkner himself and through his engagements with various publics through and in the context of this novel also a larger cultural fear, manifested in the "universal physical fear" Faulkner refers to in his most visible direct public engagement, his Nobel Prize acceptance speech.

The portal that reveals this fear comes in the oblique connection to another disabled body. After breaking the brandy glass, the French general asks to be excused from this practice because "we cannot afford to break French glasses" (947). To this comment the German general replies: "And whose fault is that? [. . .] that we have been—ja, twice—compelled to destroy French property? Not yours and mine, not ours here, not the fault of any of us all, all of us who have to spend the past four years straining at each other from behind two wire fences. It's the politicians, the civilian imbeciles who compel us every generation to have to rectify the blunders of their damned international horse-trading—" (947).

Although the German general is not aware of it, his comment about horse-trading can well connect in the reader's mind to the story of the disabled racehorse that forms a significant part of the novel's foregoing chapter. This is the protracted tale of the wonderful and expensive thoroughbred injured in a train wreck; rather than let the horse's owner turn him into a stud with no other purpose in life but to sire other race-winners, the cockney groom, the African American minister Tobe Sutterfield, and the latter's grandson "steal" the horse, heal his leg well enough that he can run, and take him all about the Mississippi watershed running him in small-time races. When the authorities finally catch up with this party, they find that the groom has shot and killed the horse, saving him at last from a fate of being installed machine-like in the capitalistic designs of his owner. The episode is problematic—Faulkner clearly means the reader to see the thieving entourage as noble in its efforts to save the horse from a particularly pernicious undead-like fate, yet their killing him shows that the horse remains colonized by the humans and their deadly ideals, with no one, including the author, giving much thought to the horse's agency or desires. Or rather the author believes the thieves understand and agree with the horse's desires. To the immediate point, the German general's reference to horse-trading links to the horse episode by associating those military figures who fight wars metaphorically with racing horses and those civilian politicians who instigate and perpetuate wars with the horse-owners, who manipulate without understanding the horse's perspective, which is wrapped up in glory and sacrifice and the other verities Faulkner espouses late in his career and articulates most famously in that Nobel Prize speech. The German general's outrage at being subject to the civilian politicians' capricious will can be read as a fear of what they will do.

These matters intrigue me because I think there may be discerned here a nexus of disability, Faulkner's public image, and his writing that finds articulation in the figure of the disabled racehorse. It would not be inaccurate to see the decade during which Faulkner wrote and rewrote *A Fable* as marking his transition into a physically and even cognitively disabled writer of disability : : the man cuts a diminishing figure in this time period, his silvering hair and growing wrinkles and failing body small in frosty soil beside hoof-tracks, eyes unfocused, back humped. This decade led into a remainder of a lifetime fraught with missed engagements from Rome to Japan, increasing jokes about his enslavement to the bottle, more and more hospital visits, and a failing heart. Much of Faulkner's disabling resulted from his alcoholism, and there were many alcohol-induced episodes during this time. Even as the germ of *A Fable* was taking root, Faulkner was in Hollywood having hired a Mr. Nielsen to be a kind of "nurse [. . .] to see that he got to work on Monday" (Blotner 456), and A. I. Bezzerides, with whom Faulkner was staying, was struggling to convince his tenant to drink less (461). Throughout the 1940s Faulkner had what he called "collapses," once uttering the chilling comment to his daughter, "Nobody remembers Shakespeare's children" when she attempted to deter a binge (473). In October 1948 Faulkner drank himself unconscious in New York where Ruth Ford and Harvey Breit checked him into the Fieldstone Sanitarium (498). And Faulkner was actually sick with pneumonia and, in his fear of such a public event, almost incapacitated with drink on the trip to Sweden to accept the Nobel Prize in 1950, for he dealt with a painful shyness and phobia of public speaking by drinking, a practice that led to more and more collapses as he became a more public figure both during the time of his writing *A Fable* and for the rest of his life.

Faulkner's alcoholism in fact registers a vexed aspect of ability-disability. Not all drinking was equal. It seems clear that consuming and handling large amounts of alcohol was an *ability* Faulkner prized as a measure of masculinity. This kind of robust alcoholism formed a major part of Faulkner's identity and his sense of physical and mental strength. He commented once that "When I have one martini [. . .] I feel bigger, wiser, taller. When I have a second, I feel superlative. When I have more, there's no holding me" (Blotner 227). Alcohol consumption also seemed to be a kind of crutch for Faulkner to use for help in handling social situations that were awkward for him. In these senses, alcoholism was hardly a "weakness" created or brought on by disability but was rather for him both enabling and a signal of abledness. Medical discourse now might well look to underlying physical factors, including genetic ones, to help explain the alcohol addiction, pointing to a foundational disability that fueled the drinking. Indeed, the very ability to drink led to disablement, and Faulkner along with Fitzgerald, Hemingway, and others might be provocatively examined as cases of this curious ability-disability dynamic. This disablement in Faulkner's case included not only situations of disabled drunkenness but also a general physical and cognitive deterioration.

In addition to episodic as well as an increasingly general disabling alcoholism, Faulkner suffered much during this time from horse-riding injuries, which actually served to fuel his alcoholism further. On a trip to Paris in May 1952, Faulkner experienced incredible pain, most immediately, he claimed, from being thrown from a horse in the city. This was actually the most recent of many horse-falls, and at the Clinique Remy de Gourmont "nine x-rays revealed the problem: he had a broken back" (Blotner 555). On September 18, drinking to ease the back pain, he had a "convulsive seizure" (560). Joseph Blotner offers the gruesome details of an unhealthy man: "Now he was suffering from spasms of the deep spinal muscles all the way from his humped upper back down. His range of spinal movement was only seventy percent of normal. Though a set of x-rays showed no new fractures, they revealed other old ones: mild compression fractures of dorsal vertebrae 8, 9, and 10. For some years now he had been walking around with five broken vertebrae in various stages of natural splinting, complicated by bone-lipping, spur formation, and moderately severe hypertrophic arthritis" (560).

Faulkner would also claim head injury from the fall (567), and these injuries continued. In a terrible cycle, Faulkner would self-medicate with alcohol, painkillers, and tranquilizers, which deepened the damage to his system. These efforts were then necessarily followed by dry-outs. Blotner observes that, by 1953, there "was pain and discontent in nearly all his letters" (560); what became a pattern during the composition of *A Fable* finally culminated in a fall in June 1962 followed by self-medication which brought on the coronary occlusion that killed him.

While the disabling pain and alcoholism vivify Faulkner's experiences of disability during this time and later, I am especially struck by Blotner's use of the word "normal" in the quotation above. The field of disability studies has well shown the many coercive implications of the term and the construct it identifies, and it seems clear that Faulkner was to some degree a disabled writer of disability when working on *A Fable.* In the months following the above-mentioned x-rays, Faulkner experienced a number of medical encounters. He was fitted for a back brace, not the first time in his life (Blotner 561). Then he was examined and allegedly administered electro-shock therapy by Dr. Eric P. Mosse at Westhill Sanitarium in the Bronx (563). In March 1953, Faulkner was examined by psychologist S. Bernard Wortis and claimed Wortis declared his brain to be near the borderline of abnormality. In Wortis's view, Faulkner told his wife Estelle (herself an alcoholic), his alcoholism resulted from oversensitivity, which made him less resistant. At Gartly-Ramsay Hospital, Faulkner's file carried the label: "An acute and chronic alcoholic" (574). While some of this material is admittedly anecdotal, it nevertheless points to Faulkner's status as a physically non-normal specimen due directly to alcoholism during the composition of *A Fable*. And this status results from destructive behavior that constantly begat more of its kind.

Disability and horses intersect in a different way too. Horse racing was much on Faulkner's mind in the years of *A Fable*'s writing and until his death. Numerous references to horses and racing appear in his writing, professional or otherwise. There are a few memorable examples. When Malcolm Cowley ventured that Ernest Hemingway might write the introduction to *The Portable Faulkner* in 1947, Faulkner said no, adding, "It's like asking one race horse in the middle of a race to broadcast a blurb on another horse in the same running field" (*Selected Letters* 229-30). In 1955, Faulkner wrote a *Sports Illustrated* article on the Kentucky Derby. The climactic event of his final novel, *The Reivers,* is a horse race. But it is the context of disability that I want to focus on by citing his comment in a letter to Bennett Cerf in 1947 about his need to return to Warner Brothers to write because "I want to buy another horse since pretty soon now I shall be too stiff in the joints for anything except old man's riding" (*Selected Letters* 255). There is a striking proximity in this comment between horse riding and Faulkner's obsession with his aging and what he saw as the diminishment of his power and energy as a writer. Very often his commenting on this matter pertained to the progress or lack thereof on *A Fable*. The novel did not come easy to him, and over and over again he would characterize himself as someone getting old and slowing down, simply unable to write with the energy he once had. The writing's "a slow thing compared to the speed I had once," he wrote Harold Ober in 1947 (*Selected Letters* 248–49). Discussing his writing in a letter to Saxe Commins in 1953, Faulkner wrote, "The initial momentum ran out, and it is getting more and more difficult, a matter of deliberate will power, concentration, which can be deadly after a while" (345). Again, other instances appear in the correspondence, using language evoking the idea of running a race, showing a link-up in Faulkner's mind, conscious or unconscious, of being analogous to a slowing, aging race-horse. Blotner at one point observes that, "In a sense, the creator of this tale had himself been a stud, spending his seed in Hollywood to produce offspring for which he cared little" (486).

It seems to me that here is a simultaneity of elements—Faulkner the more and more disabled man and writer, the disabled racehorse still running, the disabled German general upset that he is being manipulated by civilian-politicians the way they would a race-horse, maneuvered about at the whims of forces with imperial visions different from his own. Again, what I find myself wanting to read as part of the flypaper to which these elements stick is an underlying fear. This is a complex fear with many dimensions: fear that Faulkner's writing powers are hopelessly diminished or lost, fear that such things as riding he will not be able to do anymore, fear that his sexual power is failing, fear of public speaking, the fear of what the world will do or worse not do with his life's work. Although his written response to *The Partisan*

Review's rejecting the "Notes on a Horsethief" excerpt from *A Fable* he'd submitted for publication essentially attacks the magazine culture of his moment, it clearly shook his confidence as he indirectly asked for reassurance from his agent and publisher. Even in 1953, with the novel nearly finished, he wrote to Joan Williams, "I know now that I am getting toward the end, the bottom of the barrel. The stuff is still good, but I know now there is not very much more of it, a little trash comes up constantly now, which must be sifted out" (*Selected Letters* 348).

These latter comments of course come after the Nobel Prize speech, in which fear plays such a central role, and which helped to exalt Faulkner to the level of a figure about whom myths would not only be created but fixed as he transformed into a very abled Citizen Faulkner. "Our tragedy today is a general and universal physical fear so long sustained by now that we can even bear it" (*Faulkner at West Point* 118–19), Faulkner says in a speech his stage fright rendered inaudible at the actual Nobel Prize ceremony and which was only readable in the papers the next day. Faulkner explains in the address that the fear is that of the atomic bomb, expressed in the question, "When will I be blown up?" (119). It is this fear—not personal fears—that has caused young writers to forget about the things they should be writing about, Faulkner asserts. And so the writer now "must teach himself that the basest of all things is to be afraid and, teaching himself that, forget it forever, leaving no room in his workshop for anything but the old verities and truths of the heart [. . .]" (119). Lawrence Schwartz has limned the ways Faulkner's writing and image became appropriated by proponents of conservative U.S. values during the Cold War leading to his winning the Nobel Prize, and Michael Kreyling in *Inventing Southern Literature* explores the idea of Faulkner the person writing and "Faulkner" the Nobel Laureate. This Nobel Laureate Faulkner, mythologized within a larger notion of U.S. cultural value that feeds into cultural imperialism differs significantly in his rhetoric about fear from the real aging writer wracked with back pain and the physical limitations brought on by years of heavy drinking and horse falls. The public mythologized Nobel Laureate can be an unafraid preacher of fearlessness, while the person struggling to put words on pages and, worse yet, to speak them is an outrage to the ideology of ability that pervades the very individualistic notions of Faulkner's speech—the idea that "man" figured as humanity but interestingly in the singular, will "not merely endure he will prevail" (119). The "enduring" of "man" comes because he can still talk, and the "prevailing" comes because "man" is "immortal, not because he alone among creatures has an inexhaustible voice, but because he has a soul, a spirit capable of compassion and sacrifice and endurance" (120). This ideal "man" Faulkner envisions can stand alone because of his capabilities.

And yet the writer, in Faulkner's conception, is "one of the props, the pillars to help him endure and prevail" (120). This closing line of the Nobel speech strikes me as a move away from the autonomy and individuality most of the speech propounds. Instead, Faulkner closes with a vision of interdependence, with the writer capable of providing a crutch for "man." It seems to me that here we find an acknowledgment of what another disability theorist, Lennard J. Davis, calls "dismodernism" or the vision of a cultural moment when the disabilities of all bodies can be observed and not held against the constructs of normality driven by the ideology of ability—a moment when interdependence is not only the norm but the ideal, with autonomous ability revealed as an exclusionary lie. This crutch function of the writer in the Nobel Speech which Faulkner actually rewrites into *A Fable* can lead us back to that novel. At its very end the old general has died and is being buried in martial glory that confirms the many myths of power surrounding him, myths themselves implicit in the service of the country's imperial power. The funeral procession gets interrupted, however, when a man on crutches, with "one arm and one leg, one entire side of his hatless head [being] one hairless eyeless and earless sear" (1070), bursts into the crowd holding his military decoration aloft and screaming, "Listen to me too, Marshal! This is yours: take it!" (1071). This man is evidently the runner, who knew the Cockney groom and heard the tale of the horse from Tobe in the racehorse's entourage of thieves. The designation of "the runner" fits the context of the racehorse, for this now disabled man shouts against the cultural machinery that glorifies the dead who fight for the advancement of gain on so many levels. Although knocked in the gutter and thus physically as well as socially marginalized, the runner finds himself comforted by another old military man. In this moment when the public—a public—is engaged in the lionizing of an empire's hero, it is away from the crowd that the actual interdependence of humanity's prevailing is wrought.

This situation of being apart from the crowd blindly steeped in and following the directives of the deeply embedded ideology of ability figures in significant ways into the spatiality and disability resonance of the novel. It is significant that Faulkner shifts the scene to the

U.S. South in the part of the novel designed to offer an alternative way of channeling the ideology of ability. Although the novel does not offer an explicit gloss on what it means that the story of the disabled horse takes place there, the reader may nevertheless understand the South as signifying and readable. Again, there is a self-referentiality at work here in which Faulkner arguably draws on the very portraits of southern life and the South as a site of alterity he himself has created. This alterity pervades multiple levels, one of which being a framing of the South as a space able to facilitate the enabling of a body or mind otherwise shut out of participation in a system driven by the ability not of an individual but of that individual's ability to contribute to and further a larger social-political-economic system. The "standard" capitalistic view of the horse's value lies not in the individual horse's potentials for and realizations of accomplishment but rather of that horse's owners' potential for gain. Again, the horse's status as both nonhuman and disabled render his agency unthinkable, unreadable, and unwritable within the larger hegemony of normality. It is only when the entourage moves outside the reach of dominate culture that a new kind of ability can be realized. The space outside of that reach is as it were a South itself marked by an array of disabilities, whether cultural, economic, social, political, or even bodily (the South Faulkner writes of here faces challenges of geography and transportation limitations).

That U.S. southern places can enable disability emerges in the other major reference to the South in the novel. When the old general is trying to convince the corporal to escape his impending execution, he tells the younger man a story that takes place in "a remote place called by an Indian name I think: Mississippi" (990). He tells the corporal about how a man convicted of murder is about to be hung but sees a bird alight in a tree branch and hearing that song shouts his innocence because he realizes what the old general tells the corporal, "that nothing—nothing—nothing—not power nor glory nor wealth nor pleasure nor even freedom from pain, is as valuable as simple breathing, simply being alive even with all the regret of having to remember and the anguish of an irreparable wornout body" (990). The old general's comments uncannily verbalize a core tenet of disability studies that "quality of life" is a concept appropriated by capitalistic culture to mobilize bodies and minds within the superstructures of production. It is not unusual for disability-studies theorists to promote women's choice regarding abortion but vehemently fight abortion carried out because of an infant's expected abnormality; the same can apply to euthanasia due to disability, for disability studies remains vigilant against anything smacking of eugenics. The old general offers little in the way of a gloss on what is significant about this hanging event's taking place in Mississippi, but even the little bit he recognizes—the "remoteness" and the "Indianness"—reveals the kinds of alter-Western/alter-normal mentality at work in the story. The old general's conclusion is to tell the corporal "take that bird" (992) just as he earlier urged him to "[t]ake the earth" (987) and "[t]ake the world" (988). In one of his effective conflations of mythic material, Faulkner manages to make the old general both God and Satan, as he offers the corporal a salvation that is at the same time a temptation, both spewed from the complex emotions of a father. When the runner echoes the "take it" statement at the end of the novel, he is offering an utterance within the poetics of enabling of disability established in this scene.

Combined with and extending this disability-informed spatial alterity is another kind connected with race and ethnicity. Not only is the horse literally disabled but the entourage itself is marked by disabled elements. With the sentry as a Cockney and the other two as black Americans, the humans in this group are disabled by their social status and their speech. Here the reader encounters a more subtle kind of disability status in which both the mind and the body are involved but in which the markings are part mystified and part abstracted into behaviors. The situation recalls Lennard Davis's discussion of cultural deafness, which is especially intriguing because of its implications for the potentially disabling aspects of dialects of whatever regional, class, or racial variety. In his essay "The Rule of Normalcy: Politics and Disability in the U.S.A. [United States of Ability]," Davis observes that language is laced with constructs of normality because the very development of the concept of standardization in language historically coincides with the Enlightenment and its notions of normality. As he writes, "When we think about normality, people in disability studies have generally made the error, I would say, of confining our discussions more or less exclusively to impairment and disease. But I think there is really a larger picture that includes disability along with any nonstandard behaviors. Language usage, which is as much a physical function as any other somatic activity, has become subject to an enforcement of normalcy, as have sexuality, gender, racial identity, national identity, and so on" (104–5).

* * *

This enforcing homogenization of language became particular painful for Davis when one of the English reviewers of his first book, *Enforcing Normalcy,* criticized him for using the term "normalcy" instead of the preferred "normality." Davis makes the point that this comment worried him because he feared that his working-class background might here be showing through, not to mention that he had come from a Deaf household and that he was "in fact culturally Deaf" (103). The sort of anxiety Davis experiences is the same as a person who speaks in dialect, a performative matter intimately connected to the body. Of course all speech is a performance and all speech performances are dialects, but certain dialects bear the stamp of normality approval where others signify otherness and even stigma—again, remembering Goffman's litany of the ideal normal U.S. citizen, part of what makes one not northern or not white or in the cockney groom's case not American is speech.

As many disability scholars have noted, race as well as gender figure into configurations of disability. Garland-Thomson in *Extraordinary Bodies* asserts that disability is inherently feminizing and also shows how blackness has at times in history been conceived of as a disability. Interestingly, Faulkner often presents disability as pressuring whiteness and maleness, and much of this book will focus on white male characters whose disabilities push them into a status of otherness. Along these lines I might here interject however that it is an odd aspect of Faulkner's writing that, while many of his African American women characters conform to deep cultural stereotypes, their bodies can defy expectations. One of the foremost white imaginings of black female bodies is that of a fat Mammy, yet Faulkner modifies this image with his most famous Mammy character, Dilsey. He writes, "she had been a big woman once but now her skeleton rose, draped loosely in unpadded skin that tightened again upon a paunch almost dropsical, as though muscle and tissue had been courage or fortitude which the days or the years had consumed until only the indomitable skeleton was left rising like a ruin or a landmark above the somnolent and impervious guts, and above that the collapsed face that gave the impression of the bones themselves being outside the flesh" (1081). Faulkner's characterizing maneuver here accomplishes a complicated redefining, at once preserving the Mammy image (to which Dilsey once conformed) while casting her as being now the opposite of that image. Her physique now actually seems to suggest *un*healthiness, an aged and infirmed body that once was comfortable and "normal" according to "normal" white rac(ial)ist conceptualizations of a Mammy's imagined body.

Yet Dilsey is such a powerful figure, arguably the true leader and maintainer of the Compson as well as Gibson families. Bound as Faulkner allowed himself to be to so many preestablished notions about race, his bodily depictions are complicated, and this complicatedness becomes even more pointed in light of Andrea Elizabeth Shaw's argument that the image of the fat black woman's body can become a site of both oppression and resistance. Tracing large black women's bodies from Sarah Bartman to Queen Latifah, Shaw writes, "Superimposing fat onto the black female body doubles its representative status as the antithesis of white femininity since the dominant perspective on fatness in Western culture replicates the view of what blackness is already understood as denoting: bodily indiscipline and rebellion" (50). In Shaw's eyes, this indiscipline and rebellion ultimately becomes empowering, embodying a ruthless ability to deny white control through ideals of normality. Viewed in the context of Shaw's argument, Faulkner's denying Dilsey a fat body seems an attempt to rob that body of its resistant power even as the novel cannot finally suppress her power.

Such is an example of the complicatedness of Faulkner's renderings of race and gender in the context of disability, and other cases will be addressed throughout this book; in this "horse-thieving" episode of *A Fable,* Tobe and his grandson along with the Cockney groom are implicitly disabled by race, ethnicity, and speech, creating a small moveable society with the horse that features an enabling interdependency of un-independents as they move through spaces themselves marked by a poetics of disability connected with the region's systems of stigmas and abnormalities. To be in a "remote" place as a person of non-normal race and class status and behavior is to be an agent affected by and affecting disability. This group, in other words, represents a type of complex embodiment in which a larger contextual definition and policing of normality and abnormality, ability and disability serve as the pervading backdrop of the specific physical experiences of a (to some extent itself disabled) body of bodies themselves disabled. This spatial-physical, microcosmic-macrocosmic relation epitomizes practically any case of disability considered in its many aspects and is an important structural fact at work in thinking through Faulkner's writing disability. I do not mean this relation in a crude dynamic of "United States South versus United States North" or any other simple binary but rather to understand that spaces in their fluid definitions and redefinitions resolve in binaries even as they promote a freeing and enabling potentiality for dis-rupting—which is to say that the binary forms as an opposition to a given incarnation of hegemonic forces, which may be deployed on the grandest or smallest scales. These could take the form of a kind of imperialism and can be seen so in the most abstract sense, and here I am speaking in the terms I outlined in my earlier book *Faulkner's Imperialism* in which center-periphery dynamics configure themselves in multiple and constantly changing scenarios, doubling themselves in simultaneous moments and place.

CUT TO:

IMAGE OF FAULKNER SILVER-HAIRED IN SUIT FADE TO FAULKNER IN WORN CLOTHES BY BARN AT ROWAN OAK

WILLIAM FAULKNER
Between grief and nothing I will take grief.

The paradoxical situation of Faulkner's becoming more abled and yet more disabled at the same time—this matter gets at why I believe a single-author study of Faulkner as a writer of disability to be significant not only for Faulkner studies but also for disability studies. In a moment when single-author monographs can meet with scholarly and even press resistance and when disability studies is so keen to show the extent of its relevance, some readers might consider a book such as this one to have less usefulness. But just as Faulkner in his Nobel Prize speech declined "to accept the end of man," so I decline to accept the idea that understanding an individual author's engagement with, experience of, and writing about disability has less importance precisely because such a focus on an individual allows for an exploration of the kind of complex embodiment Siebers and others see as the way to draw together the humanities view of disability as a social-cultural construct and the medical view that focuses on individual experiences of disability. What better way to account for the individuality of disability experience than to home in on an individual; and what better way to see the wide impact of disability constructs than to focus on an individual with such visibility and influence? Examining Faulkner, whose life was and work is so filled with disability in so many different ways provides a way to prod deeply into the workings of disability as an ethos, a technics, and an ethics.

Furthermore, focusing on an individual author so given to experimentation in form and content allows for an intense investigation of how bodies and minds are constituted in literary texts. This matter presents significant problems: certainly "the body" is something literary critics have been able to prod and focus on, seeing how it can extend metaphorically into the farthest backwaters of texts, but disabled bodies demand a certain ontological materiality that can create some embarrassment for a literary scholar. Dealing with actual tactile bodies—that is to say bodies that require a theoretical presence as material configurations—presents challenges for literary texts in ways they do not in, say, theater where bodies provide constant visual cues in making meaning. Not that everything from gestures to descriptions does not contribute to the forging of prose narratives, but the fact is that by nature fiction demands that a reader formulate an imagined body for a character, and that body is highly changeable, attenuating even the normal slipperiness of a signifier. Constant reminders of a deformity might maintain a given disability in the reader's mind; at the same time, less demonstrative disabilities might even be lost in the reading process. For example, how often do readers and scholars think about the passing reference to Jason Compson's having been a fat child and consider how that plays out in his adult personality as Simone Puleo has recently argued in an essay anchored in fat studies.

This latter example illustrates part of the problem with bodies and minds in literary texts, which is an extension of the general problem of bodies and minds and disability studies, which is that bodies fluctuate. This is one of the things that sets disability identity apart from supposedly more fixed subject positions generally associated with race, ethnicity, and gender (the many exceptions noted): not only is it the case that disabled people fail to form a homogeneous group or even groups because of the great variety of disabilities and the different kinds of experiences they cause but also people's bodies can change from disabled to abled and back again by all kinds of means. Meanwhile, the memory of disability, like the phantom-sensation memory of lost limbs, can play a significant role in the actions and reactions of people who have managed to bring their bodies close enough to the ideal of normality and abledness to change their *public* status, at least, of disabledness. What disability studies does is to bring into question the limits or potentials in the scope of what a character is or can be. This problem is not new, of course, as both critics and writers must often if not always struggle with just what kind of existence a character has; whether or not a character can do or think things beyond the control or even vision or understanding of the author; whether external factors can affect characters or whether characters respond to them in ways that conform to some kind of deep logic or backstory that exists outside of the written. Again, can a fat pathos be read in Jason Compson? An author might well write a story about the psychological factors at work in a person who was fat as a child, but if an author merely gestures to this fact in a character, a problem arises in thinking about the role of that fact in the character's actions and existence.

Disabled bodies and minds throw these matters into high relief. They can demand a high visibility according to their varying markings. Likewise, they can find themselves enslaved to a functionality in which their aberrations (a term that begs the question of normality) must serve metaphorical, allegorical, or symbolical purposes. Moreover, they can be fixed within an overarching logic of ontology difficult to police but insistent in its thematic purposes. An author placing a disabled character in a literary text very often requires a reader to maintain a manifest signified of that body or mind theoretically at all moments in and in the extreme absence of visibility, which is to say the ways of making such a body or mind visible in words. The strategies for achieving such a presentation of a disabled character are problematic: one, which Faulkner somewhat employs, is to offer up such a figure according to clinical, academic, or popular notions as to what such a person should "be like" or "look like," but such notions are of course historical and being thus embedded historically suffer when notions change, sometimes even to the extent of making their presentation meaningless to later readers.

Ultimately, many of the issues disabled bodies and minds raise about the ontology of characters coincide with matters connected with Faulkner, Nobel Laureate and writer of disability, himself. Even as Faulkner, like all humans, evolved with maturation into a state of disability, in his case with his back pains and heart troubles brought on by riding injuries and alcoholism, he and his work grew more deeply inscribed in a poetics of the ideology of ability. This movement produced a curious public-character Faulkner, a man who presented himself as a small-town white southerner man given to some involvement with farming who also wrote incredibly difficult and felicitous prose and plumbed the most profound depths of humanity and culture. As a writer of and about the South he could be seen as embodying that region's abnormalities, yet he was also a Modernist writer of and about the United States and even the world. Through television, photographs, public appearances, and even audio recordings, Faulkner was able to present himself as a presence, a visible body and mind that could seem both abnormal and normal, abled and disabled, as these appearings could range from tuxedoed gentleman to patch-sleeved drunken little tramp—a man at times overwhelmingly abled and at others heartbreakingly disabled. Such paradoxes, again, key into the paradoxes of disability and into Citizen Faulkner, the Nobel Laureate, who would go on to write disability again during his tenure as public intellectual just as he had done throughout his career, which was shaped in contexts and dynamics of disability from its beginning.

A Fable appears in a critical moment in that career. Written in a style so dense as to be itself disabling to readers, the novel is deeply saturated in disability. It is a novel of failure, of momentary enablement of military forces to transcend their grim task only to have their superiors disable them again, of a gesture that calls for cooperation for full actualization. Its characters marked by physical disability are not major ones as some of Faulkner's disabled characters in other works are, but they serve integral purposes as other minor disabled characters do in his writing. At the same time that the novel acknowledges personal achievement, including implicitly its author's, it also recognizes the importance of an interdependence of individuals who need others in order to achieve good and great things. These matters make up the conceptual foundation of Faulkner, writer of disability, that the rest of this book explores.

CUT TO:

WILLIAM FAULKNER
The basest of all things is to be afraid.

FADE TO:

INT. JOHN FAULKNER'S HOUSE

JOHN FAULKNER
Bill was my brother

Fa(u)lkner's Wounded,

BEING A DISERENT BIOGRAPHICAL APPROACH

The great-grandson described it thusly at the end of *Flags in the Dust*:

> He stood on a stone pedestal, in his frock coat and bareheaded, one leg slightly advanced and one hand resting lightly on the stone pylon beside him. His head was lifted a little in that gesture of haughty pride which repeated itself generation after generation with a fateful fidelity, his back to the world and his carven eyes gazing out across the valley where his railroad ran, and the blue changeless hills beyond, and beyond that, the ramparts of infinity itself. The pedestal and effigy were mottled with seasons of rain and sun and with drippings from the cedar branches, and the bold carving of the letters was bleared with mold, yet still decipherable:
>
> COLONEL JOHN SARTORIS, C.S.A.
> 1823–1876
> Soldier, Statesman, Citizen of the World
>
> For man's enlightenment he lived
> By man's ingratitude he died
>
> Pause here, son of sorrow; remember death

One sees it most easily while driving north on Highway 15 through Ripley, Mississippi. You have to know to look to the right as you are approaching and then passing *Fred's* and *Jitney Jungle* and the venerable *Pizza Hut*. It is the highest statue in the cemetery, although from a distance you still have to know where to cast your gaze. The great-grandson took some license. The writing on the actual monument is not so dramatic: simply the name and the life-and-death dates. Stacked behind the figure's leg are the volumes representing those the great-grandfather wrote in life, one of the activities his great-grandson would emulate. After all, the child was named for him. And that is not all he would emulate.

Instead of resting on a pylon, the right hand of the statue standing this very day in the cemetery in the town of Ripley, Mississippi, is thrust forward, and time, weather, or some drunken or funseeking honkytonker has blasted the fingers from it. The other hand is tucked away in his vest in fixed and breathless Napoleonic grandeur. Ironic. For that was the hand from which digits had in real life been missing.

I

Wherever they may choose to begin telling the story of the Nobel Laureate, all biographers acknowledge the great-grandfather as the starting point of the Fa(u)lkner saga. His arrival in the young north Mississippi town of Ripley set into motion what came to fruition in the Nobel legacy. Not that the town always remembers: recently a Colonel Falkner Week has been established, but the signs that greet visitors passing through or coming to First Monday Trade Days *or* taking a tour (once under the able guidance of Tommy Covington, town archivist and Faulkner extraordinaire, and now by the talented and knowledgeable Bruce Smith) tell only of the young men who have attained the status of playing in the National Football League.

But Faulkner scholars know how the boy arrived in Tippah County, Mississippi, probably sometime in 1842 from East Tennessee to live with his uncle. They know he may or may not have met a young lady who passed through his life at that time and then again later to become his wife. That he fought in the Mexican War and wrote an epic poem about it. That he raised his own Company to fight for the Confederacy. That he returned to play a role as a town and railroad builder. That on the eve of his election to the state congress his rival and ex-business partner shot him on the square not far from the corner where many years later stood Renfrow's Café until it burned down. Many even know that early in his life this man deformed his own name, removing the "u" before pasting that name on the land itself as a station on his own rail line north of Ripley: Falkner, Mississippi, a kudzu-choked hamlet also very proud of its high-school athletes. Scholars know and often repeat these things. But many readers and scholars have either forgotten, never known, or attached little significance to something else, despite its importance to the course of so many lives . . .

April 14, 1847, was presumably a hot one near Monterey, Mexico. The Second Mississippi Volunteers had made the journey from home, starting in January and going through New Orleans to the Island of Lobus and to Matamoras, Mexico, arriving at their encampment near Monterey on March 6. They had been encamped for a month, an eternity to a young man anxious for glory, or perhaps wishing for something else—maybe the taste of a local brew or just the whipping feel of free time and space and carelessness. Maybe the heat and tedium were such to provoke him to think of long ribbony dark hair and heaving breasts and other exotic pleasures of these new environs—such amorous possibilities as might be shaped by storybook ideas of a faraway land; at least one of his fellow Ripley citizen-soldiers claimed he had a naughty reason for the escapade, having "made some indecent and improper advances upon a Mexican female, which was resented by some Male Mexicans" (qtd. in Duclos 317). Such tedium in a military camp, such a surfeit of men all around. There were orders not to leave the confining military encampment, and there is what some people always know, which is that the gift of breath and movement realizes its own desperate way. After months of traveling to Mexico, Lieutenant Falkner had had enough chewing long grass and smelling horses and their excrement and sweat and smoke and gun oil and leather and canvas. He had always taken his own way, always looked out for himself. The difference between camp and jail was getting to be mighty fine. He was going to get out, at least for a little while if not for good.

The details are lost to us now. Perhaps he bribed a guard, or maybe he struck one and dashed away. It *is possible* that he was out in the line of duty, but he had not obtained the requisite written permission. Either way, surely on April 14, 1847, which must have been a hot day in Monterey, he felt the breeze rushing against his face, whistling in his ears. He must have felt very smart and even braver if defying orders, riding free in enemy territory. Although he may have practiced caution in this escapade, it is more likely he was reveling in his recklessness, joying in the dust churned into swirling clouds by his steed's thundering hooves. Enough of all this West Point maneuvering and waiting—this is what a warrior does, riding out disdainful of danger, laughing and determined.

Or maybe he had something different in mind. Maybe he was tired of Mexico and camp life and fighting altogether. Maybe he wanted to get back to Ripley with its warm trappings of home. Perhaps that still-frontier town was not as settled as some, but it was still a place of at least the promise of stability for the orphan youth moving into a time of his life when came stirrings of the idea of being in one place and establishing himself there. Maybe he was sallying forth precisely so he could be punished by being sent back home. Maybe he even felt he could assure such a result by receiving the right kind of injury, by doing what others have done—literally shoot himself in the foot.

The official report suggests that the event was not in the line of duty but also not conspicuously violate. There were "Aquas Colientes" about four miles from the camp where officers often went, according to one W. E. Rogers, also of the Second Mississippi, "to visit the springs for [. . .] health owing to so much infection and disease in the camp at that time" (qtd. in Duclos 316). Whether for physical cure, amorous involvement, spiritual joy, or line of duty, the young lieutenant was, according to his own testimony (again he was alone), ambushed by Mexicans. He received two wounds—one in the left hand and one, indeed, in the left foot. A posse was formed to find him when he had not returned by afternoon; the soldiers brought him back, and he had lost much blood. The report filed by the regimental surgeon, Thomas N. Love, said:

> I have carefully examined this officer, whose condition renders him unable to perform the duties of his office. I attended L. Falkner for Gunshot wounds of the hand and foot, received from the hands of Mexicans concealed in ambush near Monterey on the 14th day of April last. A ball passed through the left foot between the first and second metatarsal bones, shattering the bone of the second. . . . He has not recovered from his wound, owing perhaps to loose fragments of bone which may yet work out. . . . From the injury done to the tendonous expansion of muscles, he will always perhaps be lame. . . . The other ball took off three fingers of the left hand at the first joint. . . . The stumps are yet tender and give much pain when exposed. Owing to

> his present condition, he is incapable of performing his duty, and therefore in the opinion of the undersigned is justifiable in resigning his commission from the service of the United States. (qtd in Duclos 40)

If the plan was to get back home, it worked. He was sent back to Ripley to convalesce until August. By the time he got back to camp in Mexico in September he was applying for discharge, which Dr. Love's report helped him to get in October. The wounds were severe enough, and after all he had been attacked, said the official report. By the way, he was returning to his bride, whom he had married in July.

He was returning to the promise of something else as well. In 1849, he applied for pension and bounty land for disabled veterans. The doctors who examined him and wrote on his behalf at this point were William McRae and Benjamin Jones of Ripley, and their report included the following comments: "[He is] entirely incapacitated from following any occupation requiring the use of his hand. And we are informed and believe it to be true from their appearance, that both his foot and hand are exceedingly sensitive to the effects of cold, inflaming, swelling, and becoming very tender upon the least exposure. Upon the whole, we consider said Falkner not only incapacitated from military duty from the effects of said wounds; in his hand and foot. But in our opinion he is totally disabled thereby from obtaining subsistence from manuel [*sic*] labor" (qtd in Duclos 41). He was approved for the pension and land eventually—it took him until 1851 to succeed in getting them. The amount was $204 a year for life and 160 acres of land. Quite a bit for the once-penniless orphan. He was set now—a veteran, a landowner, a married man in a town that could be on the make. Depending on how things had or had not been planned (he had either attained success outright or had made the most of bad luck), he had turned disability to his advantage.

Either way, what the blues singer Albert King called "real bad luck" finally found the lieutenant out. It turns out that Falkner in his efforts to increase his status and belonging in town became part of a group with the dashingly coy name of the Knights of Temperance. One Robert Hindman attempted to join this group but was blackballed. Inquiries were made. Someone claimed the wounded veteran Falkner had committed the deed.

Enraged, embarrassed, frantic, Hindman met the lieutenant on the steps of the courthouse and fired a pistol point-blank in his face. It misfired once. He tried again, failed again. The young Lieutenant Falkner did what certain kinds of people in certain times and certain places will do. He pulled out a knife and stabbed his assailant.

Robert Hindman's tombstone still stands in the backyard of a home on the edge of town. It rather dramatically proclaims that the one buried therein was "Killed by W. C. Falkner" (changed from its original inscription of "Murdered by W. C. Falkner"). The sight of it moved the great-grandson, who would work it into his fictional world. More importantly, it is emblematic of the passions that naturally ran high in the Hindman family following the death. The family did not see their relative's death as the result of a rash deed but rather as an extension of something the lieutenant had started when (they thought) he had cast his vote against Robert's application for membership in the chivalric order. Thomas Hindman Jr. could not stand it, the way everything had gone down. The very site of the lieutenant drawing breath irked him to the point that he too tried to kill him. He also failed, and the very lucky Falkner retaliated again and ended *his* life.

Now a kind of one-sided feud had begun, and any Faulknerian worth her salt knows of this. What most Faulknerians may *not* know is that this Hindman's attacks were not all just gunslinging ones.

Brooding over his son's death and his own growing hatred of Falkner, Thomas Hindman Sr. took upon himself to write a letter to Congressman Jacob Thompson arguing that Falkner was not eligible for receiving disability compensation on the grounds that he was *not* in fact disabled. He wrote that Falkner's "wounds have long since became [*sic*] sound, from his foot he suffers no inconvenience whatever and the loss of so small a portion of two fingers on his left hand can cause but little if any" (qtd. in Duclos 41). When Thompson sent Hindman the official doctors' reports, Hindman pressed on, writing:

> Mr. Falkner now, and for a long time back, walks, runs, jumps, and dances, with as much activity and apparent ease as any young man in our county, and uses his hands with no apparent inconvenience whatever—I see him frequently and have not been able to discover any halt or lameness in his walk—During a snow in January last—I was at Ripley when I seen [*sic*] him

> engaged for several hours in breaking wild horses to run in a sleigh. The day was cold, he wore no gloves, and seem'd to use both hands equally well; there not being the slightest appearance of soreness or swelling, neither did I hear him complain of any sensitiveness from the effects of weather. At Monterey, on his return to the United States, and but a few days after he had obtained the Certificate from Surgeon Love, he attended a Fandango, and in my presence danced a considerable time, without any apparent inconvenience—From New Orleans to Ripley, and at all times since, that I have noticed him he wears either a tight fashionable boot or shoe—I have seen his wounded left foot bare and never discovered any contraction of the toes, as stated by McRae and Jones. [. . .] And as regards the true situation of William C. Falkner—he is unquestionably a stout, active, athletic young man, able to earn his living by use of an axe, mattoc, maul, or any other tool used by labouring men, was he a shade darker and belonged to me, I could now easily sell him for one thousand dollars, after showing his wounds, and exhibiting the affidavit of McRae and Jones also. His true situation is well known in and about Ripley—he engages freely in all the exercises and sports, common with stout, active young men such as dancing, jumping, riding, and breaking wild and unruly horses to harness, &c, &c.—most of which he excels at. (qtd. in Duclos 44)

A remarkable letter. I must confess that I find it hilarious to try and envision a long-bearded man attired in somber nineteenth-century garb "jumping." On a different note, the letter is very disturbing, the comment about Falkner being a shade darker carrying with it a particularly stark tone, hinting at ways race and ability intersect in the antebellum South. Besides its obvious racializing and objectivism, it is part of the incriminating sheen of the letter's text that Hindman does not write that Falkner would need to be not two or three but just one shade darker for him to be able to put him on the auction block. The comment amounts to a rather astounding conflation of racial passing with passing as disabled: the equation has been drawn by disability studies theorists who are keen to argue that bodily abnormality is constructed whether talking about skin color or bodily variation. Incidentally, there is no Falkner-the-writer here, as Hindman is more concerned to stress Falkner's more, shall we say, "animal" skills, the athletic abilities that make him able to play unfettered and to labor, also without fetter. Hindman in essence is arguing that to take care of Falkner is tantamount to supporting a person of color who is perfectly capable of working as a slave.

I would pause to discuss disability and gainful free (non-slave) employment as uneasy compatriots at best. Among the abled, especially the abled involved in manual labor, there persists a tendency toward a mixture of suspicion and envy regarding coworkers who receive disability compensation. For the steel-mill welder whose hands have been burned beyond all use there is likely to be much support and even outrage if compensation is not secured. For the welder who complains that blinding headaches are preventing her from performing her duties, there is often a suspicion of fraud. The same goes for back problems—a muscle-bound man receiving compensation for back pain better make sure he and the welder with headaches never seem to be pain-free when not at the workplace. Such easy money is simply too tempting not to provoke chicanery, but taking on such a performance requires extending it to other aspects of life where being perceived as disabled could itself be disabling in ways that work against the very freedom that the evasion of labor offers. Meanwhile, for people who are disabled, such compensation, while vitally helpful, may at times seem small compared to the opportunities offered by not being disabled.

At work in the issue of disability and employment is a psychological crisis. Writing over a hundred years after Hindman on laws regarding disability and employment, Cheryl Rogers ponders the matter. She observes that at the heart of disability and employment lies the paradox that a certain level of disability must be met in order for one to receive compensation, but then that level prevents any reentrance into the workforce. As Rogers notes, two different notions prevail regarding disabled people and labor, "one contending that the disabled are to be pitied and not expected to work and the other demanding full integration into society, including the opportunity to work" (120). Interestingly, the latter is often embraced by disabled people themselves. Paying close attention to the lack of fixed definitions and the catch-22 in which disabled people find themselves, Rogers writes that the

> very process by which disabled applicants become eligible for benefits leads to learned states of helplessness. For example, disabled claimant's [*sic*] must prove total and long-term disability to become eligible for SSDI

> [Social Security Disability Insurance] and/or SSI [Supplemental Security Income]. As a result, a disabled "mindset" sets in and the applicants may inevitably come to view themselves as totally dependent and unable to work. This situation is even worse for those disabled who do not qualify for cash benefits under existing programs: after identifying those disabled individuals who appear to be capable of work and therefore ineligible for disability benefits, we do nothing further. The message once again is: If you can work, don't expect any help; if you cannot, the government and/or the private sector will take care of you as long as you remain invalid. (122)

There is, then, quite separate from whatever physical condition should prevent the carrying out of duties in a given labor situation, a compulsion to posturing. And the pressure on this posturing is immense.

Rogers's use of the word "invalid" is especially striking to me, presented as it is without an indefinite article. Simi Linton spends some quality time with that term, brilliantly asking, "Are *invalid,* with the emphasis on the first syllable, and *invalid,* with the emphasis on the second, synonyms or homonyms?" (28). Linton observes that "[b]oth *invalids* share the Latin root *invalidus,* which means weak. It could be argued that some disabilities do result in weakening of the body, or, more likely, parts of the body, but the totalizing noun, *invalid,* does not confine the weakness to the specific bodily functions; it is more encompassing" (28–29). To be not valid requires a context: as I noted before, being blind is disabling in a world of light, but when the lights go out the visually impaired person has an edge over the sighted. Yet Linton is definitely onto something in observing that the designation of "invalid" as a judgment of validity is a generally unproblematized blanket one. There is a chasm between the designation of "healthy" and "invalid" that is as wide and deep as the lack of parallelism in the two terms; I believe I am approximating common parlance in evoking the two terms this way, as I do not know of anyone speaking in English referring to a nondisabled person as a va*lid.* The problem with this blanket term meaning "not valid" is precisely that the context is often left undefined, kept as invisible as the empowered center always is, whether that center is whiteness, maleness, or "able bodiedness."

In the case of William Clark Falkner, Hindman inscribes his validity within an infrastructure of physical labor. Falkner does not deserve compensation because he is not rendered invalid in a context in which he is able to perform physical labor as well as recreation. The recreation propensity is particularly damning, adding another level of scandal (as recreation, sadly, often does) to the charge of fraud. Receiving free money while being able to work is galling enough, but the recipient's having the nerve to play around too is more than Hindman can bear. Hindman's evocation of Falkner's recreational capabilities plays also into his racialization of Falkner. The man jumps and dances just like slaves do yet does not work as slaves should! And that tight fashionable shoe—why, he is a black man dandied up no less! Included here perhaps is a condemnation of a poor white (which is to say, not-quite-white) man making good. The tone of disappointment and regret in Hindman's voice is really very intriguing, for he is actually upset that he could have made as much as a thousand dollars on the likes of this man. The line of argument is impressive if morally shocking: Hindman is writing to show that Falkner is in fact valid as a man in society yet he simultaneously shows him to be invalid as an independent subject because he is essentially a black man. There is just no winning with Hindman.

As we know, Hindman was biased, and he actually acknowledged this fact in his writing to the congressman. Just keeping things straight. But while admitting his animosity, he failed to explain another problematic thing. When Falkner applied for the disability pension—which happened prior to Falkner's killing Robert Hindman—Thomas Hindman Sr. *had actually himself supported Faulkner in doing so.* This reversal of his own former testimony along with the evidence of the ill feelings resulting from family conflict in the end destroyed Hindman's credibility. Falkner's pension was suspended for a short time until everything was sorted out and then was reinstated, although he would lose it again during the Civil War when the southern states were dropped from the roll (it was later paid to him again at the rate of eight dollars a month).

We might conclude, as Thompson did, that Falkner's wounds were disabling. Yet the story does not end there, for Faulkner's involvement in the War Between the States makes the whole matter thorny again. Whatever disabilities he had did not prevent him from raising his own company and participating in significant action. Some even claim it was he and not Old Blue Light Jackson who actually stood like a "stone wall" that fateful day at

Manassas. Certainly his rising to the role of colonel is an unqualified one, as I know of no documents that say he succeeded despite his disability. In the bizarre convolutions of the Hindman saga, was Hindman actually correct when noting that Falkner was not so terribly disabled and was actually disentangling himself from a hoax that he had himself helped to create? Perhaps Hindman had come to see clearly what a charlatan Falkner was, albeit at the precious expense of his family members, and now was determined to set the record straight. Donald Duclos, Faulkner's lone "factual" biographer, does not clear up these muddied waters, for after all he suggests that the Colonel's disabilities were both known and remembered, marked in marble no less, and even commemorated in souvenirs of sorts: "As mementos of his narrow escape from death, in addition to the possible silver coins, Falkner also had the stubs of his fingers on his maimed left hand, which, according to legend, he always kept tucked in his vest or pants pocket, perhaps because they served—to him at least—a constant reminder of the danger of excessive daring and recklessness. Also, he brought home with him two other souvenirs which yet remain in the Fau(u)lkner family: an ornately carved walking stick and a Mexican machete bearing the inscription 'Not to be used for cutting trees'" (51). Duclos adds the observation that I have already noted—that Falkner's statue in Ripley preserves the Colonel's legendary pose, with his left fingers tucked in one of his vest pockets.

Just how disabling Colonel Falkner's wounds were must forever remain a mystery; likewise, and as a result, there perpetually haunts about his legacy the possibility of fraud. I have in the past employed the concept of the "Counterfeit Other" to describe characters in the great-grandson's writing who are white people performing as or made black. They do this in order to glean the sympathy accorded to the victimized. In fact, they are often themselves oppressive victimizers or representatives of a victimizing group. Their masquerade as other thus becomes a cruel diversion that obfuscates the true plight of the oppressed, which is often perpetrated by the masquers themselves. Just as passing as abled may be equated with passing as white, so the concept of the Counterfeit Other may apply in a disability context.

The Colonel's wounds may even be seen as empowering. It is a curious thing that disability can be wielded as a positive thing. In *Extraordinary*

Bodies, Garland-Thomson even points out that at times disability has been presented as a mark of nobility, for example in the case of Melville's Captain Ahab, whose missing leg hardly weakens him, barely disables him, and ultimately lifts him to the heights of tragic heroism. While one should not fall into the trap of "mythologiz[ing] disability as advantage" (Siebers 63), it is useful to see how disability can be appropriated as a luxury of a normate (see the Note for explanation of this Garland-Thomson term) under such circumstances. Indeed, I have and now again suggest the term "disabled normate" for such figures. Perhaps the Old Colonel was parlaying his disability into the seizure of a higher class status. Perhaps he attained a certain nobility, too, although clearly not with everyone in his world—his killer, Richard Thurmond least of all. At the very least, the Colonel's memory was a checkered one . . . the great grandson would later say, "I can remember myself, when I was a boy in Ripley, there were some people who would pass on the other side of the street to avoid speaking—that sort of thing. . . ." (qtd. in Duclos 282).

II

And that sort of thing—the memory of the Colonel and the many conflicting emotions it provoked—must have been an inestimably large thing to the great-grandson at the same time that it must have felt natural, normal. To those born on the inside, what seems beyond explanation or desire or decency to those on the outside is simply part of life. Yet that fact makes it no less significant, looming, and desirable, if differently so.

The great-grandson was born in New Albany, Mississippi, but spent his earliest years in Ripley. He would have ridden on his family's railroad through the area—certainly he heard the trains rumble and screech through Ripley on it parallel with Main Street and would know that his people had built it. His parents gave him the illustrious Old Colonel's name, with the different middle name of Cuthbert, arguably more sonorous than the great-grandfather's underwhelming "Clark." The Colonel's house was still standing at the time as it had when he lived there and before it would be renovated outside and in and turned into a medical clinic and years later the offices of the internet provider Dixie.Net.

The new William displayed an interest in active robust living just as the man he was named after had. This tendency became apparent as he grew older and the family moved to Oxford. He loved horses and aeroplanes, even attempting to build a flying machine as a child. He like to play ball, too, and would get a broken nose from his high school gridiron heroics. In many ways he was living up to his grand name . . . he even, so the story goes, claimed early on that he wanted to be a writer like his great-granddaddy.

There were some problems, though. For one, he did not stand up straight enough. His mother fretted over this fact, for she believed Falkner men should carry themselves with excellent posture. She struck upon the solution of ordering a horrific brace for the boy. In the words of his brother John:

> It was about this time that Mother put braces on Bill. For some reason he got sloop-shouldered all at once. Mother was afraid it might be his lungs. She took Bill to the doctor and braces were ordered for him. They were sort of like a corset without a front. There were two padded armholes for Bill's arms and the back was stiffened with whalebone and laced crossways with a heavy white cord.
>
> At first Mother laced Bill into it, with the knot in the cord about at his belt line in back. But Bill could reach that. So she put the lace in from the bottom and tied the knot between his shoulder blades. I remember he complained about the thing being too tight each morning when Mother laced him into it (of course, Jack and I stood there and watched and laughed) but tight or not, it sure cured his stoop. (72–73)

Indeed. And John knew the score, as a sibling does. Knew how much this straight-back business had to do with an ideal, as he went on to write that "[m]ost little men rear back and take long strides, but with the exception of Grandfather, I've never seen a man with a straighter back or firmer stride than Bill's. It lasted him all his life too, so I guess Mother knew what she was doing" (73). John's comment includes mention of the other "problem" with the new William Falkner model. The great-grandson never had that growth spurt that would make him physically as large as the Colonel. "Little" would always be a word used to describe the great-grandson. He would spend the rest of his life trying to maintain perfect posture in order that he might have that noble mien that Meta Carpenter (Wilde) would later write was peculiar to white southern men of his class and generation and that she so liked about him. He was also making sure to achieve his greatest possible height. These things he did even when his back was broken (necessitating another brace) and, finally, humped.

Can we look at this posture and height situation and begin to think of the young Falkner—not the older pained Faulkner—as being able to relate firsthand to the experience of a disabled person from an early age? In both cases, it might be a stretch (pun not intended) since these things seem not to have kept him from doing what he wanted to do either as a child or an adolescent. Both posture and height pertain to bodily ideals, but also to the ideal of the local aristocracy and to some extent even narrower pressures of an admittedly haughty family. Perhaps his mother's corrective might be seen as an instrument to educate the great-grandson in the dynamics of Counterfeit Othering, in manufacturing a disability or imagining a nonnormal body as being socially disabled rather than physically so, substituting the social for the physical. Intended or not, the great-grandson learned the lesson well, and at the very least he may have gained insight into the machinery behind the curtain of the ideology of ability if not the concerns and even experiences connected with disability.

If the great-grandson was not going to stand as straight and tall as the Colonel, at least maybe he could live up to his ancestor's immense reputation by getting on in life and, as they say, making a big man of himself. But that did not seem likely as he reached late-adolescence/young-adulthood. By that time he had dropped out of high school and was spending his days walking in the woods in Lafayette County and writing not-memorable poetry. He even lost his girlfriend to a man with better prospects. It seemed the boy just could not act right. He could not even keep his image consistent, acting like a bum but dressing like a dandy.

It is now well known that the young man was posing. He was certainly neither the first nor the last young person in history to do so. James G. Watson has written at length on this posing, tracing Faulkner's various poses through to his fiction, observing the ways the author would refract them in his characters. Posing was a practice the writer would never grow out of: one of his most memorable photos is in some ways one of his most ridiculous—himself as a grandfather remaking himself once again as a Virginia fox-hunter, a photo that now hangs in his house in Oxford

Rowan Oak. We might wonder what his poses would have been like had he lived. Would he now look like Snoop Dog? More important, the refraction Watson describes plays out in significant ways in the disability-informed biographical context of Faulkner's writing.

What was perhaps the great-grandson's most famous and outrageous pose is one that holds particular significance in light of the great-grandfather and disability. Although the connection is hardly discussed among scholars, the similarity between Faulkner's military experience and subsequent performances are uncanny in their resemblance to the stories surrounding his ancestor. The story of the enlistment is well known: !DESPERATE FOR GLORY IN COMBAT! young Billy Falkner seeks to enlist. Anecdotal evidence has him claiming he attempted enlistment in the U.S. Army's Signal Corps only to be rejected because of his height. So he told a girl, Eula Dorothy Wilcox of Clarksdale. Joseph Blotner notes that the official requirements of that time did not stipulate a required height and besides there is no record of William Falkner's ever having attempted to enlist (60). The great-grandson's alleged comment to Wilcox, "do you know anything that would make me grow tall?" (60), is most significant for his own consciousness of the disabling nature of his less-than-ideal body—or perhaps Wilcox's idea and/recollection of that body and/or Faulkner's insecurities about it.

It seems though that his true desire was to be in the Royal Flying Corps, which had just been renamed the Royal Air Force. Where better for someone to go who is desperate for glory in these modern times? But how does a person not a subject of the crown pull off this preposterous pose? He fakes the British accent—not as difficult for a white Mississippian of the planter class as you might think, a southern accent transformed from stigma to enablement in a different cultural environment. He succeeds in enlisting through this enabling fiction, and off to Toronto he goes. Makes his way through the paces of cadet training, taking copious notes with detailed drawings of Sopwith Camels and soldiers and diagrams and tactics. Writes letters back home to his folks about the experience. Prepares for a first flight. Never happens. War ends. Out of luck.

But here is where the fiction and fun really began for the young man (after all, he was a member of a class and race of a region that had built a vast glorious fiction out of its own military defeat). Listen to John, with his mixture of sibling admiration and knowing irony: "When [Bill] got off [the train from Canada] we saw that he was limping. As soon as we greeted him and got him in the car he told us that some of the graduating class had gone up to celebrate getting their wings and he had flown his Camel halfway through the top of a hangar. The tail of his ship was still outside and they got Bill down from inside the hangar with a ladder" (124). Limping! Was Faulkner reliving his great-grandfather's war-induced disability? We have no way of knowing whether such was a conscious imitation, although it was certainly more easily performed than pretending to have lost a couple of fingers. There is a dashing photograph of the young Faulkner in uniform leaning on a walking stick, and it is delicious to think that it could have been the walking stick the family had inherited from the Colonel's Mexican War experience.

Even more intriguing is that the great-grandson should represent his wounding as being the result of a pointless joy-ride much like what his great-grandfather's injury may have resulted from. Joseph Blotner concatenates several of these stories:

> His brother Jack said Bill told him how he celebrated the armistice: "I took up a rotary-motored Spad with a crock of bourbon in the cockpit, gave diligent attention to both, and executed some reasonably adroit chandelles, an Immelman or two, and part of . . . a nearly perfect loop." Its chance of perfection was spoiled because "a hanger got in the way and I flew through the roof and ended up hanging on the rafters." [. . .] Later, Estelle's son, Malcolm, would say Faulkner told him he broke his nose in the accident. He told Phil Stone there were actually two of them in the plane and that they both hung from their seatbelts "trying to drink from a bottle upside down." Several years later he told Calvin Brown, Jr., that he had crashed in France, falling uninjured through a thatched roof and landing in the soup tureen of a peasant family's Sunday dinner. A dozen years later Faulkner would write that he wrecked not one but two aircraft. No newspaper of surviving official record took note of such a crash. (64)

Interesting to see Faulkner developing his multiperspectival, myth-building narrative technique. He was also beginning to *write* as well as *tell* fiction about aviators.

It seems also worth mentioning that, like his great-grandfather, the RAF "veteran" was keen to dance and celebrate upon his return home, however much he may have limped from his war experiences. Again, we can look to the little brother for some tattletaling: "Bill wore his uniform for some time after he got home. He liked it; besides, I had worn out all the clothes he left when he went in service. I had worn out Jack's too. Bill and I went to several victory dances at towns around Oxford and Bill did all right in his British officer's uniform, his slacks and RFC wings. He lent it to me several times. I liked it too" (124).

The great-grandson did not attempt to get disability compensation for his alleged injuries, and over the course of time he distanced himself from this particular self-fictionalizing altogether. His brother Jack's actual wound in combat and his brother Dean's death in a plane crash sobered him. By the time Malcolm Cowley was preparing *The Portable Faulkner,* the writer was very reticent on the topic. In an early draft of his introduction to the book, Cowley quoted from a source that alleged that Faulkner had crashed his plane in Europe and had been wounded. Faulkner began an uneasy dance in which he tried to distance himself from his earlier claims. In a series of letters, he attempted to convince Cowley to reduce all details about his service to the simple comment that he was in the RAF. Blotner finally gave the world the true details of the writer's war experience, and viewed across the history of all that was said about it and everything military experience clearly meant to the great-grandson and his family, the reality is painfully galling. Blotner tells us that in fact he "was discharged 'in consequence of being Surplus to R.A.F. requirements,' and the column headed 'Casualties, Wounds, Campaigns, Medals, Clasps, Decorations, Mentions, Etc.' was simply stamped NIL" (66).

III

But long before he let the fiction of his RAF experience go, the great-grandson blended it into both his writing and his persona as a writer, all of which was further blended with and mediated by the legacy of the great-grandfather, with its embedded aspects of disability. Indeed, the waters of this period of the great-grandson's writing and self-presentation are muddied when viewed broadly. For example, the first "biography" of him was arguably Sherwood Anderson's "A Meeting South," a piece that itself blends fiction and nonfiction. The protagonist is a wounded war veteran from Alabama, a poet named David. In the story, David tells of his illustrious grandfather and drinks heavily to neutralize the pain from his wounds. Meanwhile, he spends most of his time bumming around polishing his verbosity.

Such characterization on Anderson's part accords with the great-grandson's autobiographizing. He composed the following biographical statement for his first book publication, *The Marble Faun*:

> Born in Mississippi in 1897. Great-grandson of Col. W. C. Falkner, C.S.A, author of "The White Rose of Memphis," "Rapid Ramblings in Europe," etc. Boyhood and youth were spent in Mississippi, since then has been 1) undergraduate 2) house painter 3) tramp, day laborer, dish-washer in various New England cities 4) Clerk in Lord and Taylor's book shop in New York City 5) bank- and postal clerk. Served during the war in the British Royal Air Force. A member of Sigma Alpha Epsilon Fraternity. Present temporary address, Oxford, Miss. "The Marble Faun" was written in the spring of 1919. (*Selected Letters* 7)

The things the young poet finds to be worth mentioning are noteworthy; they may be compared with the statement he sent to be published with "A Rose for Emily," this time as William Fa*u*lkner, having restored the "u" the great-grandfather had removed (a deformation of a deformation restoring normality or merely throwing deformation into a great glaring light?):

> Born male and single at early age in Mississippi. Quit school after five years in the seventh grade. Got job in Grandfather's bank and learned medicinal value of his liquor. Grandfather thought janitor did it. Hard on janitor. War came. Liked British uniform. Got commission R.F.C. pilot. Crashed. Cost British gov't £2000. Was still pilot. Crashed. Cost British gov't £2000. Quit. Cost British gov't $84.30. King said, "Well done." Returned to Mississippi. Family got job: postmaster. Resigned by mutual agreement on part of two inspectors; accused of throwing all incoming mail into garbage can. How disposed of outgoing mail never proved. Inspectors foiled. Had $700. Went

> to Europe. Met man named Sherwood Anderson. Said, "Why not write novels? Maybe won't have to work." Did. *Soldiers' Pay.* Did. *Mosquitoes.* Did. *Sound and Fury.* Did. *Sanctuary,* out next year. Now flying again. Age 32. Own and operate own typewriter.
> [no signature] (*Selected Letters* 47)

Interestingly, neither bio mentions a wound, although the fiction of two crashes would imply such. The second biography excludes the ancestor, as if by restoring the "u" and coming into his own the great-grandson had somehow replaced the Colonel. The new William Fa(u)lkner had now arrived. It is noteworthy that both statements present Faulkner as a rogue, as possibly being guilty of chicanery. Perhaps the young writer was keying into the legacy of fraud that belonged, rightly or not, to the great-grandfather. The great-grandson's version foregrounds laziness, a romanticization of the idea of the tramp, a kind of Chaplinesque pose that fits with the great-grandson's appearance.

We might cast everything in disability studies rhetoric by observing that Faulkner is keen in these statements to walk a line between normalcy and stigma, and he employs the tension arising from this line-walking in his early writing by creating wounded characters who conform to one or more of these self-presentations. Such is the case in his "New Orleans" sketch entitled "Mirrors of Chartres Street," which deals with a tramp who is wounded in the same way the great-grandfather and great-grandson both claimed to be. The story's narrator tells of a character whose voice is marked by "the hoarseness of vocal cords long dried with alcohol, and he was crippled" (*New Orleans Sketches* 15). The narrator describes the man as being "apelike" but juxtaposes that description with the comment that "his neck muscles [moved] as smooth as an athlete's to the thrust of his crutch" (15). Two interesting things appear in these descriptive items. First, we can see Faulkner's uneasy (or perhaps too easy) equation of disability with animality. This equation appeared in Faulkner's earliest work—the faun in *The Marble Faun* is disabled in the sense that his movements are absolutely constricted not only by the built environment of the garden he stands in but also by the fact that he himself is "built" of a static substance. The sculpted faun represents a physical incarnation of a mythic figure that exists as an ideal only—this creature may not have variations and still be recognizable—and, intentionally or not, Faulkner well shows the irony that while the faun represents fluidity of movement, sexuality, and identity that figure is also fixed in identity just as he is fixed physically. The faun's being part nonhuman animal exemplifies the problems of identity and its fixedness in the context of disability, a paradox of identity stability and disability I will take up in detail later. For now, I stress that disability, especially deformity, can eject a human from the ranks of humanness, and the narrator's description of the man in "Mirrors of Chartres Street" as ape-like conforms to this idea of disabled-human-as-animal.

Yet the narrator also focuses in on the compensatory bodily feature that makes the man the opposite of disabled—his neck muscles suggest localized superhuman strength. This move is not surprising or original, for literary history is replete with disabled people with compensatory powers, the physically blind Tiresias's tremendous prophetic insight being an example that immediately comes to mind. The young Faulkner, attuned as he is to the store of literary and mythic materials from centuries before, assembles then a somewhat classical disabled figure, animal-like, movement-constricted, yet possessing greater power in one aspect than that of norms. Because of these things, the character possesses a point of view different from that of normal humans, and Faulkner takes advantage of this perspective as the man speaks: "Say, you are a young man now, and you got both legs. But some day you may need a bite of bread and a cup of coffee, just a cup of coffee, to keep the damp out of your bones; and you may stop a gentleman like I'm stopping you, and he may be my son—I was a good one in my day, fellow" (15). The man not only offers his perspective of life but insists on thrusting it upon the narrator, explaining what disability activists have since stressed, that everyone is only a step away from disablement and is even evolving into, maturing into disability. The narrator immediately registers his anxiety about the threat of disablement, explaining that "I had prided myself at the time on my appearance; that I did not look even like a prospective bum [...] but who knows what life may do to us?" (15). With this realization, the narrator moves into sympathy with the man, commenting, "Anyway, to have such a breath fondly on one's neck in this nation and time was worth a quarter" (15). With the money the narrator gives him, the man goes to see a movie, prompting the narrator to say, "Truly, his was an untrammelled spirit" (16).

Later, the narrator sees "him for the last time" (16), watching from a gallery in the French Quarter. The new placement carries significance: not only does it signify access to society, presumably a home or apartment, it also implies the ability to climb stairs, get through doors, and pass through rooms to a space above the street. It suggests re-established safety of the normate within a built environment that privileges a normal body and signals a new, more contemplative, less overtly anxious perspective. Not so the disabled man on the street below. Standing near a policeman, the man with his crutch "described a rectangle upon the pavement and within this rectangle he became motionless with one movement, like a bird alighting" (16). The man then speaks again to those around him: "This is my room [. . .] now, how can you arrest me, huh? Where's your warrant for entering my room, fellow?" (16). Quite a remarkable thing Faulkner realizes here, for deprived of the advantages of the normate-privileging built environment the man in essence builds his own more fluid room. The act contrasts with the narrator's evoking another animal, a bird, to describe the man, achieving a paradox of which Faulkner himself may not have been fully aware—at the same time the man's disability gives him a kind of freedom it also shuts him out of sheltering aspects of civilization. The man then skillfully works to regain access to civilization's built safe harbors, albeit via a distinctly non-normal route and to a distinctly non-normal destination, for he shouts:

> Arrest me in my own room! Arrest me! Where's laws and justice? Ain't I a member of greatest republic on earth? Ain't every laborer got his own home, and ain't this mine? Beat it, you damn Republican. Got a gov'ment job: thinks he can do whatever he wants. [. . .] Listen, men. I was born American citizen and I been a good citizen all my life. When America needs men, who's first to say 'America take me?' I am, until railroad cut off my leg. And did I do anything to railroad for cutting off my leg? Did I go to railroad president and say, "Say, do you know you cut off my leg?" No, sir. I said I been good American citizen all my life—all my life I worked hard. I been laboring man, and ain't every laboring man got his own room, and ain't this mine? Now, I ask you, one gentlemena to 'nother, can damn Republican come in laboring man's room and arrest him? (17)

The man's claim for American citizenship comes off as outrageous in light of the tenuousness of his status even as human. Yet his argument proceeds according to strong (and ironically) "republican" logic: he has been a good laboring citizen, has not even challenged the system that disabled him. Moreover his disability results from his participation in the furtherance of ableism as he ironically loses individual mobility while working on a project designed to increase national-scale mobility.

If "Mirrors of Chartres Street" has not already sufficiently telegraphed its conclusion by now, both the conclusion and the implications of its obvious antecedent become clear when a police car arrives to take the man to jail. The man quickly changes his tune, saying, "Yes, sir [. . .] I'm American citizen and laboring man, but when a friend sends a car for me, why, I'll go. Yes, sir, never refused a friend in my life, even if he's rich and I ain't nothing but self-respecting American citizen" (18). Clearly jail is the briar patch and the disabled man Br'er Rabbit, an implied casting that brings out the racial implications at work in the description "ape-like" (blackness may also be signified in the comparison to a third animal, "a water beetle" [163]). Although evidently a white man, this disabled character emerges in the vein of black trickster represented as an animal, another gregarious animal, that is, who in his attempts to perform as a sociable good citizen becomes ensnared with the Tar-Baby and finds his mobility destroyed. In this striking reformulation of Joel Chandler Harris's story, the disabled trickster might be seen as a hero of the cultural margin. The story's closing lines promote this heroism, seemingly lifting this anonymous disabled street-person to a stupendous height: "And one thought of Caesar mounting his chariot among cast roses and the shouts of the rabble, and driving along the Via Appia while beggars crept out to see and centurions clashed their shields in the light of golden pennons flapping across the dawn" (18). Of course the tone comes off overdone, leaving the reader (at least this reader) to wonder finally if the narrator is simply making a mockery of the disabled subject of the story.

The narrator—elusive, deflecting attention from himself—may well haunt the reader as much as or even more than the articulate disabled man. Are we to see a silent, observing young William Faulkner withdrawn in the shadows of Chartres? Are we to understand that the "mirrors" of Chartres reflect back to him his own history (familial and personal) with disability real or otherwise? Like his great-grandfather, the disabled man is involved in building a railroad, although unlike the Old Colonel he actually labors in the job. At the same time, the disabled man figures his work as a service to the country as though it were the equivalent of military service, and he now flaunts his disability in the face of the authority, as Chartres Street was then the location of the Second City Criminal Court and Third District Police Station, a building of Romanesque arches that may have inspired the Caesar imagery. The mirror distorts, turning the ancestor of high estate into a bum, making his left-right movements right-left ones, so to speak. But what of the image of the great-grandson himself? Here he crabs as far away from bum status as he can get, his anxiety the only thing that keeps him from practical normate invisibility. There is a marked Oedipal situation in the great-grandson's literally standing above the stand-in for the Colonel, but that anxiety of influence seems hardly defeated by the fact of its achievement through a retreat into normalcy. The uneasiness makes itself felt even on the vaguest levels, most especially in the needless cruelty of the mock-heroic closing. While the story may be read as a case of Faulkner's having a disabled person speak, its artfulness and importance may lie in its accurately capturing the lurking doubts and fretful efforts of individuals, with their variations, to stay within and police the borders of white male human normality.

I insert gender into the list of identity issues at this point because the specifics of wounding are, at this point in Faulkner's thinking, conditions pertaining to men and masculinity. Disabled "legs" naturally comprehend the gamut of literal and metaphorical impairments of what all one can suppose a man to be and do, and even if we disregard biographical implications in the story, it is plain to see that, on the most superficial level, the narrator perceives himself as a man facing the prospect of disability reflected back, which conveys an anxiety of castration. At work here is a blend of proximity and distance, sympathy and competition, although the competition manifests in anxiety born of the precariousness of the mismatch of ability, not just that of the disabled man and the narrator, but of ability as a thing in itself.

The competition aspect becomes much more pointed in another early story, "The Leg." The story is one of the strangest pieces in all of Faulkner's oeuvre, being a kind of Gothic horror melodrama infused with Lost Generation psychological tendencies. The narrator's name is apparently David (he is referred to by his friend George as "Davy"), an American in England at Oxford who goes to fight in the Great War. The name is significant: as already noted, it was the one Sherwood Anderson gave the Faulkner character in "A Meeting South"; at the same time, Faulkner would use it often in his work for characters with an artistic flair who resemble himself. But here Faulkner is not just meeting a disabled person or standing on a balcony down at him as he rails against the government. Instead, he actually imagines what it is like to occupy the position of that man and his body.

The story opens with the narrator in a skiff with an Englishman named George in a lock on the Thames owned by the father of a young woman named Everbe Corinthia. The young woman is operating the lock and opens it while George flirts with her, with the result that the skiff shoots through and George goes overboard. He is unhurt, but Everbe feels badly about it. Meanwhile, David is envious of George's vamping. The scene is an idyllic one for David nevertheless, a moment that transpires before the war when the greatest injury one experiences is a spill in the river, wounded vanity, and the ache of a smitten heart.

Different from the war experience, which brings such a severe injury that David's leg must be amputated. The second section of the three-part story features a nightmarish dreamscape, with both David and George apparently suffering from posttraumatic stress disorder (the word "shellshock" would likely have been used at the time). George moves in and out of sanity as David passes in and out of consciousness. At the same time, George goes back and forth from England to Belgium, where David is convalescing, although David appears to leave too. David thinks them both on the same errands. When awake, he is obsessed with his lost leg because he does not know where it is or its condition. Before the surgeons amputate it, David pleads with George, "I want you to be sure it's dead. They may cut it off in a hurry and forget about it. [. . .] I couldn't have that, you know. That wouldn't do at all. They might bury it and it couldn't lie quiet. And then it would be lost and we couldn't find it to do anything" (830). When the leg is gone, replaced by a wooden and leather prosthetic, David begs George to find it for him until George is no longer there. In fact, David has stated that George is dead, and perhaps he only imagines George is talking to him and searching for his leg throughout section two. The plot has, by this point, become terribly obscure, and as Robert Hamblin has written, from beginning to end the story "leaves ambiguous the question of whether key incidents represent supernatural occurrences or merely the imaginary products of an unsettled mind" (225).

Part three of the story has David talking to a padre concerning Everbe's brother's attempt to kill him. David cannot understand why the brother has acted so violently, but the padre explains that after their father died Everbe would run away in the night to meet a strange man who would jeer from the bushes. When she dies mysteriously after one of these trysts, the brother vows to kill the man. He thinks the man is David, and in fact the padre produces a photograph of David that had been in her possession: "it was my own face that looked back at me. It had a quality that was not mine: a quality vicious and outrageous and unappalled, and beneath it was written in a bold sprawling hand like that of a child: 'to Everbe Corinthia' followed by an unprintable phrase, yet it was my own face [. . .]" (841–42). It is difficult to read the situation. There is a suggestion that in the throes of despair after the amputation David had gone on midnight-somnambulist or crazed excursions as a kind of Mr. Hyde, so terrorizing the young girl in his jealousy as to bring about her death, although this scenario is doubtful since he is in a different country and even land mass. More likely is that George was encountering her on his trips back to England. The most disturbing suggestion is that the leg itself was able to get to Oxford and is the agent that frightens the girl to death—at one point David tells George his leg is "jeering" at him, and it is that word Everbe's brother uses to describe the masculine laugh from the bushes, although he is never able to locate its source, using only the photograph to hunt down whom he imagines to be the hated culprit.

The latter reading, whether taken literally or metaphorically, is particularly rich as well as surprising. The phallic implications are unmistakable, of course (as Lisa Paddock and James Carothers have noted)—the defeated and presumably limp amputated leg as compared with the perpetually hard prosthetic wooden one he receives, the former overcoming the latter by means of intentionality. Still in the Jekyll and Hyde vein, the leg channels the monstrous jealous side of David and carries forth that murderous emotion as its own monster. Hence the reason David literally does not have a leg to stand on when confronted by the padre. Metaphorically speaking, the latter seems true no matter who the actual culprit is, for himself, George, and the leg are affected by his covetous rage. At the same time, the true reason for Everbe's mysterious death may be a rape that is physical, emotional, and metaphorical—a rape she is perhaps marked by from the beginning, as her name, Corinthia, may well evoke a style of column (another evocation of Greek marble), an association with the phallus.

Aside from the bizarre in the story that makes it an intriguing read along with its other thematic possibilities (we might also read the leg's being lost as a literal comment on the Lost Generation, making David a refiguring of Hemingway's Jake Barnes in *The Sun Also Rises*), the story is significant for its attempt to understand the internal, personal experience of a wound. Faulkner's fascination with the experience of amputation and of wearing a prosthetic as well as the remaining sensations of ghost limbs with their phantom sensations is evident, and it perhaps makes for the central energy of the story. David says that "my nights were filled too, with the nerve- and muscle-ends chafed now by an immediate cause: the wood-and-leather leg. But the gap was still there, and sometimes at night, isolated by invisibility, it would become filled with the immensity of darkness and silence despite me" (*Collected Stories* 833). At another point he says that "I rose from the cot, the harness of the leg creaking with explosive loudness" (837). He also writes that "I swung my foot to the floor and rose, holding on to the chair on which the artificial leg rested. It was chilly; it was as though I could feel the toes even of the absent leg curling away from the floor" (841). The interest in phantom pain leads me to wonder if there were apocryphal Fa(u)lkner family stories about the Old Colonel's experience of missing digits. Certainly the sound of the prosthetic might well have resulted in some way from Faulkner's own experiences with the back brace.

Particularly interesting in this story is Faulkner's working out an aesthetic of absence. He obviously wrote the story long before Derrida's time, much less David Wills's channeling of poststructuralism's deferral of meaning into the specific context of prosthetics as completions of idealized bodies (signifiers to the signifieds that are imagined normal bodies).

Nevertheless, Faulkner delves into the overwhelming presence of the absent leg: its phantom sensations serve David as the stimulations that define his consciousness whereas the possibly homicidal leg itself with its literal sensations throws back an image of himself as homicidal that is unrecognizable to him. In Faulkner's hands, the body precipitates a Lacanian crisis when it is so literally fragmented because not only the reflected image but the body itself takes on multiple roles of estrangement—estranged others instead of an othered consciousness. Consciousness becomes dispersed and multi-intentional throughout different parts of a fragmented body, parts not necessarily controlled by a central, single consciousness. As David says to George, "You'll find it some day. It's all right; just a leg. It hasn't even another leg to walk with" (831), suggesting that a single leg's natural reflected other sets up a kind of separate Lacanian situation from a single person's consciousness. We might follow David's logic out further to consider what his one still-intact leg thinks of the false one, which is to say, does that leg really have another one to walk with? This binary of walking proliferates throughout the story, as George and Everbe die, leaving David literally with no one to walk with. The padre's final comment, "May God have mercy on your soul" (841), is chilling in its reducing David to a single entity when in fact he is so many parts. It is hardly appropriate for God to have mercy on such a binary thing as a body + spirit = soul when in fact his body is made up of so many more fragments. To appropriate Luce Irigaray's language, there is a riveting horror of masculine oneness about this story in which to be is at least to be two. This fragmentation terrifies by outraging ableist hopes of independence, singularity, and autonomy.

As with "Mirrors of Chartres Street," then, in this story reflections bound off reflective surfaces, provoking a similar welter of mixed emotional responses. George as both friend and rival elicits a sharper response from this story's narrator than the other's, but this narrator too hides just outside the reader's ken just as he (or his leg) hides in the bushes jeering. The big difference comes in the narrator being the wounded and disabled figure in this story, and the rage and competition he feels come from a position of inferiority instead of superiority. Again, I find it important to see these reflections also snaking back to Faulkner's own sense of self, which includes always haunting in the background the Old Colonel, Faulkner's own originary identical reflected other. The Old Colonel may also be seen as a kind of leg or column for the novelist, an absence who is a constant overwhelming presence. In light of this connection, it is especially interesting that the novelist's deformation of his own name could well be read as a prosthetic—the letter "u" added to provide completion, a kind of "you" acknowledged and incorporated for the achievement of wholeness that is merely a tenuous holding together of disagreeing parts.

Faulkner expands these reflective processes into a more extensive if not more complicated arrangement in his first novel, *Soldiers' Pay.* Here again the biographical features emerge: the title is propitious, given the Old Colonel's history with disability pensions, and Clifford E. Wulfman well links the great-grandson's alleged wounding with that of Donald Mahon's in the novel. As Wulfman notes, the great-grandson not only limped upon returning from Canada but also told some people he had a steel plate in his head. Mahon's head is wounded truly (strange to write in the warp of actually wounded characters and real-life people who pretended to be so), and he is dying, as the novel transpires largely over the course of his last days. He returns home in the care of Joe Gilligan, a fellow soldier who takes him into his keeping, and his wound and imminent death become the catalysts that drives the novel's action.

The novel's significance regarding disability lies overwhelmingly in its presentation of ableist-framed responses to Mahon's wounding. Faulkner launches into the dynamics that whip into swirling melee around the largely static and unresponsive Mahon right away on the train ride where Gilligan together with an untried cadet named Julian Lowe encounter Mahon and later Margaret Powers. Faulkner establishes a clever triangle disabled (unwittingly) by the disabled character himself, for both Gilligan and Lowe instantly fall in love with Margaret but find themselves paired outside of their own triangle by Margaret's sympathy with Mahon. Although Faulkner's writing ability may not have yet matured in this novel, his deft shifting of dynamics among this foursome bears note: Gilligan and Margaret soon bond in sympathy with Mahon while Lowe sees himself in competition with Mahon for Margaret—a competition he feels he cannot possibly win. If Mahon resembles the play-acting Faulkner's wounded-veteran act, Lowe likely displays Faulkner's true anxieties. While Margaret's patronizing dismissal apparently does not replicate Estelle's apparently more conflicted breaking off her relationship with Faulkner to marry another, it takes little imagination to see a lovelorn Billy Faulkner in Cadet Lowe. Likewise, the young Cadet Faulkner who never fought surely must have seethed as Lowe does, "To be him, to have gotten wings, but to have his scar too!" (34). His jealousy coupled with his sensing Margaret to be in love with Mahon drives Lowe to pine for the ultimate disablement, "I would have been killed there if I could, or wounded like him [. . .]" (39).

Faulkner himself sees the dangerous petulance in such disability mythologizing, having his narrator rhapsodize, "But what was death to Cadet Lowe, except something true and grand and sad? He saw a tomb, open, and himself in boots and belt and pilot's wings on his breast, a wound stripe. . . . What more could one ask of Fate?" (39). The final sentence places the proper cloak of irony around the comments, but the passage is more significant when viewed as an early note in a score on the various faces of ugliness shaped by the ideology of ability.

One of the ugliest of these faces for many readers is surely that of Cecily Saunders, the girl Mahon left behind in Georgia. Faulkner establishes more triangles with Cecily as a part, whether she is actively competing with Margaret for Mahon, unwittingly competing with Emmy, or finds herself caught between Mahon and George Farr. Each of these triangulations keys into ableist fantasies hobbled by Mahon's status as severely disabled. However much her regional identity might have been made to stigmatize Cecily, Faulkner avoids doing so: in the context of the novel, she and her family represent a distinctly unmarked middle-class respectable status. While she might rebel against it in her flirtatious behavior and sexual adventurousness—her father asks her if "nice girls sit around half-naked" (102)—she nevertheless knows nothing less than commitment to maintaining that status in her marriage. Her disgust and horror at Mahon's scar even take on enough strength to dissuade her from the otherwise enviable and romantic position of marrying a war hero, an inducement that tempts her before she realizes the severity of the wound itself. Where Mahon once represented middle-class status, now George Farr seems more appealing; as Gilligan says, "Fellow's got money, I hear, and no particular brains" (243), although the ever perspicacious Margaret assures him that

Cecily regrets having deprived herself in the end of the chance to be a war widow. It may be difficult to sympathize with the spoiled Cecily, but in taking a broad view of the situation it can be argued that she is pressed into a gamut of gambles by the deeply operating ideology of ability, and however frivolous she seems the necessity of making the right guesses and moves carry very real consequences in her implied quest to succeed as a woman of optimum social worth. Whether commendable or not, Cecily lives according to her full and unquestioned indoctrination with the ideology of ability and can be seen as taking an active role in assuring a non-stigmatized future, choosing the very able George as her mate. Lest her situation be too quickly dismissed, the tenuousness of her status shows through in the chorus-like comments of "The Town": "That girl . . . time she was took in hand by somebody. Running around town nearly nekkid. Good thing he's blind, aint it? Guess she hopes he'll stay blind, too" (209).

Faulkner himself may not seek to deprive Cecily of all sympathy, but his juxtaposing her with Emmy contributes to the negative connotations surrounding her. Janaurius Jones often refers to Emmy as Cinderella, whom she in many ways is not (she never claims her Prince Charming Mahon), yet the fairy tale aura surrounding both her and Jones the faun informs Cecily's image as well. In all her melodramatic repulsion with Mahon's scar, she emerges as a character straight out of a Grimm brothers fairy tale, a failed beauty to Mahon the beast, her interior ugliness a betrayal of her beautiful exterior. She is a very conventional character in this respect, as Margaret is the conventional beauty who *does* love the disabled man. Cecily's response represents one common normate sexual response to disability, and her revulsion at Mahon's scar—her initial response a melodramatic faint—Faulkner exaggerates to the point that it raises her to a quintessential embracer of ableism.

The "good" characters in the novel on the other hand maintain that status partly by their attitude toward disability (one gets the sense that the Caddy Compson–like Cecily might have redeemed herself by sharing the later-created character's sympathy with disabled people). Again, Margaret's obsessive martyr-driven sympathy with Mahon along with her kindly if condescending treatment of Lowe and (less condescendingly) Gilligan install her in the moral center of the novel. Her active and successful efforts toward orchestrating the lives of Mahon and everyone around him ironically lift her even above Rector Mahon as an agent of benevolence, confirming the "power" signified in her last name and all she does. Gilligan's sympathetic interaction with Mahon along with his generally likeable nature also put him in a positive category. In Gilligan, Faulkner conjures another mirror reflecting his own image not as lovelorn cadet but as rebuffed but still-loyal lover and friend; where Cadet Faulkner might romance other ladies in the wake of his jilting and subsequent war experience, hometown Faulkner remained at Estelle's beck and call. Both Margaret and Gilligan, along with other disability-sympathizing characters, nevertheless also display what can be taken as a disturbing general concern with their own affairs. Haunting her constant thoughts of Mahon are memories of her own dead husband, and Gilligan's motives for hanging around are lashed tightly to Margaret and his hopes of possessing her. Even Rector Mahon's preoccupations tend to veer from his wounded son. I point this out not to hold characters or real-life people to some impossible standard—no condition of another can be expected to keep one's attention to complete exclusion of self—but rather to note Faulkner's placement of his disabled character as being relevantly irrelevant.

Concerning Mahon and his wound, it is clear that in this early phase in Faulkner's career he is fascinated with ways wounds can both literally and figuratively fragment the body, but with Mahon's wound, Faulkner explores a different kind of visibility from that in "Mirrors of Chartres Street" and "The Leg." Perhaps because of his awareness of the possibilities for counterfeiting leg injuries, Faulkner presents the scar as an irrefutable mark of trauma. A killing-off and mangling of tissue, Mahon's scar represents an inescapable inscription that validates the less-provable blindness also resulting from the injury. Unlike Faulkner and his great-grandfather, Mahon clearly lacks any desire or intention to hoodwink those around him. Yet his blindness is something they are unsure about that requires the confirmation of medical experts. Not so the scar, which in turn horrifies Mrs. Burney, endears Margaret Powers, confuses Cecily Saunders, enrages Julian Lowe, depresses Joe Gilligan, and fascinates young Robert Saunders. It defines a place within the space of Mahon's face, its evocative power coming from its placement on a space that largely does most of the work in establishing familiarity, since one might well be identified by the way one walks but the face certifies recognition. For the characters who knew Mahon before the wounding, the scar disrupts the face familiar to them, fragmenting it into familiar and unfamiliar parts, with the tension generated by the memories evoked by the familiar and the shock brought by the unfamiliar provoking the varied responses tinged by their own internal make-ups and anxieties.

To whatever extent Faulkner both in this text and in his own life capitalized on the romanticization of wounding, he also shows that the truly wounded person or character's own experience is far from wonderful. Mahon has little grasp of the doings around him, no real idea of the emotions and attractions his scar generates. Faulkner could have been more detailed, more relentless, more scatological as he would be later in presenting disabled people, but he makes clear Mahon's immobility and the monotony of his life as a disabled person. We do not get much of Mahon's perspective—Faulkner's focus rests too much on the experiences and attitudes of the abled, the soldiers' pay ironically poor even from the narrator, in terms of narrative attention—but Faulkner at least gestures to its existence to show how little ableist viewpoints and concerns can have to do with disabled people's actual experiences and situations, the ways, again, a disabled body can so readily be made to serve as a mirror to reflect the panoplied preoccupations of people identifying/self-identifying as normal.

When Faulkner finally got around to creating characters that closely resemble those in his own family—including the great-grandfather—it is not surprising that disability from war wounds as well as other causes plays a significant role: the Sartoris family in *Flags in the Dust* is full of aches and pains. In the novel, Faulkner foregrounds infirmity in remarkably prescient ways for a youth whose days of illness lay before him. Partly, the Sartorises' many physical difficulties serve a metaphorical function: long an empowered family of the old order, they face a changed environment of new science and economics that disables them in ways their impairments symbolize. Beyond these things, though, this novel that Faulkner saw as the germ of his apocrypha features many elements of disability and abnormality that appear throughout his career.

Before enumerating the details of disability, literal and otherwise, among the Sartorises and those closely associated with them, I would note some of the disabled figures woven into the novel's descriptive thread. One of these appears when young Bayard arrives at home and encounters old Bayard sitting on the porch; as young Bayard talks about his brother John's death when his plane is shot down in the war, "[l]ocust drifted up in sweet gusts, and the crickets and frogs were clear and monotonous as pipes blown drowsily by an idiot boy" (576). I will be focusing on the so-called "idiot" characters in the next part of the body of this book, and I do not want to over-reach in reading significance into this quickly drawn image. Still, in this novel written just before the one featuring Faulkner's most famous "idiot," the evocation of a meaningless arbitrary sound connected with cognitive disability is striking. It is a figuration that seeks the sublime in disabledness, for Faulkner seems to want to approximate a kind of terrible aural beauty powerful in its lack of order or control. The connection here again is with animality, with the "idiot" standing on the border of human and animal constructs.

Another arresting disabled figure appears as an actual character. Again, young Bayard is present in a situation in which sound is connected with disability. As he walks on the square, he encounters "[a]gainst the wall squatting a blind negro beggar with a guitar and a wire form holding a mouthorgan to his lips, [who] patterned the background of smells and sounds with a plaintive reiteration of rich monotonous chords, rhythmic as a mathematical formula but without music" (638). Here again a disabled person creates non-signifying sound, although in this case it is ordered and mathematical instead of disorganized and wild like the idiot boy's sound. Both cases include that word "monotonous," which again can be read in relation to the human-animal border as a marker of unreason signifying an animal construct. Unlike the idiot boy, whose lack of racial markings presumably presents him as white in Faulkner's logic, this African American character leaps from the background as a character also positioned on race and gender borders. He wears a kind of fake military uniform—"filthy khaki with a corporal's stripes on one sleeve and a crookedly-sewn Boy Scout emblem on the other, and on his breast a button commemorating the fourth Liberty Loan and a small metal brooch bearing two gold stars, obviously intended for female adornment" (639). The description's implications haunt on multiple levels: the blind man might be trying to present himself as an injured soldier, but a fake one with military decorations as fake as his author's. The uniform seems also a bid for whiteness in a novel that accords authentic, serious warrior status to white men; a reader may not be off the mark in reading pathos into the veteran Caspey, but it is clear that his military experience cannot mitigate against his blackness for the Sartorises.

Just as the pseudo-military-garbed blind black beggar is a caricature of Caspey and the young William Faulkner, so he grotesquely mirrors young Bayard, who in turn can be seen as representing his author. Bayard interacts with the man, giving him a coin. Faulkner describes the encounter: "Bayard sought a coin in his pocket, and the beggar sensed his approach and his tune became a single repeated chord but without a break in the rhythm and the meaningless strains of the mouthorgan, his left hand dropped groping a little to the cup and read the coin in a single motion, then once more the guitar and mouthorgan resumed their monotonous patter" (639).

The tableau is Lacanian broken-down, Hegel-short-circuited, disabled by a mutual blindness, with the beggar having no idea who has given the money and Bayard presumably unaware of his similarity to the man. The beggar's race illuminates Aunt Jenny Du Pre's calling Bayard an Indian (602); she does so apparently to describe his uncouth ways in polite society, and in terms both of behavior and social interaction he outrages white aristocratic mores. Bayard and the man also resemble each other as types of beggars, the latter for money, the former for emotions, experiences, danger. Neither fits well into the standard labor structures of their environment, much like Caspey, who had "returned to his native land a total loss, sociologically speaking, with a definite disinclination toward labor, honest or otherwise, and two honorable wounds incurred in a razor-hedge crap game" (588–89). Neither seems to profess gratitude in a conventional sense. Obviously, the scene realigns that in "Mirrors of Chartres" to view the ostensibly normal white observer and the disabled figure marked either by literal or figurative blackness and animalness from a third-person vantage. Here again Faulkner demonstrates an awareness of economics of and in relation to disability—he would again present a coin as a conspicuous object in the context of disability in *As I Lay Dying.*

Although there are other vivid background (at times foreground) elements of disability that take their places in the overall tapestry of pain in the novel I will discuss later, I would make my transition to the foreground proper via the character Simon Strother, who represents a bridge from these background disability elements to the novel's main and Fa(u)lkner-like family, the Sartorises. This black character holds an important job with the Sartorises, yet it is a position moving toward the social periphery and ultimately extinction. As the driver for the family, he enjoys a level of privilege, albeit one a number of the younger generation of African Americans distain, especially Caspey. As an old man, Simon has a "mis'ry in de back" (562) and a disabling fear of automobiles, physical and metaphorical kinds of disablement that combine with the social and labor disablement of his race in early twentieth-century Mississippi. He thereby emerges as a symbolic figure who keys into the vanishing-world theme of the novel as a conductor of the dying aristocracy's ailments in a manner similar to the blind beggar's mirroring young Bayard. Positioning black characters in such a way is not original to Faulkner, but using pain and fear as disabling markers to whatever degree is the world of a writer of disability. Like many white southern writers before him—most notably Thomas Nelson Page—Faulkner's faithful black retainers occupy both background and foreground, a figure not altogether controllable for the author or the white aristocracy. Certainly Simon has a mind of his own.

The Sartorises themselves are undergoing the painful shift to dispossession emblematized in Simon's "unemployment" resulting from old Bayard's riding in the automobile. They maintain an outmoded sense of normality and ability. For example, Jenny Du Pre resembles Faulkner's mother in her obsession with posture, and the role of the body's orientation and attitude represent class. Aunt Jenny is described as having "cold affability, and with her delicate replica of the Sartoris nose and that straight grenadier's back of hers which gave the pass for erectness to only one back in town—that of her nephew Bayard—she stood at the steps" (565). In the words of Blotner, Faulkner's mother "sometimes appeared arrogant, brusque and self-assured, like the Old Colonel" (18) and told her eldest "You've got a back just like the Old Colonel, but you've got to be a better man than he was" (19). The class and race pride and potency implied in this erect-back value speak to an ideal of bodily abnormality and ability itself plugged into a vanishing social hierarchy, the last echoes of which *Flags in the Dust* is determined to examine if not enjoy.

Of course, the bulk of the ability-disability problems devolves on the Sartoris men, toward whom Aunt Jenny has such a love-hate attitude. As has been well documented, Faulkner models these men on real-life Falkner men, including himself. Caught in both a changing environment and their own disabling destructive habits, the Faulkner and Sartoris men display what James Watson has described as "sensory confusion and dissociation, a literal self-fragmentation fully appropriate to his preceding sense of self-dissolution" (4–5). This business of "self-dissolution" becomes particularly noticeable in young Bayard, who most obviously parallels Faulkner the novelist himself. Although less dramatically than the autobiographical David in "The Leg," young Bayard seems to suffer from some degree of posttraumatic stress disorder. The first mention of him in the novel is revealing: Simon tells old Bayard that he saw the young man: "Jumped off de wrong side and lit out th'ough de woods. [. . .] Wouldn't even git off at de dee-po [. . .]. De dee-po his own folks built. Jumpin' offen de bline side like a hobo. He never even had no sojer-clothes. Jes a suit, lak a drummer er somethin'. And when I 'members dem shiny boots and dem light yaller pants and dat 'ere double-jinted backin'-up strop he wo' home las' year. . . . [. . .] Cunnel, you reckon dem war folks is done somethin' ter him?" (546). To this monologue, Old Bayard replies, "What do you mean? [. . .] Is he lame?" (546). Latent in the question is the larger question of "lameness" and all it signifies about masculine potency, a concern that haunts the young Faulkner spurned by his childhood sweetheart and struggling to compete with a legend bearing his own name.

Wracked with grief over his brother's death, young Bayard seeks to assuage his survivor's guilt with life-threatening activities. Immediately after encountering the beggar, Bayard starts drinking with McCallum and soon ominously states, "I've been good too damn long" (643). Inebriated, he goes to ride a powerful unbroken stallion that promptly throws him. After bandaging his head, Dr. Peabody sends him off toward home with V. K.

Suratt and a young man named Hub, who stop along the way to drink more moonshine (these events eerily foreshadow Faulkner's own future with horses and drinking). The occasion represents a social-class breakdown for Suratt, who takes Bayard's drinking with working-class people such as himself and Hub as a sign of good character. After sobering up back at the restaurant in town, the proprietor of which tells Bayard, "You'll kill yourself" (657), Bayard, Hub, and a man named Mitch go to get Bayard's car, at which point they drink again and find a band of black musicians to serenade Narcissa. Not long after this night, Bayard wrecks the car, resulting in his being placed in a body cast that renders him motionless. Disabled thusly, he must lie passively as Narcissa reads to him. He remains passive and quiet and feminized for a time after he heals. But eventually the guilt leads him to another ride in a plane, which crashes and kills him.

Aunt Jenny sees the disabling behavioral tendencies in young Bayard not as a localized war-wounding but an underlying personality element passing through generations of Sartoris men. This behavioral disability is a curious thing—an ultimately confining blend of "glamor" and "disastrousness" predictably part of "a game outmoded and played with pawns shaped too late and to an old dead pattern" (875). The condition apparently originates three generations back from young Bayard and John to the old Colonel John Sartoris and the original Bayard. Again, this generational pattern harkens back to Faulkner's family. Although Colonel John Sartoris is most closely modeled on Colonel Falkner—it is his gravesite statue that resembles the one of the Old Colonel in Ripley—the "Carolina" Bayard actually makes the ill-fated anchovy run that resembles the great-grandfather's injurious excursion in Mexico. However, when John Sartoris does appear in connection with disability, he is actually faking injury. Old man Will Falls tells of Colonel Sartoris's clever escape from a Yankee patrol when a group of northern soldiers confront him on his front gallery asking for Colonel John Sartoris; he explains that the colonel is away fighting. They order him to lead the way to where the colonel is, which he gets up to do. In Falls's own words, the colonel "got up slowly and tole 'em to let 'im git his shoes and walkin' stick, and limped into the house, leavin' 'em a-settin' thar waiting" but "Soon's he was out of sight he run" (558). Of course, Faulkner casts Colonel Sartoris's performance in a totally different light and context from that which Thomas Hindman alleged of Colonel Falkner: this ruse is an adroit maneuver of wartime rather than a deliberate conning of the government under the noses of knowing civilians. At the same time, though, it is worth mentioning that Colonel Sartoris otherwise looks and behaves in the ways Hindman describes Colonel Falkner looking and behaving, for John Sartoris "was always giving dinners, and balls too on occasion [. . .]. For with his frank love of pageantry, as well as his innate sensibility, he liked to surround himself with an atmosphere of scent and delicate garments and food and music" (586). One imagines that John was very much given to jumping and dancing with a tight fashionable shoe.

Arguably the fulcrum figure in the Sartoris generations is old Bayard. His age has brought certain disabilities to him, the most conspicuous being his deafness. Not having fought in a war, Bayard has no wounds, but the deafness serves a significant function, presented at the very beginning of his characterization when he and Will Falls are talking "into one another's deafness" (543). Viewed in the context of the Sartorises' falling from prominence in a changed world, Bayard's deafness represents his inability or refusal to attend cultural changes. This aspect of the deafness becomes salient in the context of his other physical abnormalities when Jenny takes him to Dr. Alford concerning the wen on his face. Dr. Alford is "in the youthful indeterminate thirties; a newcomer to the town and nephew of an old resident. He had made a fine record in medical school and was of a personable exterior, but there was a sort of preoccupied dignity, a sort of erudite and cold unillusion regarding mankind, about him that precluded the easy intimacy of a small town [. . .]" (618). As both a progressive and an outsider, Dr. Alford represents the antithesis of Bayard (things that bring Jenny's respect), and he promptly declares that the wen should be removed before it becomes cancerous. At this point, Dr. Lucius Quintus Peabody appears, much to Jenny's chagrin, whisking Bayard away from Dr. Alford, examining him, and explaining that while the wen is probably not dangerous Bayard's heart is weak and likely to fail him, especially if he keeps riding in the car with young Bayard. Dr. Peabody too represents the old order, which Jenny despises, and while he tells her not to let Will Falls put his famous salve on the wen he also admits that "Will has done some curious things with that salve of his" (621).

In this sequence of events and those that follow, Faulkner sets up old Bayard's body as registering a number of cultural and narrative elements within the novel's framework of old versus new science and culture. On one hand, the lines between old and new are drawn clearly along the wall of Bayard's deafness. Where he is deaf to new medical developments he can somehow hear Will Falls, whom he lets treat him with the salve. Jenny and Dr. Alford take Bayard to see a specialist in Memphis, and when he touches the now "blackened excrescence" Will has treated, "the thing came off in his fingers, leaving on old Bayard's withered but unblemished cheek a round spot of skin rosy and fair as any baby's" (745). The point seems to be that Bayard's deafness is a shield to protect him from the new order. I might add here that Blotner sees Faulkner himself as having harbored a similar view of medical technology, writing of his balking at "surgical fusion" to cure his broken back in his fifties, "A man with a lifelong distrust of doctors, he treated his farm animals with turpentine, and for humans, favored Epsom salts or silver nitrate. The most he would agree to was a few days of bed rest in a hospital" (555). It was not long after this moment that Faulkner may have had electroshock therapy and undergone psychiatric examination, but he generally seems to have conformed to a kind of old Bayard "deafness" concerning medical technological advancement.

At the same time, though, old Bayard's deafness (like Faulkner's "deafness" later in life) is not absolute. He is not, for instance, oblivious to all new technological developments. However much he may be a typical male Sartoris, as Jenny might put it, young Bayard's association with planes and cars casts him as being also part of the new order, and old Bayard's fascination with the car and refusal to quit riding in it finally bring the demise of a heart attack Dr. Peabody predicts. Leaving the protection of deafness to change kills old Bayard, and this chink in the armor can well be read as a commentary on the inevitable and deadly breakdown of the old before the march of the new. The flexibility of his deafness registers another significant aspect of disability too, which Faulkner introduces early on—that is, a kind of disablement created by the confines of physical existence itself. Returning to the novel's opening scene, it is clear that Colonel John Sartoris, "Freed as he was of time and flesh [is . . .] far more palpable than the two old men cemented by a common deafness to a dead period and so drawn thin by the slow attenuation of days" (543). The description continues: "John Sartoris seemed to loom still in the room, above and about his son, with his bearded, hawklike face, so that as old Bayard sat with his crossed feet propped against the corner of the cold hearth, holding [John's] pipe in his hand, it seemed to him that he could hear his father's breathing even, as though that other were so much more palpable than mere transiently articulated clay as to even penetrate into the utter-most citadel of silence in which his son lived" (543).

The moment is remarkable for the remembered sound of breathing's ability to overcome Bayard's deafness and the concept that a legendary, Colonel Falkner–like existence after death achieves an abledness finally more powerful than a disabled physical life. The pipe stands as the material marker signifying both the limited physical and unlimited nonphysical lives, bearing as it does John's teeth marks, "the very print of his ineradicable bones as though enduring in stone, like the creatures of that prehistorical day that were too grandly conceived and executed either to exist very long or to vanish utterly when dead from an earth shaped and furnished for punier things" (543). There is an inescapable dialectic of the material and nonmaterial, physical and nonphysical in this passage and in the legacy of Colonel Falkner and his disability upon which it and so much of the great-grandson's writing of disability are built. It is the same dialectic that drives the phantom sensations and actual material prosthetic limbs of "The Leg" as well as the legend and grave statue of Colonel Falkner described as Colonel John Sartoris's quoted at the beginning of this part of the body of the text. It is a dialectic aimed at immortality as ultimate ability, the great material monument of which appears in the form of art—for William Cuthbert Faulkner, writing.

By this point in his life and career the great-grandson was poised to come into his own, creating characters with less overtly biographical connections, for which he would become famous. Not that the biographical context ceases to be significant, for it lurks within Faulkner's disabled characters in vital ways as does the context of southern identity generally. In fact, that biographical context can be discerned in characters that represent the very antithesis of the Sartoris-Faulkner clans.

IV

In a short biographical essay, Franklin E. Moak makes an intriguing assertion about the extent to which the great-grandson channeled the Old Colonel and his legacy in his writing. Moak writes:

> There are general similarities between the Sartoris and Falkner families. They remain general because there is also a decisive difference between the two family lines. While in *Sartoris* the fictional family is viewed as aristocracy which, through generations, decays, the story of the Falkner family is one of success. J. W. T. Falkner, for example, the Young Colonel, far exceeded his father: he was a bank trustee and legislator. Murry Falkner served as business manager and financial secretary of the University of Mississippi and lived in what was probably the best faculty house on campus. His son, William, won the Nobel Prize for Literature.
>
> Still, the decadence which is portrayed in *Sartoris* is not unlike what the Falkners in Oxford certainly observed from day to day and year to year. It is only natural that as some of the Snopeses began to strive for and achieve upward mobility, their values, particularly the negative ones, became more visible, thus giving the illusion of increasing decadence among the older families, when, in fact, that decadence had been for generations built into that stratum of society. A case could be made for the decadence, as William Faulkner viewed it through the Sartoris family, that existed in the early part of the twentieth century being merely the residue of an earlier period when the social and economic structure of the Old South was undergoing radical changes. The alternative to decay would be a kind of ruthless ambition or a kind of shoddiness that Faulkner portrays in the Snopes family. It is just possible, in fact, that the other side of Colonel Falkner would be the making of a Snopes tradition [. . .]. (266)

Moak rather puzzlingly goes on to write that this "Snopes tradition" is "something that William Faulkner did not live long enough to pursue" (266). Oddly, Moak seems to have missed the very brilliant thrust of his own observation . . . that the rise of the Snopeses *is* a portrait of the rise of the Sartorises, a relation of a different phase in the history of that rise, and that the Snopes trilogy is a Snopes tradition that will eventually come to the same end as that of the Sartorises.

I am particularly impressed with the idea that the Old Colonel may be seen as the inspiration not only for Colonel Sartoris and the decaying aristocracy the Sartoris family represents but also, incredibly enough, the aristocracy's arch enemy—the rising nouveaux riche, the rapacious Snopeses: the wrenching, squeezing, scraping poor white bane of Yoknapatawpha. The diametric opposite of the highfalutin Sartorises. It seems counterintuitive even to suggest, but as Moak shows, the Old Colonel himself was just as much if not more a man on the rise, more an investor in railroads dealing in fluid capital than a hard-nosed conservative holding on to the old order. Instead of being a descendent of a moneyed pillar of the community, the young William Falkner was an outlander come to make good on the frontier. He was much more a figure along the lines of Sut Lovingood, a poor white. In short, Moak's observations imply that it is a fitting legacy that the Old Colonel's statue should be surrounded by the likes of *Pizza Hut* and *Jitney Jungle* . . . he may well have brought such establishments to town himself had he lived a hundred more years.

Moak's observation takes on particular luminosity when considering the business of wounding, for we find two conspicuously wounded figures bookending the Snopes lineage. The first is Ab Snopes, the man who was shot by none other than Colonel John Sartoris himself. Ab, the "Father Abraham" of the family (as one early attempt to tell his story is entitled), who was shot in the leg for trying "to steal [Sartoris's] claybank riding stallion during the War" (*The Hamlet* 744), and who limps for the rest of his life. The oedipal implications become all the more obvious when we consider that "Barn Burning," the first work in which Ab appears, details the coming of age of his son Colonel Sartoris Snopes, named after the very man who wounded him.

Ab is most immediately recognizable in the story "Barn Burning" as a classic disabled villain. Leonard Kriegel offers a schematization of crippledness in literary representation, identifying three types of literary mobility-impaired people: the Demonic Cripple, the Charity Cripple, and the Realistic Cripple. The first of these is exemplified in the character of Captain Ahab, as Kriegel thinks of this character as someone who has had something to done to him or her which maddens this character. Kriegel offers the following comments on this kind of figure.

> The Demonic Cripple burns with his need for vengeance. Because of this, he frightens the "normals." He is too singular, too focused on his wound and the needs that wound has created within him. As a consequence, he threatens to unleash a rage so powerful that it will bring everything down in its wake. The visible fact of his infirmity offers no solace to other men, because he himself is quite willing to accept the idea that his accident is his essence. His image becomes, both for him and the "normals," the very center of the threat he embodies. His accident gnaws at his insides, leaves him no peace, consumes his every breathing moment, so that he cuts himself off from ordinary pursuits and ordinary men. Indeed, he despises their values, questions their successes, holds fast to the center of his own existence, the wound he so visibly bears. (26)

Ab (Ahab?) Snopes is decidedly a Demonic Cripple in his initial appearance, but as Faulkner prods deeper into his character in subsequent works we can read him in more complicated ways. In *The Unvanquished* he emerges as a poor man simply trying to get by, a person unconcerned about the political sides of the war and more concerned about trying to better his lot in life. By the appearance of *The Hamlet* we see Ratliff presenting him as practically a victim, saying, "Ab aint naturally mean. He's just soured [. . . because of] that business during the War. When he wasn't bothering nobody, not harming or helping either side, just tending to his own business, which was profit and horses—things which never even heard of such a thing as a political conviction—when here comes somebody that never even owned the horses even and shot him in the heel. And that saved him" (756).

In recasting Ab as a victim, Faulkner greatly broadens the significance of his wound, turning it into a sign that might be productively read in the context of what Jeffrey C. Alexander calls "cultural trauma." In his essay "Towards a Theory of Cultural Trauma" Alexander observes that "the gap between the event and representation can be conceived as the 'trauma process'" (11). For Alexander, trauma is not the wounding event itself but rather the developed and contextualized narrative of the wound. Ultimately, Alexander sees trauma as not a personal but a collective cultural phenomenon, explaining that trauma "is the result of [. . .] acute discomfort entering into the core of the collectivity's sense of its own identity. Collective actors 'decide' to represent social pain as a fundamental threat to their sense of who they are, where they came from, and where they want to go" (10). This representation finds creation and facilitation in the hands of what Alexander identifies as "carrier groups" such as those who generate media, literature, art, and education (11). Alexander goes on to trace the typical development of the trauma as narrative.

This "cultural trauma" relates to Faulkner's South on at least two very obvious and significant levels. First, there is slavery, an event that itself registers as a cultural trauma in two different ways. On one hand, as Ron Eyerman argues, building on Alexander's work, slavery functions to define African American identity; on the other hand, it serves as what Bernhard Giesen calls the "trauma of perpetrators," shaping white southern identity in the guilt of having committed crimes against humanity. The second level on which cultural trauma functions in Faulkner's South is that of the trauma of defeat, which has defined white southern culture in ways that Wolfgang Schivelbusch details in relation to French and German military defeats in his volume entitled *The Culture of Defeat: On National Trauma, Mourning, and Recovery.* The Faulkner character who perhaps best exemplifies all of these forms of cultural trauma is Quentin Compson, the young aristocrat burdened with the tragedies of slavery, miscegenation, incest, and defeat who finally finds himself reduced to the tortured final words in *Absalom, Absalom!* regarding the South: "I dont hate it! I dont hate it!" (303).

Ab's wound however signifies a different cultural trauma. The narrative of the impudent, wronged, and seething poor white man was not a new one when Faulkner began recording the Snopes saga: the Southwest Humorists and later Thomas Nelson Page created their own versions of Ab Snopes–type characters in the South both before and after the Civil War. When Ab appears in "Barn Burning," *The Hamlet,* and in *The Unvanquished,* his role is a distinctly subservient one in relation to the aristocratic Sartorises. And the traumatized cultural category of which Ab is a part and which the specific narrative of the wound his body bears is that of poor whiteness. Like a plate of ham and eggs in which the chicken was involved but the ham was committed, the poor white Ab was involved in the Civil War but far from committed to its racial or regional politics. The pragmatist later hunted down for his shady economic forays by white aristocrats and

African Americans alike, Ab finally rates, like so many of his white-trash ilk, lowest on the social scale.

In the end, Ab Snopes's receiving a wound is significant because the cultural group of which he is a part has neither an identifying mark nor a primal moment from which to generate a narrative of trauma. His whiteness cannot count against him as the blackness of an African American can (however non-biological racial constructs may be), and while Theodore Allen and Grace Elizabeth Hale have aptly described the development of poor whiteness as a racial construct as well as a class distinction, poor-white history follows a somewhat different trajectory from that of aristocratic white or African American southerners. From the beginning of their presence as a political entity in the 1830s, poor white men and women have steadily risen from one level of degradation to a higher one; dubious though this development may be, it is nevertheless distinct from the aristocratic history of wealth destroyed by civil war and subsequent decay or from the African American history of enslavement, depravation of civil rights, and march toward true equality. But Ab Snopes does have a mark, a wound. And he is "soured," or traumatized. What seems significant about Ab in terms of history and trauma is that his wound represents the visible narrative of the invisible other. Ab, with his limp, functions as a conspicuous sign of a narrative of poor-white oppression, and V. K. Ratliff serves as a "carrier" who conveys the narrative that articulates the social pain of poor-white history. This significance represents a very different imagining and inscribing of Colonel Falkner's wound—as is clear in his biography, he had no illustrious military family or history of education to draw on. His wounding came from a lone act, possibly of disobedience and even self-destruction, that may well be read as being prompted by class anxiety and the desire for upward mobility.

The striking thing about a wound is that it should emerge as a perversely positive entity, the catalyst that facilitates the generation of narratives ultimately meant to solidify culture. In an attempt to make profit, Ab Snopes gets shot by his social superior and as a result, in the words of Ratliff, "Ab had to withdraw his allegiance to the Sartorises" (*The Hamlet* 756). In his hurt and anger, he silently rebels against that social class, tromping on Major de Spain's rug (de Spain another aristocrat) and burning the barns on the land he works. At length, he goes to work for Jody Varner in the small rural community of Frenchman's Bend; Varner plans to scam Snopes himself by letting the man and his family work the land until the harvest and then threaten to tell the authorities that Snopes is a barn burner, believing that once Snopes realizes the game is up and he will be ratted out he will leave town. But things do not work out that way; instead, Ab's son Flem plays Jody just as Jody plans to play Ab, and from this start Flem systematically takes over not only Frenchman's Bend but Jefferson and before long the Snopeses rule all of Yoknapatawpha County. Flem is a pure capitalist where Yoknapatawpha economics tend to work on a modified version of capitalism the rules of which are dictated more by family connections than by profit margin. While it is true that Flem comes to an ignoble end (shot by his own relative in a house formerly owned by de Spains—the family his father worked for in "Barn Burning"), he and his family represent the rise of poor-white political power (Flem's cousin, Clarence, actually gets elected to the state senate in a poor-white political power move reminiscent of Huey Long's). And so Ab's ugly wound emerges as the piece of grit around which has grown the pearl of the Snopes-dominated community, an alternative view of this recuperative depiction of disability as ultimately empowering as it was for the Old Colonel although not in the same way or with the same results in terms of the two men's ultimate social standings.

The other wounded Snopes character I want to discuss is unique on two counts that both seem at first glance to break with the diserent biographical Fa(u)lkner-Sartoris-Snopes lineage I have been looking at. The character is a woman, and her wound has nothing to do with either her legs or her back. That Linda Snopes Kohl is remarkably different on so many levels from anyone or anything Yoknapatawpha County has seen before is clear from Charles "Chick" Mallison's astonished comments about her at the beginning of the "Linda" section of *The Mansion.* Quoting those comments as a block should pretty well establish the parameters of the subject under examination.

> You aint even going to meet the train? [. . .] Not just a new girl coming to town [. . .] but a wounded female war veteran. Well, maybe not a new girl [. . .]. Maybe that's the wrong word. In fact maybe "new" is the wrong word all the way round. Not a new girl in Jefferson, because she was born and

> raised here. And even if she was a new girl in Jefferson or new anywhere else once, that would be just once because no matter how new you might have been anywhere once, you wouldn't be very new anywhere any more after you went to Spain with a Greenwich Village poet to fight Hitler. That is, not after the kind of Greenwich Village poet that would get you both blown up by a shell anyhow. That is, provided you were a girl. So just say, not only an old girl that used to be new, coming back to Jefferson, but the first girl old or new either that Jefferson ever had to come back home wounded from away. Men soldiers yes, of course yes. But this is the first female girl soldier we ever had, not to mention one actually wounded by the enemy. Naturally we dont include rape for the main reason that we aint talking about rape. [. . .] I'd think you'd have the whole town down there at the depot to meet her. Out of simply sympathetic interest, not to mention pity: a girl that went all the way to Spain to a war and the best she got out of it was to lose her husband and have both eardrums busted by a shell. (429).

Unpacking Chick's comments is a study in watching the water-wall of Faulkner's career-long male privileging crest if not curl forward and crash. Chick could well be speaking of his own creator when expressing how unthinkable a wounded woman veteran is to the male mind of Yoknapatawpha. Even his mercilessly recursive way of talking cannot get in the way enough to stifle the power of Linda's existence. She so outrages and upsets the construct of "normal woman" in this northeast Mississippi town that Chick cannot even figure out what kind of language to use to describe her. New, old, an old girl that used to be new—all terms that struggle to discern and define her *use* as frantically as (in Ratliff's imagination) clothes once strove to cover her mother Eula's Amazonian body. As Keith Louise Fulton argues, Linda defies the mythology of women as symbols of nature to be controlled, land to be plowed. That she stands outside of normal male Yoknapatawphan notions of the use of women's bodies resounds in her being war-wounded and not raped, a kind of wounding that merely comes with a misogynistic imagining of a woman's utility. Chick's final sentence reads as rather a weak effort to try and box her back in to a "normal" woman's use and place as he suggests she deserves pity for losing her husband as well as her hearing. But the comment rings hollow even to Chick in light of his realization that her husband himself was not a Yoknapatawpha ideal of a caregiver and that even their marriage had hardly been normal.

What Chick and everyone else discovers upon Linda's return is that she is not only deaf but that when she tries to speak her voice emerges as a harsh quacking sound. It is a curious maneuver on Faulkner's part: one of the most memorable things in the novel and in fact all of Faulkner's work for me. It seems a strike at the very defying of norms she achieves, a price that must be paid to the male gatekeepers of Yoknapatawpha, perhaps even to Faulkner himself. It is a nuanced disability—as Claire Crabtree points out, although "Linda's beauty is marred by her inability to speak except in a toneless 'duck quack,' her maiming also serves to intensify her significance. Faulkner's animal metaphor suggests a reduction of her power, but also a spiritualizing of it" (533). This spiritualizing is frightening to male characters, and Crabtree notes that while "Chick's description of the potential of sexual love is perhaps the most positive characterization of sexual union in all of Faulkner" the fact is that "'ecstasy and excitement' would be marred by Linda's injury, by her inability to speak in a way appropriate to romance or even to humanness, as here again disability produces animalization. More important in Chick's considerations, however, is not Linda's injury but the injury imposed by her power on the male lover" (536). Pursuing this give and take, positive and negative vacillation in the male response to the disabled Linda, Crabtree writes, that "in Linda, Faulkner creates an admirable, idealistic woman character capable of moral choice and sacrifice. Linda is unpossessible, an object of a somehow purified desire" (537). At the same time, Crabtree acknowledges that "the violence Chick abjures is simply reversed; if the male does not treat the woman with sexual violence, she will instead suck out a part of his being and leave only a husk or shell" (538).

Crabtree's ideas concatenate nicely with Diane Roberts's reading of Linda. "Linda is a freak, an anomaly" (170), Roberts says outright. But she goes on to write,

> Unnatural as she is, "monster" though she is called, there is something great about Linda. Her voice does, as Hee Kang says, break "the 'vault of silence'" that has reduced and bound women in this world. That "ugly" quacking insists on being heard, even though she cannot hear what is said in reply, an inversion, maybe a parody, of the quiet woman whose real voice is ignored by the world of men as they make of her a fantasy figure, writing her story for her as Gavin tries to write words *for* Linda—words she usually rejects.

> Her quacking (Faulkner's description an attempt to link her, however grotesquely, to some residual animal quality?), her "mannishness," so unlike her ultrafeminine mother, and her intelligence overturn all the inscribed feminine of Faulkner's earlier work. (175).

All the above points to something clearly derived from the Colonel's legacy, which is the way that a disability can be turned into an empowering thing. Linda is the flower of the Snopes ambition. She can attain social status that even her remarkable father can hold only as a façade, and in so doing herself embodies the self-made *man* the Old Colonel sought to be. Linda and her disability link back to the Fa(u)lkner-Sartoris heritage in other ways too. Her wound seems of a different kind, but she parallels Old Bayard: his deafness and weakening heart symbolizing the dying heartbeat of the old order and his generation's inability to hear the pounding footsteps of change and progress. Now, years later, Linda, who is a product of that tide and change and in fact a member of the tribe that wrought these things, is herself deaf, but deaf in the other direction, retroactive, able to turn away from the voices of the male-dominated past.

For the record, Faulkner even allows the business of fraud and disability to creep into the narrative. When making his way to Jefferson to kill Flem, Mink Snopes talks to a man he is staying with the night before going on into town. Mink's object is to make sure he has his facts straight. Regarding Linda's deafness he says "A woman in a war. She must have ever body fooled good. I've knowed them like that myself. She jest makes claims and ever body around is too polite to call her a liar. Likely she can hear ever bit as good as you and me" (689–90). Mink is trying to make sure he will be able to shoot Flem without Linda hearing it, and he succeeds in getting a rise out of the man, who confirms the truth of her deafness. I mention the matter, again, because of the fraud that haunts about wounds in Faulkner's ancestry, life, and writing.

The final overall observation I would make is that from the great-grandfather's individualistic struggling to Linda Snopes's quacking something changed and developed in Faulkner's writing. Linda's wound is the most easily faked, yet it is more real than his great-grandfather's apparently were and his own certainly could ever have been. Other strong women can be found in Faulkner's oeuvre, including Jenny Du Pre, but few of them are quite like Linda, for Linda seems to represent a voice altogether more distinct even than the one Faulkner envisioned in his Nobel Prize speech and that the old general speaks of in *A Fable.* That "puny inexhaustible voice" was *man's;* the quacking voice of *The Mansion* is a *woman's.* If we compare the wounded runner's status at the end of *A Fable* with that of Linda's, we see in fact the contrast between an ineffectual voice and an effectual one, for the disfigured and—it should be acknowledged—crippled runner is only one man screaming his futile complaints against a system, where Linda is able to coordinate the men around her in a successive campaign marked by interdependency. In fact, however true Crabtree's observation that Linda reverses male violence, her presence and power differ in the way that Irigiraray argues feminine being differs. The Old Colonel presented himself as *one,* the individual, the hero. Linda is more than one, operating through multiple channels, through multiple manipulations, in a dependency that is not one of subservience but equality, in ways even superiority, to the men who help execute her plot to have her father killed. At times she communicates with a notepad, at times without it. Hers is a fluid existence that marks an accomplishment for Faulkner not only in presenting women characters but also disabled ones. She is in this respect one of the crowning achievements of a career spent exploring a legacy of disability set into motion before he was even born.

From: disfaulkstudies@listserv.net
Date: Sept 25, 2010
Subject: Smart Idiots in Faulkner

In a recent book exploring the role of the "idiot" in Faulkner's writing, Frédérique Spill sees Faulkner's alterity in self-presentation as being a way for him to perform or at least participate in the performance of the role of "idiot." Spill's argument is that Faulkner himself had experienced the kind of marginalization that Benjy Compson <benjy33@jefferson.com> and other such characters experience partly because he himself was acting in a way that created such perception, a self-imposed "idiocy" as it were, different from an externally imposed disability status such as that created by, say, his childhood backbrace. To Spill's thinking, Faulkner performed an "idiot" role throughout his life in the sense that he often pretended to be simply an ignorant farmer who miraculously wrote amazing fiction. Spill amusedly writes,

> He was loath all his life to be away too long from Oxford, Mississippi, to the point of neuralgia in the creation of Yoknapatawpha County, where he lies today in the company of a bottle of Bourbon perched on his tomb as a floral arrangement. Faulkner had always so well succeeded in passing for an idiot that the critic, disconcerted, often asks, by what miracle this was the same man who composed novels that were inspired by genius. (translation mine 17)
>
> {Il répugna toute sa vie à s'éloigner trop longtemps d'Oxford, Mississippi, point néuralgique de la creation du comté du Yoknapatawpha, où il repose aujourd'hui en compagnie d'une bouteille de Bourbon, juchée sur sa tombe en guise d'arrangement floral. Faulkner a, pour ainsi dire, toujours tellement bien réussi à se faire passer

> pour an idiot que la critique, déconcertée, s'est souvent demandé par quel miracle c'était bien le meme homme qui composait des romans aussi manifestement inspires par le genie. (17)}

With Spill's comments I would move from one kind of biographical approach to a more attenuated one in examining Faulkner's engagement with disability. Connection has been drawn between Faulkner's "idiot" characters and a cognitively disabled neighbor of Faulkner's childhood named Edwin Chandler, providing at least one example of the writer's encountering such an individual. But as Spill shows Faulkner's concept and experience of "idiocy" was something he also internalized. In fact, discussing his "idiot" means in part witnessing an extreme prodding of Lacanian self-other dialectic through a fragmentation he first explores in "The Leg," with its efforts to understand the alienation of experience in the context of disablement, with specific attention to a prosthetic situation. Attendant upon the Faulknerian idiot character stand the large issues of fiction's contribution to understanding of and even approaches, clinically as well as socially speaking, to disability.

The Faulknerian idiot is cognitively disabled in ways that affect his (all of these characters are male) speech, his movements, his emotions, and the look in his eye. This character seems to lack a level of intelligence that would make him normal, with the peculiarities of his intelligence generally being seen by readers and other characters as inferior. Such a character first appears in another of Faulkner's sketches from his New Orleans apprenticeship days entitled "The Kingdom of God." The description of the nameless disabled character in this story sets the precedent well. Faulkner writes that the "face of the sitting man was vague and dull and loose-lipped, and his eyes were clear and blue as cornflowers, and utterly vacant of thought; he sat a shapeless, dirty lump, life without mind, an organism without intellect. Yet always in his slobbering, vacuous face were his two eyes of a heart-shaking blue, and gripped tightly in one fist was a narcissus" (*New Orleans Sketches* 55). There is a strong inner-outer complementarity to this description: the character's appearance is meant to convey his internal characteristics, his cognitive disability.

Faulkner would play with this complementarity in later incarnations of the character, disrupting its synergy at major points. In "The Kingdom of God," this character whom another character calls "loony" and the narrator refers to as an idiot precipitates the story's action, although not through any awareness of his own. He must go with his brother while the latter loads illegal liquor. When the third man in the group upsets the "idiot" by breaking his flower, the latter begins to scream. This screaming brings the normal brother to the rescue as he leaves off his distracting the police from the loading of the liquor to attack the culprit. Once the flower is fixed, the disabled brother stops howling, but in the meantime the police have spotted the illegal cargo and take the men into custody. Although the normal brother calls the disabled one "a kind of luck piece" (56), he turns out to be bad luck for the accomplishment of their crime.

Much like Donald Mahon in *Soldiers' Pay*, the cognitively disabled character in the story serves as a prop, a kind of ticking bomb that serves Faulkner in constructing narrative. Faulkner would rework this automaton-like character into Jim Bond in *Absalom, Absalom!* The final progeny of Thomas Sutpen's hoped-for dynasty, the mixed-race Bond is "*hulking slack-mouthed saddle-colored*" (177). As Sutpen's Hundred burns to the ground, "there was only the sound of the idiot negro left" (309). These characters in both stories are passive. Their very presence as disabled people brings about actions and response, but they themselves do not act. Bond, particularly, assumes a symbolic presence, containing in his body if not his "blood" the pieces of Sutpen's and the South's villainous and tragic racial oppression and the horrible things its accompanying attitudes have led to.

At the same time, the cognitively disabled character in "The Kingdom of God" anticipates a character who is both passive in the dealings of other characters but active as a narrator. An informed reader can hardly envision the idiot brother's blue eyes without thinking of those much more famous eyes of Benjy Compson. Less well known but very similar in appearance and also cognitively disabled is Ike Snopes <ikemope@frenchmansbend.org>. Along with these two stands another character who differs in that he tends to register a normate outer appearance and is not cognitively disabled in the same ways but who nevertheless closely resembles Benjy and Ike. All three of these characters are vital ones in the texts in which they appear, revealing much about Faulkner's art and the intricacies of representation of disability generally.

Benjy:

I am of course responding to much published critical work when writing about these characters, some of which I will address here and others I cite in the note at the back of this book. In dealing with the first section of *The Sound and the Fury* "narrated" by ~~Maury~~ Benjamin "Benjy" Compson I am dealing with one of the sacred cows of Faulkner's canon. It has received a great deal of strong textual analysis, and yet there are certain questions that have not been asked regarding it, perhaps because it has so dazzled readers as a technical achievement. I want to ask some of those questions—questions about just what it means that Faulkner employs a cognitively disabled narrator, about what exactly this narrative does, what its functions are, and most importantly about what Benjy the character may be up to in his narrative and in the action of the novel. Following these questions leads to some unorthodox answers: specifically that this text, so long celebrated as a radical experiment, is actually surprisingly conservative in its essential form as well as in its sociopolitical assertions and assumptions, and that Benjy Compson, Faulkner's most famous disabled person, is not only much more intellectually complex but also more prescient, conscious, and skillful as a narrativist than Faulkner scholarship has conventionally thought.

My reexamination of Benjy is in part a response to Maria Truchan-Tataryn's 2005 article, "Textual Abuse: Faulkner's Benjy." Truchan-Tataryn lowers the boom on Faulkner and Faulkner critics alike for their treatment of Benjy, and I would like to quote liberally to present her premises. She opines that the "critical cliché" that "the first section of *The Sound and the Fury* is applauded as Faulkner's most remarkable achievement" has "resisted notice" (159). Faulkner criticism, she writes, "manifests not only an overwhelming admiration for the unparalleled skill with which Faulkner produced such a plausible idiot in the character of Benjamin Compson but also an ignorance of changing concepts of disability" (163). "Despite the growth of a global disability rights movement and the development of the discipline of disability studies in the humanities," she continues, "the figure of Benjy's mindless, voiceless subhumanity continues to resonate through Faulknerian scholarship as a believable portrait of disability" (160). Scholars thus need to take another look at Faulkner's famous "idiot," for "[r]einterpreting Benjy, problematizing the idea of absence of thought in a conscious individual as a realistic possibility, invites a deeper consideration of the need to engage with diversity in human experience and its textual representation" (172). Ultimately, she explains, Benjy "illuminates not the (lack of) subjectivity of a cognitively impaired individual in lived experience but rather imaginings projected upon a population denied agency and voice by authors of public policy as well as narrative texts" (163). Truchan-Tataryn's "intent is not to add yet another variation to the established themes of explication of Benjy but to demonstrate how unquestioning acceptance of him as a successful representation of intellectual disability reveals an underlying ableism in the literary critical endeavor and an academic acquiescence to dated socio-cultural constructions of disability" (159–60).

Truchan-Tataryn's criticism of Faulkner scholars is in some ways harsh—there are many powerful, original, and sensitive studies of Benjy—but the ableism at the heart of literary criticism is quite real and obviously a matter of concern to this author. Also, the matter of authenticity she puts her finger on—projected imaginings versus what a cognitively disabled person is really (not) thinking—lies very much at the heart of disability representation. Representing cognitive disability puts especial stress on authenticity in that there exists an implication of fundamental alterity and even otherness in the possibility that an individual not the self has a mind and/or emotions that simply function differently. The kind of paradoxical recognition of the self in the other that simultaneously depends upon the separateness and alterity of the other necessary in creating as it were recognizable human (or in many cases even nonhuman) characters falters when trying to grasp an identity foundationally different. To the postmodern eye the layering of fictions required to establish a strategic universality that enables such recognition brings the crisis of authenticity and authentification endemic to the Lacanian exchange that is a character to the brink. Faulkner often unabashedly acknowledged that people tell their own stories, and that of course goes for authors too, but with Benjy perhaps Faulkner really is asking too much. Unless of course a character can somehow transcend his or her text, which is to transcend her or his very ontology, and exist within the ontology of a living, breathing biologically, socially, politically, and culturally imbricated being in the world. Prodding this kind of material makes for a messy undertaking. Taking my cue from Truchan-Tataryn, I want to roll up my sleeves and delve into the ways these issues of disability and representation find embodiment and en-mind-ment in Benjy.

To begin my exploration of these matters I first want to point out that Faulkner realizes Benjy's marginalization on several levels and hinges that marginalization on the recognition of his disability. When Benjy's name is changed from Maury to Benjamin, Versh explains that he has been turned into a "bluegum," which is something that in this novel happens to black people. Benjy's crossing over into African American spaces on Easter Sunday testifies to the fact that he "belongs" in the marginal space of the other. It is precisely his disability that signals the name change, the transformation into "bluegum," and his being placed among African Americans, making him "less" white, perhaps even nonwhite, in the sense that lower-class white people are raced as well as classed as "poor white trash." A case could also be made that he is marginalized as *too white*: with "dead looking and hairless" skin, "pale and fine" hair, and eyes "of the pale sweet blue of cornflowers," Benjy seems conspicuous for his paleness (1088), something like the albino in Erskine Caldwell's *God's Little Acre*. His silence, broken only by animal-like moans, mixes with his conspicuous whiteness to render him a figure of a kind of horror not unlike the terror associated with whiteness in the context of Poe's *The Narrative of Arthur Gordon Pym*. Finally, his disability emasculates him practically (he does not possess the power of other white men) and literally (by way of his castration), so that he is further marginalized in terms of gender. Whether figured as nonwhite, too-white, feminine, or even an animal (compared as he is to a horse and a "trained bear"), Benjy is a figure of inaccessible otherness in the novel.

Which is, of course, what makes Benjy's section so radically daring—Faulkner invades the inviolate, and lets us come with him. The chiaroscuro effect of juxtaposing what is "inside" Benjy's head with what his "outside" looks like is what allows Faulkner to up the ante in his own game. Almost as if he were writing his own review, Faulkner wants his readers to know just how good he is and so gives us an image of Benjy later in the text designed to shock the reader as it does Donald M. Kartiganer, who writes that the image seems that of "another idiot from another novel" (339). Like a good magician, Faulkner has enhanced the contrast between the possible and the impossible, the expected and unexpected, the concealed and unconcealed. He gives us the "secret" world of Benjy Compson's consciousness—life as seen by the inscrutable other. And what is perhaps *most* shocking about it is what Leslie Fiedler argues is so shocking about the "freak," which is the possibility that the self resides in the other marked by human variation, that ultimately the freak is "one of us." Put another way, the surprise of Benjy's monologue is that he is so *normal.* Not just normal, in fact, but more—an accomplished architect of narrative.

In order to delineate the specific beams and braces of Benjy's narrative, I want to revisit the text of the first section of *The Sound and the Fury* as if it is *the first time I am reading it.* Recapturing the experiences of reading any book is as difficult and perhaps as impossible as new historical critics have taught us that any attempt to peer through the lens of the present into the past is. But whether it is possible to remember my own first reading accurately or not, I would like to try and (re)create as best I can an initial engagement with the text and try to ponder the questions that could arise in an uninitiated reader's mind. At the very least, the questions I want to raise in such a process will hopefully help illuminate aspects of the text that years of lauding it have tended to obscure. One of the foremost of these aspects is just how wrought this text actually is. In many ways, it is a skillfully constructed narrative masquerading as a mess.

As with any text, the opening paragraphs of Benjy's section establish the rules of reading peculiar to this specific text. To quote, for the sake of convenience:

> Through the fence, between the curling flower spaces, I could see them hitting. They were coming toward where the flag was and I went along the fence. Luster was hunting in the grass by the flower tree. They took the flag out, and they were hitting. Then they put the flag back and they went to the table, and he hit and the other hit. Then they went on, and I went along the fence. Luster came away from the flower tree and we went along the fence and they stopped and we stopped and I looked through the fence while Luster was hunting in the grass.
>
> "Here, caddie." He hit. They went away across the pasture. I held to the fence and watched them going away. (879)

These paragraphs present the reader with certain clues. Immediately, the reader can see that there is a first-person narrator whose sense of identity is consolidated enough for that person to offer up utterance from the position of the self. The person is an "I." Also from the first sentence, we can see that the narrator is capable of presenting a somewhat sophisticatedly modified lexical unit: "the curling flower spaces." The image is strikingly visual, strikingly poetic.

Another thing that happens beginning in the first sentence and continuing throughout the first paragraph is that the reader is bombarded with a series of pronouns without antecedents and verbs with no direct objects. "They" who are being watched through the "flower spaces" of the "flower tree" are "hitting" while "Luster" is "hunting." Who are "they" and what are they "hitting"? Who is "Luster" and what is he "hunting"? We are not kept in suspense long: already we know that "they" are approaching a "flag," and when we find out that "they" "took the flag out," then we can pretty safely assume that they are golfing. Indeed, we quickly hear one of the "hitters" say, "Here, caddie," and we can now set our mind at ease that this initial mystery is solved. It is a little strange that the narrator should call the golf course a pasture, but it is early in the text and the reader is probably in a hurry to get to the bottom of the mystery of the narrator and of the story the narrator has to tell.

But what effect has been established at this point on the reader? Accepted knowledge says that Faulkner presented all of these awkward lexical items to show that the narrator lacks the sophistication to present facilitative engaging prose. And Faulkner teachers as well as Faulkner scholars have often promoted the notion that the various linguistic codes are to be interpreted as signs of cognitive disability. It may be, however, that such approaches overdetermine the text's implied reader, for it could just as well be argued that the text's refusal to be engaging and facilitative actually makes it highly engaging precisely because of that refusal. There is not necessarily any reason to think after the first two paragraphs of *The Sound and the Fury* that we are not in the hands of a capable, if unreliable, narrator. Moreover, the first eight paragraphs give us what is, in terms of formatting, a very traditional narrative. The paragraphs are organized logically and organically. The dialogue is properly set apart in quotes. No words are misspelled. There is no reason to think there is anything unusual about this text beyond the language being odd. But "odd" in stream-of-consciousness writing is not unexpected—James Joyce's *Portrait of the Artist as Young Man* features similar strategies—and does not necessarily signal a mind that is abnormal. :-)

However, the third paragraph alerts us to the fact that something is indeed not quite "normal." Luster speaks, letting the cat out of the bag in his usual trickster way, saying, "Listen at you, now. [. . .] Aint you something, thirty three years old, going on that way. After I done went all the way to town to buy you that cake. Hush up that moaning. Aint you going to help me find that quarter so I can go to the show tonight" (879). Again Faulkner presents a situation with Lacanian undertones—the problem of recognition of the self in the reflected image of the other—for we find out something about who the "I" of the text is from another character. We now know that the narrator is thirty-three and moaning and that this person Luster has enough authority to tell the person to "hush up" and to order the narrator around to help find the quarter (which Luster apparently is hunting). Arguably, the first shock might come to the first-time reader *now* and *not* in section four. The juxtaposition of the age of thirty-three and the action of moaning are clues that immediately signal the narrator as disabled, and this revelation causes the reader to review what she already knows about the narrator. The credibility of the text now changes because the narrator's reliability is brought into serious doubt, which forces the reader to look to other characters for help in negotiating what is "really going on" in the text.

The foregoing might have seemed like a bit of unnecessary "lemon-squeezing" reader response–led close analysis (as Terry Eagleton says of William Empson's style), but I wanted to slow down the reading enough to consider some things. First, I think it worth noting again that stream of consciousness as a style in itself does not automatically signify cognitive disability—certainly it does not later in Quentin's monologue. Second, I would state again that, if Luster does not drop these hints here in the third paragraph, then there is no reason for the reader to make the assumption of disability; if anything, the reader may well be impressed with the deftness of the narrative even if it is not as sophisticated as his suicide brother's. Third, there is a strong possibility that, if the other characters do not inform us of Benjy's condition, then the entire first section of the novel could seem not only that of a "normal" person but also a text that is extremely contrived: the reader is supposed to buy the idea that a person over the course of only a day is going to think about his entire life in a way that presents a narrative that is both discernable and meaningful, that the person's mind is going to jump *involuntarily* from point to point in a way that will add up to a story full of metaphorical and narrative significance.

In fact, the text *is* contrived in a way that has a somewhat conventional precedent, for its strategies of plot construction, radical as they seem, actually replicate in principle the forms of plotting found in classic detective fiction. Peter Hühn discusses the layers of narrative and secrecy in the plotting of detective fiction, writing that "the basic internal tension in a classic-formula [mystery/detective] novel can be conceptualized as a contest between [. . .] *writing* stories and *reading* stories. The criminal devises or *writes* the story of his criminal act, at the same time, however, protecting it against reading, composing it as an unreadable secret story" while the "detective attempts to decipher its traces and interpret their meaning, and in the end he succeeds in *reading* it" (40–41). What Faulkner gives us in Benjy's section is a chronological narrative that is scrambled and hence a variation on the same kinds of plots that appear in Arthur Conan Doyle stories or Agatha Christie novels. In this regard, the text is essentially nothing new; rather, it is an established form skillfully repackaged. What makes this repackaging different is that where classic detective fiction features a sleuth who puts the mixed-up pieces of the criminal's narrative together, Faulkner forces his readers to be the sleuths. :-/

But a significant question to raise at this point is, who exactly is supposed to have forged this narrative—Benjy or Faulkner? And to what extent does the suspension of disbelief apply in the case of the first section of *The Sound and the Fury*? Robert Dale Parker's answer is that Faulkner is the architect and that we can and must believe in his speaking for Benjy. He writes that in "the first section of *The Sound and the Fury* we get not Benjy's language, although we might sometimes call it that as a convenient shorthand, but . . . Benjy uses no language at all. In the absence of language, the more unusual words are no more radical a distortion or illusion than the use of any language to render a state of no language—what he *would* say, if he *could* say, *which he can't*. Faulkner has it both ways, forging an impossible compromise that evokes a lack of language and a minimum of intellectual complexity while also maximizing the representation of those incapacities through language" (28–29). The "impossible compromise" Parker recognizes sounds something akin to Spivak's doomed subaltern who cannot speak because she is caught between the language of the center and that of the margin. But Parker does not permit Benjy the nobility even of "subaltern" status, for he is simply *unable to speak*. For

Parker, the narrative is Faulkner's. And Parker is certainly not alone in his reading. Not a few readers tend to cut Faulkner some slack: after all, they would well argue, he is *approximating* what may be in Benjy's mind.

If we choose to read the monologue as Faulkner's "speaking for" Benjy, then we should consider what function Benjy serves. By the light of this perspective, Faulkner does not come off very well in making the decision to colonize the body and mind of a disabled person. Indeed, read this way Faulkner appears as the precocious and maybe even reckless person we know he could be, a show-off using a clever gimmick. Meanwhile, Benjy and his thoughts become the very instance of "projected imaginings" of a normate upon a nonnormate body that Truchan-Tataryn complains about. Benjy becomes Faulkner's ventriloquist dummy, a figure set up not really so much to explore his own thoughts and feelings but rather to tell the puppeteer's story. Testifying to this notion of Benjy-as-functioning-character is that Benjy's story is very lean: it serves its narrative function well and has none of the kind of subterfuge and excess that could have come closer to realizing his narrative as mere sound and fury. One can imagine Joyce writing this book and throwing in passages entirely unconnected to the storyline. But even Benjy's red herrings serve to propel the narrative, however obscurely.

In short, if we read Faulkner as the architect of Benjy's section, then as Truchan-Tataryn suggests, we learn much more about Faulkner and what he thinks and what he thinks Benjy thinks than we do about what the person born Maury Compson thinks. The specific thing we can learn about Faulkner is that his radical experiment is in yet another way tempered by a *conservative* design, for he employs a narrative tactic that uses Benjy as the other only to confirm and normalize the rhetoric of the self. Benjy stands in as a Counterfeit Other constructed for the express purpose of further marginalizing true others and reifying the narrative of the empowered, which is in this case the white southern aristocratic patriarchy. One of the most curious things about critical reception of his monologue is that scholars have not considered other ways Faulkner might have represented Benjy's thoughts. Ben Wasson might have tried to "normalize"

Benjy's time-jumps (which Faulkner promptly reversed), but these days we rarely question Faulkner's representational approach, even though he could well have shown mental disability in the text through misspelling, odd arrangement of text on the page, poor punctuation, and so on. Yet, as noted before, Benjy's style is impeccable. He does not misspell words, he puts quotation marks in the proper places, and however limited his vocabulary may be, he speaks the language of the other Compsons, which is to say that he speaks in the "invisible" dialect of the center, the white aristocratic patriarchy. This language stands in marked contrast, on the other hand, to the way that the speech of African Americans is represented: they speak in dialect, with Versh worrying about Benjy "[h]olding onto that ahun gate" (881) and Luster telling Quentin's boyfriend from the show that he does not "ricklick" seeing him before (915). Indeed, although Luster chastises Benjy for not playing "in the branch like folks" and complains that "folks dont like to look at a looney" (891), Benjy is, on the inside at least, much more one of the folks than is Luster.

The effect of Faulkner's endowing Benjy with the speech of the aristocracy is that the focus of the novel's tragedy remains securely focused on the Compson family. I do not mean to imply that Faulkner entirely excludes the African Americans in the novel from the weighty tragedy that pervades it, although I am not sure that Faulkner was as thoroughly aware of the extent of their role in it when he first wrote and published the novel as he was when he later produced the Compson appendix. But instead of realizing a way that Benjy as a hybrid figure who is both a white Compson and a black bluegum (as well as a poor white aristocrat and feminized man) can articulate a hybrid poetics, Faulkner makes him a spokesperson for empowered whiteness, who confirms rather than subverts traditional southern race and class hierarchy.

There was ample precedent among white aristocratic southern writers for this maneuver of creating an othered figure who stands in to speak the narrative of the self, most notably in the early frame narratives of Thomas Nelson Page. Collected in his volume *In Ole Virginia, Or, Marse Chan and Other Stories*, these stories use African American narrators to confirm the pro-slavery image of the Old South as a nostalgic place of peaceful race relations. For example, Sam, the ex-slave who tells the story of Master Channing in "Marse Chan," says to the white auditor, who is the narrator of the frame, that the years of slavery before the Civil War "wuz good ole times [. . .] the bes' Sam ever see! [. . .] Dyar warn' no trouble nor nothin'" (10). The logic of the story is that if this slave says that the old days were good old days then they really must have been good old days. The black narrators of Page's fiction are white aristocratic southerners masquerading as black ex-slaves, and their function is to normalize slavery and the slave-owners' propagated image of race relations as harmonious. Page's ultimate goal is to present an effective reconciliation romance, which envisions a reunion of northern and southern *whites* after the Civil War. As Karen A. Keely explains, in order to bring about these narrative visions of reconciliation, writers such as Page "deliberately ignored [. . .] the exploited and devastated black bodies on which such romance is built" (643).

There is a problem, however, with such a depiction of the other—the problem of authenticity. I am not referring to some naive notion of authenticity but rather the crisis of authenticity, or the need to instill and distill as much authority and believability in a character as possible. The crisis is that, when the other is employed in the furtherance of the desires of the self in fiction, the other must be endowed with the aura of authenticity in order for that figure's arguments to be convincing. The Counterfeit Other cannot be seen as being too obviously fake, else the entire project implodes because it is seen as the ventriloquism it is. Of course, in some ways this problem is easily solved by using marginal figures about whom the center knows very little anyway. The level of knowledge many target-audience northern white readers actually had about black people beyond minstrel stereotypes may have been generally limited enough for Page to pull off a believable act of puppeteering—not only does Ralph Ellison's *Invisible Man* retroactively attest to the "projected imaginings" of white people on black bodies, but this phenomenon is also confirmed in the fact that when Charles Chesnutt wrote stories designed to beat Page at his own game his white readers simply thought he was writing Page all over again, as Keith Byerman has noted. Turning to Faulkner, Truchan-Tataryn's very point is that he and his readers had such little understanding of disability that Benjy could be a convincing figure. Certainly Faulkner has stacked the deck, speaking for someone who cannot speak.

This crisis of authenticity ultimately allows these authors' Counterfeit Others to get out of control. It is as if because these writers do not "know" what in actuality black or disabled people are thinking they take extra measures to negotiate the authenticity of those characters. In Page's frame narratives, this crisis of authenticity emerges in his black narrators occasionally letting slip their secret *modus operandi*, revealing the possibility that their narratives of joyous ex-slave days may not be entirely truthful. These black people engage in a game of what they call "prodjickin,'" which is essentially a form of lying, a type of Signifyin[g] that, as I have elsewhere argued, is "a rhetorical strategy of harmless subversion the harmless nature of which is suspect yet convincing enough for the listener to overlook its threat" (Hagood, "Prodjickin'" 431). Thus Sam first appears talking to his former master's dog, saying "Yo' so sp'ilt yo' kyahn hardly walk. Jes' ez able to git over [the fence] as I is! Jes' like white folks—think cuz you's white and I's black, I got to wait on yo' all de time" (2). When Sam realizes that the white frame narrator has heard him talking to the dog that way, he says assures the white man that the dog "know I don' mean nothin' by what I sez. [. . .] He know I'se jes' prodjickin' wid 'im" (3). This strategy of double-speak is ostensibly contained in the benign situation of Sam's talking to the dog, but Sam admission of lying, or "prodjickin,'" has the effect of throwing everything else he says into a dubious light. Any thinking reader must wonder if his claims about how wonderful it is to be a slave are just more of his "prodjickin.'"

The perplexing thing about this "prodjickin'" in Page's stories is that one might wonder why he decided to include it as a performative strategy at all when he could have just had his narrators tell their proslavery narratives; again, the answer lies in the problem of authenticity. In his effort to create a convincing character who uses language and performative strategies that bear some verisimilitude to whatever it is that Page thinks of as authentic behavior of an African American man he somehow felt the need to include the man's conversation with the dog. Perhaps a late-nineteenth-century white southern aristocratic mentality—long accustomed to relegating African Americans and their perspectives—simply could not imagine a black person being subtle enough actually to lie to a white person about such a thing as prewar race relations. Or maybe the paternal attitude of the aristocracy was so deeply invested in its notion of the slave-and-master relationship in the U.S. South being pseudo-familial that it could not think that an ex-slave would betray that. Certainly in Page's writing there is a sharp distinction between "good" black people (ex-slaves who are "one of us" aristocratic whites—although not too much one of us) and "bad" black people who seek various types of independence. Whatever the case, the fact is that this prodjickin' opens a window not only upon these African Americans' "true" ideas but also on the secret machinery of the visible texts they (that is, Page) generate for whites to consume.

What might we learn if we consider how this same dynamic applies to the case of Benjamin Compson? What happens if we consider the first section of the novel to be not Faulkner "speaking for" the person christened Maury Compson but instead take it for what it purports to be: a true interior monologue? What if instead of yet again making the mistake of assuming that because Benjamin Compson's motor skills are impaired and that he is incapable of meaningful speech we consider the possibility that he *could* think the sort of sophisticated text attributed to him? What if we remember Derrida's insistence that there is nothing outside of text, that inscription is fundamental and antecedent to the logos? What if we consider the possibility that Benjy has his own motives that help him get out of Faulkner's control? lol

If we consider the first section of *The Sound and the Fury* in this light, then we find that Faulkner takes the opposite route of Page to achieve what is nevertheless the same effect. Specifically, the monologue of the first section is marked by a conspicuous *anti-authenticity*. To illustrate my point, I want to consider briefly what Gene Fant Jr. has referred to as "the novel's most famous linguistic pun" (104): the confusion of the signifier "caddie" with the phonetically identical signifier "Caddy." From the standpoint of authenticity, this device simply does not hold up: "caddie" just simply cannot be "caddie" in Benjy's mind. It must always be "Caddy," and a much more accurate rendering of that phoneme from Benjy's perspective is simply "Caddy," whether referring to golfing or to his sister. The whole point of the text and the device itself is that he cannot distinguish the difference between a "caddie" and "Caddy," or the monologue ceases to function according to its assumed rules.

Unless, of course, Benjamin Compson *does* know the difference between the two.

In sacrificing rather than overworking authenticity, Faulkner either intentionally or unintentionally introduces the possibility of Benjy's also working within his own secret machinery of textuality in a way that runs counter to the dynamics and assumptions of Faulkner's using him as a puppet. Intentionally or not, Faulkner gives us the possibility that Benjy is more prescient (and his cognitive disability even less quantifiable) than he has been seen as being by other characters as well as by readers. And this possibility leads the way to the further possibility that the great tragedy of Maury/Benjamin Compson is not that he is sadly and ironically confused by anything that sounds like the name of his sister but rather that the signifier itself (and the phoneme which he knows refers to the signifier) carries a much more complex set of meanings that are equally and just as deeply troubling and sad to him. Seen in this way, the signifier "Caddy" might be a very different kind of symbolic repository, the site wherein is focused Maury's frustration at his inability to articulate what is in fact a complex inner self. Consider, for example, just what sorts of dynamics are associated with the name "Caddy" beyond just its sound: toward the end of the monologue, Benjy remembers his mother talking to Caddy when they are children: "'Candace.' Mother said. 'I told you not to call him [Benjy]. It was bad enough when your father insisted on calling you by that silly nickname, and I will not have him called by one. Nicknames are vulgar. Only common people use them. Benjamin.' She said" (926).

Added to the other ways Benjy's name-change has marginalized him is this moral-tinged-with-class marginalization coming with Caddy's nicknaming him. Now he is "common." More importantly, so is Caddy, and Mrs. Compson's implying that Candace is herself "common," or vulgar, for having a nickname anticipates and highlights the labels of vulgarity applied to her later in life (and carries interesting implications about Mr. Compson). The very word "Caddy" contains the very aspersions cast upon Candace by her family, and there is every reason to believe that Benjy well understands exactly what his mother has said and its implications. In other words, the signifier "Caddy" evokes not just Benjy's love for his sister but his awareness of her marginalization, and even his own marginalization as a nicknamed person.

If we rethink Benjy's section by reexamining the text in terms of its complexity and considering how Benjy himself engages that complexity, then we find that he is "abnormal" in a very different sense than readers have generally thought. Scholars have long understood that Benjy's text is complex, and not a few first-time readers have abandoned it in disgust and frustration. But the consensus has generally been that Benjy is unconsciously complex, the complexity of his text arising from his impairments, which in turn impair the reading experience. I am suggesting, however, that however physically impaired he may be he is nevertheless consciously complex and is actually similar to another Faulkner character who constantly faces the threat of being sent to Jackson: Darl Bundren <darlb@yoknapatawpha.edu>. Part of Darl's abnormality is his uncanny ability to narrate with such power. The fact that he actually narrates his mother's death scene from miles away highlights the other extraordinary thing about him—that he can see things that others cannot. Although he is punished for his abnormality, it is a dramatic irony of *As I Lay Dying* that Darl's threat is essentially his greater ability. He knows too much, and he can present what he knows in devastating ways. If we think of Benjy in the same way, then he becomes abnormal not in the sense of being "lesser" than but "greater" than the norm—a skillful architect of a complex associative narrative. And our decoding of his text transforms into a much different sort of an enterprise that is in fact much truer to the actual functioning of the text: rather than decoders of a mess, we become assemblers of an elaborate and intentional puzzle.

This complex associative narrative in fact anticipates the internet's hyperlink model, and *The Sound and the Fury: A Hypertext Edition* uses the internet to demonstrate that functioning and even to "straighten" Benjy's section out. On this website, one can find the ways Benjy's section can be "unscrambled" and a narrative progression discerned. It is surely no accident, incidentally, that Truchan-Tataryn was one of the editors of this web-based edition and that she should write on Benjy's narrative acumen.

This possibility of intentionality resituates the locus of narrative control on Benjy rather than Faulkner, and the result is that all the deeply embedded white aristocratic attitudes become his own. He now becomes the dangerous figure many other characters perceive him to be, although not necessarily for the same reasons. Indeed, in light of Hühn's work, he now stands in as the "criminal" of the detective story, and this repositioning changes the status of certain characters, for where I earlier stated that Faulkner gives us no sleuths for *his* skillfully constructed secretive text, he does provide them for *Benjy's*. One is Caddy herself, who "more than anyone actively attempts to interpret Benjy's cries" (Roggenbuck 583). The other is Luster, an unreliable sleuth for an unreliable narrator. Hühn writes that added to the two layers of narrative in classic detective fiction is yet another secret layer of narrative, which is that "the *story* of his interpretation and reading process is also hidden from its readers" (41). Although Luster tells the man with the red tie that Benjy "cant tell what you saying. [. . .] He deef and dumb" (914), the fact is that Luster is well aware that Benjy can hear and understand when he says, "Beller. [. . .] Beller. You want something to beller about. All right, then. Caddy." he whispered. "Caddy. Beller now. Caddy" (919). It may be just too much coincidence that Dilsey promptly calls the two over and queries Luster as to what he has done, asking him, "Is you been projeckin with his graveyard" (920). Luster, the trickster with his own secret story in the tradition of the prodjickers of Page, well understands the quiet life of desperation led by his charge.

In constructing this reading of Benjy, I want to be careful not to fall into the very trap of projected imagining Truchan-Tataryn writes of. I believe Benjy's alterity remains intact. And his section is greater than the sum of its narrative parts. It is also steeped in modes of cognition, the smells, the sounds, the images that also define his being, understanding, and narrating. Faulkner mobilizes these many details to convey Benjy's ontology through his epistemology. Yet here again emerges the same crisis of authenticity representation. I would address this aspect of the crisis in Benjy actually by turning to Faulkner's second major "idiot" character.

Ike:

Although not as well-known to a general readership, Isaac "Ike" Snopes could well be Benjy Compson's twin. Certainly his character falls in line with the "idiot" character of Faulkner's work in general. The first description we get of him reveals someone uncannily resembling Benjy:

> the figure of a grown man but barefoot and in scant faded overalls which would have been about right for a fourteen-year-old boy, passing in the road below the gallery, dragging behind him on a string a wooden block with two snuff tins attached to its upper side, watching over his shoulder with complete absorption the dust it raised. As he passed the gallery he looked up and Ratliff saw the face too—the pale eyes which seemed to have no vision in them at all, the open drooling mouth encircled by a light fuzz of golden virgin beard" (*The Hamlet* 806).

For the sake of comparison, note the external description of Benjy from section four of *The Sound and the Fury:*

> [Benjy was] a big man who appeared to have been shaped of some substance whose particles would not or did not cohere to one another or to the frame which supported it. His skin was dead looking and hairless: dropsical too, he moved with a shambling gait like a trained bear. His hair was pale and fine. It had been brushed smoothly down up on his brow like that of children in daguerreo-

> types. His eyes were clear, of the pale sweet blue of cornflowers, his thick mouth hung open, drooling a little. [. . .] He sat loosely, utterly motionless save for his head, which made a continual bobbing sort of movement as he watched Dilsey with his sweet vague gaze as she moved about. (1088)

The order of presentation is reversed from that of Benjy's: where the latter first speaks to us and then is described externally later in the novel, Ike is first externally marked as disabled in the "Flem" section of *The Hamlet* while Faulkner does not give us something resembling Ike's perspective until later in "The Long Summer" section. Taking this presentation as it comes, as Faulkner gives it, we find Ike positioned very carefully in a story about turning the Faulkner world upside down. Ike emerges initially as something of a structurally and metaphorically functional character in the novel. Where Benjy is a plot device that narrates, Ike is at first only a plot device.

A noteworthy exchange attends Ike's first appearance in the novel described above. V. K. Ratliff has been explaining his plan to buy goods to sell in turn to a Yankee "goat-farmer," and he has just abruptly stopped because Flem walks out of the store and passes Ratliff and his listeners. Jody Varner is with Flem, and when Ratliff suggestively asks, "Aint you closing early, Jody?" the latter replies "That depends on what you call late" (806). It is a big warning about redefinition, which is an abundant process in Frenchman's Bend at the moment (it is tempting here to employ a Richard Goddenesque identification of a pun here—Frenchman's "Bend," where the rules are bent, where you cannot see around the bend). Ratliff has encountered plenty of these warnings already that business had changed, that things do not proceed according to "normal." Flem himself is bizarre-looking and -dressing, and his clan is an abnormal lot, from his disabled father to his fast-talking relative I.O. Yet Ratliff pays little attention to these warning signs in his self-confident—in fact, fatally arrogant—quest to be the man who bests Flem in a trade. Ratliff rather condescendingly says to Jody, "Maybe it is getting toward supper time" to which Bookwright, seeing what Ratliff cannot see—that Flem (who a later unnamed character says "don't even tell himself what he is up to. Not if he was laying in bed with himself in a empty house in the dark of the moon" [991]) has gotten wind of Ratliff's plan—tells Ratliff, "Then if I was you I'd go eat it and then go and buy my goats" (806).

But Ratliff has not yet learned to listen, merely replying that he figures he can wait and then starts to go on with his story when he notices Ike. "What's that?" he asks (806) and the above-quoted description follows. With this question, Ike's status as a "what" is hermetically sealed before even the most superficial kind of description is offered. After the reader sees Ike pass by, Bookwright says, "Another one of them" (806), meaning a Snopes. But Ratliff, too busy being cute, misunderstands and thinks Bookwright means another one of them you-fill-in-the-blank-epithet/slur-for-a-disabled-person. We then get another description: "Ratliff watched the creature as it went on—the thick thighs about to burst from the overalls, the mowing head turned backward over its shoulder, watching the dragging block" (806). In the next part of the book I will deal with the "stare" about which Garland-Thomson has provocatively written, but this is no staring encounter in the sense she describes in which a starer and staree experience and undertake a culturally and/or personally revisionary moment. This is instead pure voyeurism of a kind that grows increasingly uncomfortable as the novel progresses. Not that the voyeurism is not uncomfortable in itself, but "the thick thighs about to burst from the overalls" is a sexualized image not merely in its suggestiveness of this man's largeness in a certain area of his anatomy but also in its anticipation of Eula, whom Faulkner presents in this novel as being not much more intelligent than Ike and having an "incredible length of outrageously curved dangling leg and the bare section of thigh between dress and stocking-top looking as gigantically and profoundly naked as the dome of an observatory" (823).

So Ratliff misunderstands Bookwright. Ratliff quips, "And yet they tell us we was all made in His image," which Bookwright rejoins with "From some of the things I see here and there, maybe he was" (806). This evocation of divine-right of normality-as-construct is worth its own chapter and perhaps book, but in keeping with the lightsome spirit of the comments (which may itself deserve critique) I will merely point it out and note that the irony in Bookwright's retort is deft enough to invoke its own critique more eloquently than I can do in a thousand words. More relevant to the context of the moment in the novel is that Ratliff will not take the hint. After saying, in his eternally baffled and somewhat childlike way, "I dont know as I would believe that [Bookwright's strike against His image], even if I knowed it was true," he asks, "You mean he just showed up here one day?" (806). Once again Bookwright tries to tell him, "Why not? [. . .] He aint the first," to which Ratliff merely replies "Sho" and then adds "He would have to be somewhere," at which point we are given the news that the "creature, opposite Mrs Littlejohn's now, turned in the gate" (806–7). "'He sleeps in her barn,' another said. 'She feeds him. He does some work. She can talk to him some how'" (807). Apparently in his desire to believe in the goodness of folks, Ratliff says, "Maybe she's the one that was then" (807), meaning presumably that Mrs. Littlejohn was the one made in His image.

What Ratliff has misunderstood becomes painfully evident to him when he attempts to buy Flem's goats from him with "Snopes notes." When Ratliff presents Ike Snopes's notes, Flem goes out back to get the personage in question, and again Ratliff sees the "creature" from town described almost exactly as before only with additional details: "The mowing and bobbing head, the eyes which at some instant, some second once, had opened upon, been vouchsafed a glimpse of, the Gorgon-face of that primed injustice which man was not intended to look at face to face and had been blasted empty and clean forever of any thought, the slobbering mouth in its mist of soft gold hair" (810). The interesting thing is Ratliff's response. As soon as Flem retrieves Ike from the barn—the minute the latter emerges from there—"something black blew in [Ratliff], a suffocation, a sickness, nausea" (810). "'They should have told me!' he cried to himself. 'Somebody should have told me!'" at which point he remembers thinking "Why, he did! Bookwright did tell me. He said Another one" (810). Then

Ratliff's mind makes a defensive jump, seeking an explanation, an excuse: "It was because I have been sick, was slowed up, that I didn't—" (810). In fact, extensive mention *has* been made in the novel of Ratliff's sickness prior to this moment. The second section of the third chapter of the "Flem" part of the novel begins with "He had been sick and he showed it" (792) although only in his being thinner than usual while actually he looks "quite well, the smooth brow of his face not pallid but merely a few shades lighter, cleaner-looking; emanating in fact a sort of delicate robustness like some handy odorless infrequent woodland plant blooming into the actual heel of winter's snow" (793). His voice is also a little weaker, we are told, as he carries on with the droll men of Frenchmen's Bend. What his ailment was is not revealed, but he has apparently had an operation, prompting Bookwright to ask him, "What was it that Memphis fellow cut outen you anyway?" to which Ratliff replies "My pocket book [. . .] I reckon that's why he put me to sleep first" (794).

I must confess that I have never before made anything particularly out of Ratliff's being sick beyond it being a kind of excuse Faulkner provides for him to save face after being taken by Flem, a provision that Ratliff to his credit as an honorable person rejects. Reading with a sensibility of disability, however, I find Ratliff's temporary disability to be a deeper thing. Faulkner has Ratliff in this condition in the very same section of the text in which he introduces Ike, the *permanently* disabled person. Too coincidental not to suggest a deeper layer or layers of meaning. Indeed, reconsidering the Ratliff-Ike initial encounter, it strikes me that, however sympathetic Faulkner seems to be in providing an excuse for Ratliff's failure, he does not forget that, in his arrogance not only in his comments but in not taking especial care to allow for his temporary disablement, Ratiff has himself been an "idiot." Disability is no excuse in a Snopes world. Moreover, Ratliff's not understanding Bookwright's hinting undercuts even at the former's reliability in a manner reminiscent of the already-mentioned Darl Bundren. Like Darl, Ratliff is a skilled narrator—think of his tale about the Ab Snopes–Pat Stamper horse trade or the marvelous vision of Flem in Hell—yet he is, at least in his disabled state, not so dependable as he would seem.

Contrasting Ratliff as temporarily disabled and Ike as permanently so is fruitful. On a structural, functional level, Ike serves as a kind of mirror masquerading as a foil, a character who seeming at first the opposite of the shrewd Ratliff foreshadows and ultimately reflects back to Ratliff his own deficiencies. Of course Ike is apparently incapable of Ratliff's refined self-reflexivity, which highlights the difference between the person who is impaired but not generally classified as disabled as opposed to the person fixed in disability. Faulkner very eloquently describes the luxury of temporary disablement that might even recall the idea of passing as disabled for personal gain that lurks in his and his family's past. He writes of Ratliff:

> He was on his way to Frenchman's Bend now, though he had not started yet and did not know just when he would start. He had not seen the village in a year now. He was looking forward to his visit not only for the pleasure of the shrewd dealing which far transcended mere gross profit, but with the sheer happiness of being out of bed and moving once more at free will, even though a little weakly, in the sun and air which men drank and moved in and talked and dealt with one another—a pleasure no small part of which lay in the fact that he had not started yet and there was absolutely nothing under heaven to make him start until he wanted to do. He did not feel weak, he was merely luxuriating in that supremely gutful lassitude of convalescence in which time, hurry, doing, did not exist, the accumulating seconds and minutes and hours to which in its well state the body is slave both waking and sleeping, now reversed and time now the lip-server and mendicant to the body's pleasure instead of the body thrall to time's headlong course. (793)

This very ableist passage celebrates the survival of a brush with abnormality. It conveys a kind of romanticization of invalidism, not only in the physical sense of "relaxation" it brings but also in the sense of being literally invalid in the economic superstructure that dictates the use of time for an abled working person. However, this romanticization, like any such romanticization of the life experience of an other, springs from the owner's sense of freedom from the totalization of identity that results from the characterization of permanent disability (or, to use more recognizable nomenclature, "disability" instead of "impairment"—I outline the use of these terms in this book's note). When Ratliff suffers, he blames his mistake on his "disability," claiming it in a less touristic and more integral way—a move that is also a romanticization, albeit of a different kind. Ratliff's romanticization of disability seems to extend to the third-person narration of Ike's love affair with the cow in the second part of chapter one of "The Long Summer" section. The mere fact of this extension, incidentally, suggests just how much *The Hamlet* is Ratliff's narrative—here his voice would seem most removed, yet the "Faulknerian" narrator proceeds from a worldview heavily indebted to Ratliff's. In *The Mansion*, in which we learn of Ratliff's unusual (for Yoknapatawpha County) heritage, it is tempting to read back across *The Hamlet* and *The Town* to think how his sense of his own "abnormality" informs his viewpoint, but I am not sure there is any reason to think that Faulkner "knows" V.K.'s heritage at the time he was writing *The Hamlet*.

Mention of Ike's romance with the cow brings us back to that character, who is the proper subject of this discussion (funny that Ratliff should steal attention so adroitly). As I am reading Ratliff, Ike serves the role of completing a point about Ratliff that Faulkner intentionally or not makes. That is to say, Ike serves a two-layered function: first, his disability enables Flem to carry out a swindle of Ratliff and, second, he serves a structural function of helping to define Ratliff's character. But Ike's functional purpose continues in the cow affair, and this business with the cow serves different purposes. Despite critics' long contention that Benjy's narrative is somehow conspicuously objective, it is in fact the presentation of Ike in this section that is more in the objective style. Of course the form of the writing seems far from being so, as Faulkner presents the event in a way that borrows from the epithalamion tradition. But as far as actual presentation of events, we get little in the way of what might be going on in Ike's mind. It is as if Ike is pure function, where Faulkner had made an attempt to get inside Benjy's mind (and I might here add that declaring Benjy's narrative object is tantamount to declaring him an object when Faulkner's entire experiment is to present him as a subject). But what kind of function has Faulkner and/or the novel itself assigned to Ike? I do not mean to suggest that Faulkner's careful positioning of both Ike and the cow does not humanize both. That is certainly the case early in the narrative, but Faulkner seems to do so only to make the joke funnier when he reveals that this lavishly described love affair is actually between participants who, in the larger parlance of the book, are decidedly not human. Or is it even a joke? The tone of the entire section is difficult to read, especially if the reader does understand it to be an elaborate joke. If we read the affair as a foil for Flem and Eula (the latter of whom Faulkner describes in notably bovine terms—as well as terms of disability, as she has neither "normal" intelligence, mobility, nor "energy"), then Ike and the cow's love would seem "purer" and Faulkner's presentation of it a tender exploration of a kind of love to be lauded and embraced over the money- and position-driven romancing of Flem. So Joseph Gold sees it, writing that the affair is the "antithesis to Snopesism. Not only is the episode an idyll, and a tribute to love, which exists only in an idiot in a Snopes world, but it is also a portrait of the innocent, the anti-materialist" (29). In such a reading, Faulkner may be seen as celebrating abnormality; at the same time, Ike and the cow still operate functionally as characters. Either way one reads the narrative—either as humorous or sympathetic—the ethics of it can well leave the reader extremely uncomfortable. :-(

Having asserted Ike's functionality, I now want to turn and stress his agency, to point to his intelligence. Like Benjy's monologue, if we turn Ike's story to a different angle, we can read into it an alternative perspective in which it becomes a traditional mystery. The owner of the barn from which Ike steals food for the cow performs the role of detective in order to find Ike out. The latter is referred to, from the barn-owner's perspective, as "the thief": "the thief's dark wake lay again upon the dew-pearled grass of the pasture" (910). Like Benjy, perhaps Ike is cleverer than he seems, for the barn-owner upon trying to track Ike "discovered that he had made the same error of underestimation which Houston had made" (910). The narrator qualifies this comment with "that there is perhaps something in passion too, as well as in poverty and innocence, which cares for its own" (910), but the reader might wonder if the narrator—whether a version of Faulkner or Ratliff—gets it right. Certainly Ike achieves many of the more astounding feats of the Faulknerian canon when he somehow manages to get back inside the barn with the cow when the owner locks him out: in a version of the "locked room" puzzle that John T. Irwin so well elaborates in Faulkner's official detective stories, the reader finds that the "next morning when he unlocked the chain, the creature was inside the stall with the cow. It had even fed the cow, climbing back out and then back into the stall to do it, and for that five miles to Houston's place it still followed, moaning and slobbering, though just before they reached the house he had looked back, and it was gone. He did not know just when it disappeared" (912).

What is intriguing about Ike's amazing abilities of evasion is that they point to a kind of alternative cognition, one that is conspicuously nonhuman. We've seen Ike's connection with the cow, and you may recall that Faulkner describes Benjy's gait as being like that of a bear: I would add to that that Benjy's brother Jason constantly refers to him as being a gelded horse. At the end of the novel, it is Benjy who takes center stage, "bellowing" to use Faulkner's word, when Luster dashes in the wrong direction around the Jefferson town square. Meanwhile, in his pursuit of the cow, Ike continually foils the cow's owner and even manages at one point to perform a kind of magic trick, an amazing feat in which he enters into a locked barn where the cow is being kept without unlocking the door. I would assert that this *animalistic* embodying of cognitive disability in these characters signals an alternative sense—a "horse-sense," if you will (or cow- or bear-sense)—that is a different kind of subjectivity and agency, albeit one that is equally controlled by cognitively and physically abled humans (and here I am thinking about the literal sensibility of horses as outlined by Vicki Hearne in *Adam's Task*). Obviously, casting any person as nonhuman based on disablement, race, or anything else is a time-tested way to oppress. Yet, limited as it may be in Faulkner's writing, such agency permits a kind of mobility not otherwise available to other human characters in Faulkner: for example, Ike can move throughout woods and pastures with ease, but his cousin Mink (despite his animal name) finds his life unraveling when he combats and eventually murders the cow's owner in a different line of narrative in *The Hamlet.* Likewise, Benjy is the only member of the Compson family who as a white person can successfully enter the African American part of town. Faulkner expresses the principle of this alterity of agency when he writes of Ike "that there is perhaps something in passion too, as well as in poverty and innocence, which cares for its own" (910). The idea is a romantic one—and I am loath to descend into romanticizing especially when these characters find ablement in spaces usually abled characters don't *want* to move in—but maybe it is that passion figured in a human context as cognitive disability that manifests in a body that violates the norm and allows a different mobility. If so, then maybe Faulkner's purpose is not to seal off an identity as abnormal, but rather to offer up the possibilities of realigning the potentialities of those bodies and ultimately of human bodies in general. In fact it may well be more than coincidental that this kind of alternative agency of disability informed by nonhuman animal being should find articulation in one of Faulkner's most famous symbols: the disabled bear named Ben who is hunted but not killed by a character named Ike in the story "The Bear," which found its fullest published form as part of the book *Go Down, Moses.*

Looking back to the external descriptions of Ike and Benjy, it can be observed that Faulkner evidently seeks to anchor these characters with all their ontological and epistemological alterity in the "familiar" ontology and epistemology of childhood. Here is a mode of being that readers share universally, a stage in life marked by various kinds of physical, social, and even cognitive disability that precedes the stage of normal adulthood, which within the ideology of ability is coterminous with abledness. Childhood of course does not get figured as disability since the disabledness endemic to it characterizes normal childness. If anything a super-able child is a freak (a point Faulkner makes in his initial presentation of the knife-toting Otis in *The Reivers*). Still, this approach seems Faulkner's strong bid for universality: we have all been children is the apparent logic, only Ike and Benjy never grew past that point. Therefore, we abled (that is cognitively capable of reading [as] adults) can understand how these characters' minds and bodies work. Faulkner enlists this universality to secure Benjy and Ike's innocence for the reader if not for other characters—Benjy seems particularly dangerous to parents worried about rape. There is an innocence imputed to the animal aspect of these characters as well, but trained as Benjy the bear may be an animal is dangerous in ways a child is not. None of these ways of trying to represent cognitive or any other disability metaphorically are original to Faulkner, but he employs them to try to work his way through the authenticity crisis he cannot avoid. This problem becomes arguably most acute in a character for whom ostensibly it seems it wouldn't, the third character I want to examine.

Darl:

I have already mentioned Darl Bundren twice, and now I want to delve into a closer examination of him. He would hardly seem an "idiot" character partly because his external appearance does not so dramatically suggest an abnormal mental and emotional make-up in the vein of Ike, Benjy, and other such characters in Faulkner's writing. But he is, like Benjy and Ike, a character whose existence is marked by communication breakdowns and textual crises. Like these characters, he possesses an alternative cognition. And like Ike (Benjy too, as we shall see) he serves similar functional roles.

In discussing Darl, an immediate problem that arises is that he is not cognitively disabled in the way Benjy and Ike are, nor does his physique suggest such. Again, he lacks the vacant blue eyes, the large bear-like body. Unlike the other two he maintains a wonderful facility with language. And he has agency and plays active roles in regular human situations in ways that neither Benjy nor Ike can. At the same time, although they are much more subtle, certain cognitive abnormalities do exist in Darl, and they also manifest in external ways. There is a great deal of discourse in the novel regarding him and the ways that he is not exactly normal. At one point Vernon Tull says that the problem with Darl is that "he just thinks by himself too much" (71). "He is looking at me," Tull says at another point. "He dont say nothing; just looks at me with them queer eyes of hisn that makes folks talk. I always say it aint never been what he done so much or said or anything so much as how he looks at you. It's like he had got into the inside of you, someway. Like somehow you was looking at yourself and your doings outen his eyes" (125). It is important to note that Darl's eyes are the agents that reveal his being different. The thing they convey is merely the opposite of Benjy and Ike—he sees too much where they appear to see, or at least comprehend, too little.

As with Benjy, the reader is confronted with questions about Darl's reliability as a narrator. The novel sets up a contest of sorts—who are you going to believe, reader? All the "normal" (at least according to the society within which they operate) people who chip away in their various inarticulate ways at presenting their narratives? Or the wonderfully articulate and poetic fellow who uses all the big words and ultimately winds up declared insane? Faulkner teases us with Darl's description of Addie's death—a scene he is miles away from and never actually witnesses, although it is hard to imagine any of the other characters doing it justice. Darl seems the opposite of Addie: where she hates words and sees them as useless, pointless, and powerless, Darl seems all words. Then there is the scene in which Darl is taken away and his final monologue which follows; it is easy to read Darl's laughing and his speaking of himself in third-person and in apparent gibberish as his final breakdown, his ultimate shattering into schizophrenia as readers such as Dorothy J. Hale and John K. Simon have shown. Indeed, one wonders how to take this disabled person: is he a frightening figure who has always been on the brink of destructive behavior? Is he a figure to be pitied with a psychosocial disability that leads him to do any number of bizarre things for which he should not be held responsible? Is he a jerk when he talks to Jewel and Vardaman about their mother being a horse and fish, respectively—is Faulkner in this case presenting us the clichéd "fine line between madness and genius" with Darl constantly crossing back and forth across it? Is Darl in the end something of a hero, who realizes more fully and deeply than any other character the specific griefs and coping mechanisms his siblings, and even his father, have and so addresses each one only to be paid poorly for his services once he is no longer needed? Which of these readings one embraces probably reveals as much about the reader as the character, but I would like to pursue the latter one (perhaps minus the "hero" part, although I am still thinking about that one). For it seems to me that Darl serves more than anything else a function for the other characters and for the novel itself, and this function may be thought of as prosthetic one. Indeed, I would argue that Darl does nothing less than advance a poetics of prosthesis that also illuminates the functional qualities of Benjy and Ike.

Some significant work has been produced that considers the connection between physical prosthetics and textuality as prosthesis. A brilliant exploration of this connection appears in David Wills's already mentioned pseudofictional, pseudoautobiographical/biographical, pseudocritical book *Prosthesis*. As noted before, Wills weaves meditations on his father's prosthetic leg with poststructuralist theory of language, considering how the Derridean notion of the absence and subsequent deferral of meaning signifies a dependency, a need for an other to complete the self just as a prosthetic completes a body that is not whole, according to a given definition of wholeness. As David T. Mitchell and Sharon L. Snyder point out in discussing Wills, "*prosthesis* [is] a term that mediates between the realm of the literary and the realm of the body" (*Narrative Prosthesis* 7). This is another way of acknowledging the discursivity of the body as an imagined thing, and the disparity between the discursively created body and actual bodies is inescapable, proving that the actual physical body requires the imagined one in order to signify, to exist. Thus Mitchell and Snyder go on to write that, to Wills, "far from signifying a deficiency, the prostheticized body is the rule, not the exception. All bodies are deficient in that materiality proves variable, vulnerable, and inscribable. The body is first and foremost a linguistic relation which cannot be natural or average. The textual nature of language, be it oral or print, lacks the very physicality that it seeks to control or represent" (7).

Mitchell and Snyder build on Wills's argument to advance their own concept of "narrative prosthesis." They argue that disabled characters serve as prosthetics for the construction of literary narrative in the sense that certain narratives depend on disabled bodies for their very existence. This "discursive dependency" (47) results from Mitchell and Snyder's notion that the function of disabled people "in literary discourse is primarily twofold: disability pervades literary narrative, first, as a stock feature of characterization and, second, as an opportunistic metaphorical device" (47). Within this representational framework, Mitchell and Snyder assert that "disability has been used throughout history as a crutch upon which literary narratives lean for their representational power, disruptive potentiality, and analytical insight" (49). Stated another way, Mitchell and Snyder see "disability as a narrative device upon which the literary writer of 'open-ended' narratives depends for his or her disruptive punch" (49). By "open-ended narratives," Mitchell and Snyder evoke a structuralist notion of texts designed to promote openness consciously and self-reflexively, "texts that not only deploy but explicitly foreground the 'play' of multiple meanings as a facet of their discursive production" (48).

Darl Bundren exemplifies these aspects of prosthesis in multiple ways and on multiple levels. He is a character whose very nonnormate status literally allows him to see things that other characters do not. Whether he sees an event that happens in a place where he is not or whether he sees that his sister is pregnant or that his brother Jewel was born of a different father, Darl sees things differently. He also sees differently in narrative and philosophical senses. He provides the most compelling narratives, the ones closest to what readers think of as Faulkner's third-person narrative voice with its baroque vocabulary and syntax. He also delves into deep Hegelian and existential nuances of being—as opposed to Jewel, who "knows he is, because he does not know that he does not know whether he is or not" (80), Darl does not know what he is, working his way through the possibility that he "must be, or I could not empty myself for sleep in a strange room. And so if I am not emptied yet, I am *is*" (81). It is in Darl that we find the greatest philosophical and psychological depth as well as aesthetic finery, allowing him to fill in blanks and draw connections and even witness scenes that we would not get otherwise. The interpretive aspects of the text Darl offers, his particular seeing, provide the prosthetic role of helping to make "comprehensible that which appears to be inherently unknowable situat[ing] narrative in the powerful position of mediator between two separate worlds" and he, like certain other disabled figures in literature, "inaugurates the act of interpretation" (Mitchell and Snyder, *Narrative Prosthesis* 6).

His particular way of seeing also well situates him as a kind of figure whose own disruptive capabilities allow the novel to be disruptive. Totally unpredictable, Darl more than any other character keeps the reader questioning where the line between normal and abnormal is drawn—and that is saying something for a novel full of characters that do so. Vardaman's transference of love from his mother to a fish remains a strange and disturbing move, and even Dewey Dell's somewhat erotic encounter with the cow contains a shock element. But Darl's frank engagement with both of these characters forces the reader into a quandary—again, if a reader drawn to magnificent prose wants to rely on Darl's narrative, then his acknowledgment of his younger brother's connection with the fish either gains the power of his own narrative authority, or, as I suggested before, it is made even more ridiculous if Darl is read as making fun of Vardaman's transference. Either way, Darl represents such epistemological anxiety.

Darl does not merely serve prosthetic functions, his very visioning itself articulates a poetics of prosthesis. It is very telling that, when narrating Addie's death scene, Darl imagines that "Pa breathes with a quiet, rasping sound, mouthing the snuff against his gums. 'God's will be done,' he says. 'Now I can get them teeth'" (52). Anse is a character whose dubious status as disabled is one of his most salient features, and it is presented partly through Darl's marvelous descriptions of him. Darl is careful to present Anse's physique. "Pa's feet are badly splayed," he explains, "his toes cramped and bent and warped, with no toenail at all on his little toes, from working so hard in the wet in homemade shoes when he was a boy" (11). Not only that, Darl notes that the "shirt across pa's hump is faded lighter than the rest of it. There is no sweat stain on his shirt. I have never seen a sweat stain on his shirt. He was sick once from working in the sun when he was twenty-two years old, and he tells people that if he ever sweats, he will die. I suppose he believes it" (17). One might detect a shade of the charlatan in Anse's claim of disability, one that it might be noted at this point is not entirely unlike the novelist and his great-grandfather. Whatever the case, Darl is onto something that lies at the core of Anse's being, the notion of dependency for completion: "I reckon there are Christians here" (235), Anse tells his sons, urging them to borrow shovels rather than buy them to dig the grave at the Jefferson cemetery. Whether or not Anse actually does "say" something about the new teeth immediately after death, Darl well understands that, for Anse, Addie herself serves a prosthetic function so that the pairing of her loss and his thinking of being able to get new teeth makes sense within his logic of loss and gain. Indeed, the end of the novel brings a kind of ultimate moment of prosthetic completion in which we find that, with Addie now gone and Darl dispensed with, Anse finds a new person to "complete" him and also adds the new set of teeth. Jewel observes that his father "got them teeth" and indeed Cash (who takes over the prime narrative function) says, "It was a fact. It made him look a foot taller, kind of holding his head up, hangdog and proud too" (260).

Cash's assuming the predominant narrative control at the end of the novel is significant because he now fulfills the prosthetic role Darl has heretofore held. Darl's differentness not only provides a convenient way for the family to avoid trouble with Gillespie, it also renders him a liability in the logic of normality. The end of *As I Lay Dying* features the Bundren family's transformation from margin to center, from abnormal life to at least relative normalcy; as Patrick O'Donnell observes, they assimilate on some level to "the State and its striations, its systems of communication and exchange" (93). In the end, the family members eject Darl from their midst because he is a false limb that is no longer needed because they see him as being unable to attain normal status. They now have teeth, bananas, a graphophone, a new mother/wife, all items representative of the cultural center that is town, even if they are not themselves living in that center. All of these things are prosthetics that the Bundrens substitute for Darl and/or Addie, and Cash's taking over the prosthetic function of narrativizing is one more case of replacement. The need, the desire to excise Darl might be considered in light of a paradox inherent to disability's prosthetic function that Mitchell and Snyder discuss: at the same time that "the disabled body represents a potent symbolic site of literary investment" (49) that registers the kind of subversive open-endedness so crucial to the most provocative literature, it nevertheless depends on static forms and stereotypes that effectively stall that very discursive openness, a paradox I hinted at earlier when describing the marble faun's fixed identity, which is one that ironically celebrates fluidity. As Mitchell and Snyder put it, there is the "paradoxical impetus that makes disability into both a destabilizing sign of cultural prescriptions about the body *and* a deterministic vehicle of characterization for characters constructed as disabled" (*Narrative Prosthesis* 50). There is thus a "historical conundrum of disability" (50)—the very sort of conundrum that lies at the heart of Benjy Compson's characterization and that describes the final action taken in regard to Darl. It could be seen as bothersome that Faulkner inserted Darl's final monologue—his strange laughter and his referring to himself in third-person seem to cast him as actually having a breakdown. He seems to be performing the role of an insane person. But it also comes dangerously close to putting Darl in the same kind of conundrum that comes with Benjy—perhaps a more rational sort of monologue showing that everyone is wrong about him would have seemed a little less cheap.

Offsetting this final monologue are Cash's comments about Darl. Cash has throughout the novel been the closest one to Darl not only in age but in intelligence. Yet the reader gets almost nothing from him in the way of internal monologue until the point when Darl is removed from the family. In thinking about his brother and the way he is being treated, Darl offers thoughts that seem quite ahead of his time regarding the constructedness of normality and abnormality. He muses, "Sometimes I aint so sho who's got ere a right to say when a man is crazy and when he aint. Sometimes I think it aint none of us pure crazy and aint none of us pure sane until the balance of us talks him that-a-way. It's like it aint so much what a fellow does, but it's the way the majority of folks is looking at him when he does it" (233). Later he repeats: "But I aint so sho that ere a man has the right to say what is crazy and what aint. It's like there was a fellow in every man that's done a-past the sanity or the insanity, that watches the sane and the insane doings of that man with the same horror and the same astonishment" (238).

In the penultimate paragraph of the novel (Cash has the final word where Darl had the first), Cash is listening to music and thinks "what a shame Darl couldn't be [here] to enjoy it too. But it is better so for him. This world is not his world; this life his life" (261). Perhaps such thinking should not be that surprising for a man who champions building things on the bevel, but the comments are very interesting in light of Faulkner's thinking about the instability of definitions of the normate and whatever forms its opposite may take. It is as if Faulkner realizes the conundrum that his novel has enacted on Darl and slides Cash into his position in order to maintain the disruptive potentialities of the text. And yet Cash may strike the reader as a poor substitute for Darl—a prosthetic for a prosthetic that is twice removed from the "real," as it were. He has demonstrated nonnormate thinking and disruptive behavior (his justification for building things on the bevel and the intrusive sound of his sawing, respectively), but he lacks the narrative power and far-reaching, penetrating vision of his now-absent brother.

He also seems farther away from his mother than Darl, who at least has a clue about who his mother really is and what her innermost desires are—Addie Bundren, who if anything represents the real rather than the prosthetic. Addie's one monologue is presented roughly in the middle section of the novel, and in many ways she is the novel's center, both genuinely and in the rhetoric of the other characters (even if that rhetoric is questionable, as in Anse's case). Addie is singularly independent, noncontingent. She "takes" Anse, who is so completely dependent. "If you've got any womenfolks, why in the world dont they make you get your hair cut? [. . .] And make you hold your shoulders up" she asks him when they first meet (171). He is as alone as Addie is, but his entire mojo is to need someone, for he replies "That's what I come to see you about" (171). Addie is particularly suspicious of the prosthetic functioning of words: "[when Cash was born] was when I learned that words are no good; that words dont ever *fit what they are trying to say at.* When [Cash] was born I knew that motherhood was invented by someone who had to have a word for it because the ones that had the children didn't care whether there was a word for it or not. I knew that fear was invented by someone that had never had the fear; pride, who never had the pride. [. . .] I knew that that word [love] was like the others: *just a shape to fill a lack*; that when the right time came, you wouldn't need a word for that anymore than for pride or fear" (171–72; *emphasis mine*).

For Addie Bundren, words and the concepts they construct are prosthetics in the sense that David Wills describes. Shapes that fail to fill lacks, words themselves create the very deficiency that justifies their utility. Cash's comments seem close to Addie's, but his mother's reach much deeper into the very fabric of construction, scrutinizing the threads of that fabric itself where Cash's simply question the piece of material as a piece of material. Darl understands the ontological problems connected with words and the constructs they erect.

And yet, as I mentioned earlier, Darl is in so many ways the complete opposite of Addie, for if anything he is all words. Where Addie might be seen as being either pre- or post-Derridean in her linking words to material, Darl himself seems comfortable within the endless sea of deference that is the hallmark of Derrida's poststructuralist sensibility. Consider one of the most memorable of Darl's many fascinating passages: while Darl does not get *the* last word of the novel he nevertheless gets *a* last word. In his final monologue, he offers the following comments: "They pulled two seats together so Darl could sit by the window to laugh. One of them sat beside him, the other sat on the seat facing him, riding backward. One of them had to ride backward because the state's money has a face to each backside and a backside to each face, and they are riding on the state's money which is incest. A nickel has a woman on one side and a buffalo on the other; two faces and no back. I dont know what that is. Darl had a little spy-glass he got in France at the war. In it it had a woman and a pig with two backs and no face. I know what that is" (254). The passage is remarkable not only for its implications in the novel but for Faulkner's "idiot" characters in general. The comments occur at the moment that confirms Darl's disability. Whether we read Darl as having been mad throughout the novel, or as a person descending into insanity as the novel progresses, or as a person defined as mentally-emotionally ill and abnormal subject to changing circumstances and definitions of normality among the people of his immediate society, Darl's behavior here signals his disablement in normal society. It is a moment of radical fragmentation of self for Darl in which the inner (cognitive) person splits completely from the outer (physical) person, regarding the latter from a similar narrative space that is the site of his earlier description of his mother's death. Taken in now as a token of the state, Darl sees himself as being like the coin, "a face to each backside and a backside to each face." He is now hermetically sealed-off as disabled and thus rendered two-dimensional, the depth of his personhood collapsed into a thin metal wafer.

Darl's focus on the state's money provides what may be seen as a more vicious formulation of the processes of the formation of normality. Fully aware of the economics that have driven his father's quest to Jefferson and the ways the same economic infrastructure dictates definitions of bodies as producers, Darl cries foul. Anse does not produce: his body, disabled just as he claims it to be, has no place in the larger machine of production that creates graphophones, shovels, and false teeth anymore than it does producing cotton, corn, or tobacco. Nevertheless, Anse understands the rules of such a world and is committed to its products, finding other ways to ride the waves of the system. Darl, on the other hand, destroys. His burning Gillespie's barn, transforming the utilitarian building into a would-be funeral pyre approaches the kind of radiance-releasing destruction George Bataille envisions. To Darl, there is an incestuousness in the state's definition of normality, an inbreeding of normality, that renders a kind of monstrosity that goes by the name of normal. Such monstrosity is emblematized in the very kinds of prosthetics Anse desires. Darl identifies the false-teeth, replacement-wife-seeking hypocrite as the freak that a capitalist-driven normality-obsessed society produces, freaks such as pigs with two backs and no face. Of course, the irony of the French spyglass is that the freak inside is you, the viewer. Presumably a mirror replaces the face in the image inside the spyglass (the referent here being not just to a maritime instrument but also the carnival trick of a window promising a pornographic image only to display a picture with a mirror to reflect back the viewers face), with the Lacanian reflection of the self made strange in a very overt way, adding particular heft to the notion of the freak as "one of us" as formulated in the film *Freaks*, itself so cogently read by Fiedler, Garland-Thomson, and others. Perhaps the psychosocially disabled Darl reflects back to a reader disability itself as universal, the seeming alterity of disability as embodied in Benjy and Ike itself an obfuscation, a secret Darl reveals along with so many others. Again, I will deal with this element of universality in disability later; for now I would draw the link between the threat of disablement to the self he registers and the mirror function of the disabled character in "Mirrors of Chartres" and the self-fragmented prosthetized narrator of "The Leg."

The mention of the buffalo and pig again evokes nonhuman presences and also an alternative cognition. The buffalo nickel signals the federal government's use of Native culture—like the wooden cigar-store Indian to whom Jewel is compared early in the novel, the buffalo nickel can be seen as representing a kind of ennobling of Native Americans that in actuality glorifies the society that has vanquished them, making it more an act of self-congratulation and testimony to empowerment than a true acknowledgment of Native culture, seen as being merely worth a nickel. A woman's being on the other side represents a similar male glorification of "woman" that is only a projection of male objectivizing desire. The same kind of self-gazing disguised as celebration of the other appears in a normate's engagement with a freak. At the same time that Darl's comments imply such critiques of normalcy enforcement (to use Lennard Davis's term), they also suggest an affinity with alternative cognitions, whether they be Native, female, freak, or nonhuman animal. Like Benjy and Ike, Darl's cognition has been different from everyone else's. And like them he finds himself labeled "other" and reduced to an object in the superstructure of normal society.

Obviously not only Darl but also Ike and (as Mitchell and Snyder show) Benjy all can be seen as exemplifying the disabled character who serves a narrative prosthetic role. All serve Faulkner as important cogs in creating open-ended texts at the same time that their disabilities render their own identities static. Again, the conundrum of disabled characters. The larger conundrum in all of this however is not just the limitation of the author but the limits of a text and a character. What can be so radically disturbing about Darl's final comments is that he should have a backstory that the reader cannot fully know. But more problematic still, from a "clinical" standpoint, is that Darl actually has *no* backstory at all beyond what Faulkner has written because even the best-drawn character is arguably still a creation of words, and when a writer plunges into such a deep unknown as cognitive disability, the character's past and context must be driven to work too hard, impossibly hard. Here again the conundrum of a character's existence. How far outside of a text can a text live?

I mention the word "clinical" in its most oversimplified sense in order to acknowledge in a broad sense the hope of medical humanities that from art, writing, music, theater, and other humanities, including literary criticism, some aid can be brought to addressing disability experience. It seems to me that Benjy, Ike, and Darl would be some of Faulkner's strongest candidates for study by medical humanities, for what they reveal about the moment of their construction, the ways they "get it right" in terms of disability representation, and the ways they "get it wrong-right" by what they reveal (as Truchan-Tataryn notes) about Faulkner's own conceptualization of disability. In the layers of authenticity crises attending them, the ontological and epistemological matters surrounding these characters would seem to be most intriguing. Unfortunately, it can well be argued that Faulkner fails to create a character who might be able to serve for scientific purposes in the same way that one might furnish a cadaver—such may finally be impossible in fiction. On a different level, though, he arguably succeeds in the manifestation of these very limitations. I find the label of "Down's syndrome" Mitchell and Snyder so handily apply to Benjy just as time- and space-bound and thus as uncomfortable and even perhaps falsely totalizing as that of "idiot," even if less offensive, than Faulkner's nuanced depiction of what is actually happening in Benjy's brain, whether I find it revelatory of Benjy, Faulkner, or cultural norms. In the end, I am not sure I even buy Truchan-Tataryn's idea that Faulkner would settle for his own moment's labeling of Benjy precisely because it seems to me that he does not ultimately do so with Darl or Ike either. It is a strange thing to talk about since a writer-as-creator seems to be so in control (and so Faulkner himself claimed), but (as Faulkner also claimed, among other places in his dedication to *The Mansion*) there are limits to how well the author knows his or her own creation. What Faulkner, who is so keen to expose the processes of narrating, shows is that individuals such as Benjy and Ike and ultimately Darl are character*ized*. The materials of that characterization may differ according to scientific knowing, but it is still upon narratives that even researchers must depend even as they revise them. It is the need to pay attention to these narrativizing and characterizing processes, Faulkner implicitly tells us, when observing people who because of cognitive variations cannot themselves reliably narrate.

As if sensing the importance of backstory in presenting disabled characters whose lives and situations are sufficiently visible, in the novel published after *As I Lay Dying* Faulkner turned to an exploration of seeing in the context of disability. It is to that novel that I would like to turn. :-)

Contributor

COMING SOON . . .

BLINDNESS IN THE BACKWOODS

STARRING . . .

Nice people didn't let others know they read *Sanctuary.* Maybe they carried it about in a paper bag so they wouldn't be seen with it: so some of my relatives claim about when that book was published. Sounds like something a Flannery O'Connor character would say. I can recall my grandmother talking about it with my distant cousin, who took her MA in English at Ole Miss, writing a thesis on O'Connor under the directorship of the renowned Professor Louis E. Dollarhide (Professor Emeritus Ben Fisher cleverly says of this Mississippi icon that he taught half the state of Mississippi during his time, and the other half didn't go to school). I can hear them speak the title in that tone that means "Yes, *we* know what that one is about. That's the dirty book." My cousin does not get out much: like her mother before her, she is often bedridden, attended by her sister who once attended their mother. If you want to see her, you don't ask her to come over. You visit *her* in her small house in Ripley. You sit in the very nicely upholstered chairs in a room as airy with arches as the Roman Pantheon. My cousin's short-clipped hair is more white than blonde, and the mix is lovely and she is beautiful, with light blue eyes and a delicacy of skin, voice, and frame that is enchanting. Her skeleton, I imagine, is made not of bone but of cartilage. She wears a tiger tooth around her neck.

No, *Sanctuary* is one folks of a certain segment of society in a north Mississippi town even now laugh about in an embarrassed way, even more than *The Sound and the Fury,* which at least was about the South and aristocrats and the faded way of chivalry. *The Sound and the Fury* is tragic; *Sanctuary* is dirty. *The Unvanquished,* maybe *Sartoris* (I mean, the original, not the restored *Flags in the Dust*), and *The Reivers* are ones that fascinate many of the white literate natives of this part of the world. *As I Lay Dying* gets attention too—my cousin talks about it defensively, explaining that maybe someone not from the South tends to get it wrong when thinking Faulkner is making fun of poor whites. Actually, there is a nobility about them and the fact that the Bundrens are persevering in returning Addie's body to the resting place she requested. Yes, they do curious things, but those things make sense to *them,* and we've all known country people to do strange things, but that does not mean they're not sweet or that Faulkner was portraying them in a bad light.

But *Sanctuary* is something different. The folks at the big Frenchman's house are not good country people. Ruby might be, and maybe Lee. They might just have taken a wrong turn or two. But everything else there is sinister, sensational—not serious, not tragic.

There is much in and about *Sanctuary* to capture a reader or scholar's attention. First, there is the book itself, the history of its composition, the not-nice things Faulkner himself said about it that many people still take very literally. There is the sex, the uncomfortable voyeurism enforcing itself on practically every page. Then there are a couple of colossal characters. Temple Drake, the debutante who generally elicits *some* kind of response from readers if not from the other characters in the novel. Popeye is one of the most famous of Faulkner's villains: who cannot be captivated by this sharp-tongued, pistol-toting rounder? Robust Reba in her Memphis whorehouse, with her young nephew Uncle Buddy, provides plenty of memorable action and dialogue, and who can forget the two bumpkins from Jefferson thinking that maybe she is a seamstress because they see a woman's undergarment on the floor?

Yes, there is a great deal in this book to take center-stage, so it is probably either completely futile or completely cruel of me to parade a completely different character out to present as the Key to the novel. Still,

I really mean it when I say that one of the most if not *the* most important of the characters in the novel, when viewing its structural, thematic, and metaphorical elements from a disability-sensitive standpoint, is not Temple, not Popeye, certainly not Horace or Red but the old blind man, Lee Goodwin's father, Pap.

The who? you might ask. Lee's old blind father whom Ruby and Lee keep in their house. A minor character if ever there was one. Yet so central, so present as to be ironically invisible.

Here is Faulkner's own introduction of him. Lee leads the character onto the novel's stage by the arm,

> an old man with a long white beard stained about the mouth. Benbow watched Goodwin seat the old man in a chair, where he sat obediently with that tentative and abject eagerness of a man who has but one pleasure left and whom the world can reach only through one sense, for he was both blind and deaf: a short man with a bald skull and a round, full-fleshed, rosy face in which his cateracted eyes looked like two clots of phlegm. Benbow watched him take a filthy rag from his pocket and regurgitate into the rag an almost colorless wad of what had once been chewing tobacco, and fold the rag up and put it into his pocket. The others were already eating, silently and steadily, but the old man sat there, his head bent over his plate, his beard working faintly. He fumbled at the plate with a diffident, shaking hand and found a small piece of meat and began to suck at it until the woman returned and rapped his knuckles. He put the meat back on the plate then and Benbow watched her cut up the food on the plate, meat, bread and all, and then pour sorghum on it. Then Benbow quit looking. When the meal was over, Goodwin led the old man out again. Benbow watched the two of them pass out the door and heard them go up the hall. (187–88)

Quite an introduction. It presents a character who we soon realize is functional, a flat character Faulkner installs in the house for the purpose of heightening its horror through an attenuation of abnormality. The old man is the kind of character one is liable to find in a Stephen King novel or in *House of a Thousand Corpses* and other films of its ilk. The scene is deliberately gross, deliberately scatological. Where the man's eyes should be are clots of spit. Maybe they were put there by the man himself on a day when he had misplaced his handkerchief. His silence, his gross eating habits, the fact that he emerges for the purpose of taking his meal and then disappears behind the curtain again all attest to his being a living haint, a spook Faulkner creates to make the Frenchman's house more creepy.

We might linger for a moment on the eating habits if for no other reason than that Faulkner does. The text licenses open staring at the man as it offers up its details. His diffident, shaking hand further marks him as disabled, and his apparent lack of teeth almost turns him into something not human. We watch him suck on the meat that hasn't been cut yet. But when Ruby prepares his food at last, Benbow turns his head away—Benbow, whose eyes are the reader's eyes at the beginning of the novel. That turning away in shame approaches something of the dynamics of staring Garland-Thomson outlines in her provocative book *Staring*; it articulates a give and take from a space and position of politeness. It is because the old man cannot stare back that Horace allows himself to stare, but finally the something—perhaps the actual act of consumption (and consumption can be read thickly in light of Peter Lurie's insights on cultural consumption and vision in the novel)—dispels even Horace's fascination. It is a significant instance in looking away, which is the potent luxury of the ableist's stare, is part of the power of the stare. You don't have to look anymore once the disability stops being interesting, which is exactly the point that Garland-Thomson makes, writing that "[w]e want to surprise, but even more we want to tame that pleasurable astonishment, to domesticate the strange sight into something so common as to be unnoticeable. Those clashing impulses make staring self-cancelling, abating once we reassert the equilibrium of familiarity" (*Staring* 19). The reader might well wonder how exactly the man finally does manage to get that food down.

What heightens the eeriness of the man even more is that Lee and Ruby wait on him. He might just as easily be a wizard old and bent from life, escorted to his meal, which is specially prepared to accommodate him, and then back to his study again. As with the reading of Benjy Compson, it is difficult for me to return to my first reading of the book and recall my responses to the man although I suspect my knee-jerk response was to be not repelled but creeped out. Ruby's rapping on the table to get him to stop sucking on the meat suggests that she thinks of his actions as being repulsive, but both she and Lee cater to him, as well they would with his being Lee's father.

It happens that the young debutante with the blond legs, who early in the novel represents an ablest dream in her "perfection," finds herself after a series of misfortunes at this semi-haunted house. The situation is a weird one from the beginning, as Popeye's eyes seem to glow in the darkness, watching her after Gowan has wrecked the car with her in it. Then she tries to orient herself in the house: "She went on, slowly. Then she stopped. On the square of sunlight framed by the door lay the shadow of a man's head, and she half spun, poised with running. But the shadow wore no hat, so she turned and on tiptoe she went to the door and peered around it. A man sat in a splint-bottom chair, in the sunlight, the back of his bald, white-fringed head toward her, his hands crossed on the head of a rough stick" (207). The scene is rather like the shadow of Nosferatu stretching over the sleeping body of one of his victims. Faulkner realizes all of the Gothic potential he can, posing the shadow as threatening, building the tension that something bad is about to happen to Temple, and then releasing that tension when the shadow is shown to belong to the old man. Faulkner doesn't let the slightly easier feeling last, though. When Temple says "Good afternoon," the man does not respond. Then upon closer contemplation, she realizes something variant about him. "For an instant she thought that his eyes were closed, then she believed that he had no eyes at all, for between the lids two objects like dirty yellowish clay marbles were fixed" (208).

With this scene Faulkner nudges Pap closer to the center of the novel. So much of the novel's preoccupation, which happens to be the particular type of terror in which it deals, is to put into swirling motion around Temple a clutch of watchers. The first third or more of the novel tracks this business the way the beginning of Jack London's *White Fang* details wolves circling their prey. The constant pressure on Temple is that as she focuses on one watcher, to stare him away if not down, another veers closer to her. This is not to say Temple is not accustomed to being watched and to not returning the watching, as clearly the young men who seek to court her back at home watch her constantly. But in that arrangement she is empowered by the very act of granting and refusing her attention, an enablement resulting from her class status, that negotiates if it does not abolish the overarching frame of the male gaze. The choice to return the attention of one of these men is in her power, and they are subject to that power. But the men at the Frenchman's house are not the same (to Ruby's thinking, Lee is "a man" where the fellows Temple is accustomed to dealing with are not even men at all). Being caught unaware by one of the men at the Frenchman's house will lead to unnamed terrors, Faulkner takes care to establish from the beginning of the book. The horror of the novel depends on being trapped in a controlling unreturnable gaze. Temple's crisis is that she has been moved from the watchtower to the cell in this panoptical situation.

In a novel that therefore so foregrounds ocularity, eyes become of utmost importance. David Seed writes that eyes "receive particular attention by Faulkner as stylised objects: Popeye's are compared to rubber knobs, the blind old man's to clots of flem, and so on" and suggests that the "eye is thus thrown into prominence as an object of no visual depth, an object to be looked *at* rather than *from*" (74–75). Seed's idea, for it further layers the crisis of watching in the book, is not so much shifting the emphasis from the gaze to the specific agent of gazing as adding greater power to that agent. As we have already seen, Faulkner has posited eyes as something to be seen as well as seeing in Benjy, Ike, and Darl, and it is this layering that makes this old man so central to the novel, where a simple empowerment of the gaze would marginalize him. Garland-Thomson discusses the kind of blank stare such as those of Faulkner's typical "idiot" characters: "The visual component of people with significant disabilities—often those with cognitive, developmental, or perceptual impairments—catalogs them as blank starers. The supposed dumb look, blind eye, and idiotic expression are highly stigmatized ways of appearing that draw interrogative stares from those who are properly focused. This type of purportedly empty stare demands no response, initiates no interchange, and produces no knowledge. Blank stares function, then, as visual impotence" (*Staring* 23).

But Pap's eyes if anything make him in certain ways more frightening and even powerful. He functions to make the eye itself vis*ible* in addition to its being an entity of vision, making that organ all the more potent as simultaneous object and subject. The eye, in this novel, both "looks" and "looks like." I repackage Seed's insight (puns inevitable here and later) to get at the various dimensions of those functional dimensions of Pap's eyes and of eyes generally. Indeed, the eye is much more potent in the novel than a certain other organ normally associated with potency. The old man's eyes are unique because they only "look like." Faulkner's descriptions of them as looking like clots of phlegm or yellowish clay marbles are distinct for their simultaneous marking of both absence and presence. What are distinctly absent are glass eyes fashioned to look like real eyes although incapable of providing vision. Yellowish clay marbles are *almost* glass eyes, but if anything they make conspicuous the absence of prosthetics, by their placement where such would be. Besides, these are not marbles of the shiny variety but dull and rough. They mark their own presence by their very conspicuousness: they are monster eyes that are more mysterious and disturbing than either closed eyelids or prosthetic eyes because it is not easy to tell if they are able to "look." Closed eyelids can perhaps put others off, and glass eyes might carry the horror of the uncanny, but both make it clear that the person cannot see, a difficult enough achievement in artistic representation, as Mosche Barasch has so vividly argued, paying close attention to the ways bodily arrangement can telegraph blindness in western graphic art. The text makes it clear that Pap is not sighted, but his eyes nevertheless achieve a kind of false external looking, by which I mean that Faulkner presents them as unseeing seens. Far from the prosthetic functions assigned to the characters discussed in the foregoing part of the body of this book, Pap's not having prosthetics seems an attempt on Faulkner's part to outrage the prosthetic functioning of a disabled character if not for the construction of the text itself then for other characters. Those eyes, so powerfully visible, are elevated to metaphors, which Faulkner soon puts to use.

The fact that the old man's eyes participate in only one half of this potency would seem still to marginalize him, but it is his very ocular disability that makes him so very central. Gene C. Fant Jr. recognizes the importance that Pap's disability takes on in the novel. Arguing that Faulkner "undermines 'normal' sensory input throughout" *Sanctuary* ("The Blind Man" 158), Fant asserts that "Goodwin's father symbolizes the novel's general reader: the reader is like the invalid old man who must depend on someone else who provides everything. The reader is blind and deaf, save for the sensory input provided by the narrator, who leads the way to the story's table and provides the entire repast. Further, a passive reader forces the narrator to extrude from the narrative, to assert his or her presence throughout the construction of the narrative. Faulkner takes ample advantage of this scenario, toying with the epistemology throughout the narrative" (166).

Fant goes on to write that "'[c]ataracted eyes' have been damned, and general readers of Faulkner's fiction must realize that, when they come to the table for a fictional repast, they are completely dependent on the narrator" (166). Thus, for Fant, the reader ultimately is a figure disabled by Faulkner's own narrative manipulation, an interesting argument in light of Benjy Compson's impairments, and indeed Fant goes on to discuss Benjy. Fant's point resembles Seed's own about the limitations of visibility in the novel, as the latter writes that in "traditional Gothic fiction the hero-villain's Miltonic power is signaled through eyes which flash with power and which exert a mesmeric force over those with whom they come in contact. In *Sanctuary* eyes function, rather, to render ambivalent what is seen" (75).

In outlining the way Pap models the situation of both the reader and the narrator, Fant well shows what an important character he is, but there is more. Illustrating the centrality of the old man to Temple's consciousness is her thinking of the old man during Popeye's raping her in the barn:

> He [Popeye] turned and looked at her. He waggled the pistol slightly and put it back in his coat, then he walked toward her. Moving, he made no sound at all; the released door yawned and clapped against the jamb, but it made no sound either; it was as though sound and silence had become inverted. She could hear silence in a thick rustling as he moved toward her through it, thrusting it aside, and she began to say Something is going to

> happen to me. She was saying it to the old man with the yellow clots for eyes. "Something is happening to me!" she screamed at him, sitting in his chair in the sunlight, his hands crossed on the top of the stick. "I told you it was!" she screamed, voiding the words like hot silent bubbles into the bright silence about them until he turned his head and the two phlegm-clots above her where she lay tossing and thrashing on the rough, sunny boards. "I told you! I told you all the time!" (250)

Pap's presence in this scene buttresses the disabling situation Temple is in. There are two things going on in the scene. First, after an extended chase she has finally been cornered, but for some time leading up to this point she has been aided in this contest of watching by a watchdog, as it were, named Tommy. Tommy himself is sexually agitated by her presence, but he is her defender, and his being a defender is significant in relation to his being an "idiot" character on the order of Benjy and Ike. Like them, he serves the prosthetic function of completing Temple's deficient armament against Popeye. More than that, though, it is as if Tommy is drawn to Temple out of recognition of and then sympathy for her own situation as disabling. Her crisis, as noted above, is a disablement created by change in environment, by an abrupt transferal from what in the logic of Temple and people in her class is a world of normality to one of abnormality. The novel in a sense amounts to a retelling of Alice's experiences in Wonderland in which she is thrust through the rabbit hole by means of literal penetration not of her own accord but by the fumbling ineptness of a man (Gowan) she can nevertheless control just as she can so many of the others in her normal life. The exact opposite is true once she enters this strange new country, so that the very things that keep her entrenched in abledness in her regular life render her disabled in this one. That Tommy is attracted to Temple just as the other men are is not surprising—at least one rule remains the same in this world, that of heterosexual male lust. But again he seems to respond to her on another level too, perhaps a subconscious one for him, or (if it seems too much of a stretch to assign this intentionality to the character himself) perhaps on a level of manipulation by the author. That is to say that, even in this land of oppositional abnormality, Tommy himself is more abnormal still and so recognizes Temple's disablement. Or, again, to present this in terms of novelistic construction, Faulkner pairs the two characters—ugly, impedimented Tommy with beautiful, articulate Temple (both names start with T)—to drive home the point of Temple's new status of abnormality and disablement.

The problem is that Popeye shoots Tommy in order to get to Temple, which brings us to the second thing going on with Pap's appearance at this rape moment. With Tommy gone, Temple has no watchdog and now is confronted with the realization that her own watching, her normally potent returning vision, is ineffective and useless. Her mind then immediately goes to her father, the person who presumably stands as the last resort for her when her own powers fail, only her father is also not there, which is made all the more painfully obvious by the patriarch who *is* present not even being present in a way that can help her; he cannot fulfill the prosthetic, stand-in role she calls on him to perform. Pap in his blindness makes Temple's disablement all the more horrifyingly obvious to herself, and in cruel irony she even imagines him watching the scene without even being able to see it. Nor can he hear it. To stress the point again, Pap is a highlight marker with which to embolden in neon yellow the fact that Temple is now disabled, which illustrates his structurally prosthetic function even as it shows his failures as a father-figure for Temple. As Seed well puts it, "Whereas Ruby earlier could tell her story to Temple, Temple now reaches new heights of terror because she lacks an audience. [. . .] As Popeye gradually penetrates the space between himself and Temple, she begins to 'explain' her experience to a blind deaf-mute whose placid immobility makes a travesty of human communication" (79–80). Temple's dependence is not of the powerful Linda Snopes Kohl kind—Faulkner has not yet reached that point of envisioning an empowering dependency in his career.

Part of the reason I want to identify Pap as the Key to the novel from a disability perspective is precisely because here at the pivotal moment of the novel's action he, and his disabled eyes, are in Temple's consciousness. To some extent he presides over the scene—one might imagine a film in which the rape scene cuts to a doubled image of the sun coming together into its single self as it sets (and, by the way, why has not some director done a remake of this novel recently?) He has lodged in her consciousness on many levels that extend beyond this moment—later she calls Popeye "Daddy" and although she does not necessarily keep Pap on the surface of her memory he nevertheless stands in for the failure of replacement and the absence of her father. Perhaps it is as unwise to try and prod too deeply into the psychological make-up of a character as it is to try and identify the nature of a character's backstory or cognitive disability, but it seems reasonable to assert that after the experience at the house and her transferal to Reba's Memphis brothel she has, as it were, "gone crazy." She may be seen as resembling Darl in this sense: her slavish, nymphomaniac attachment to and involvement with Red, her trying to kill Popeye, may be read as ailments resulting from the trauma of her nightmarish experiences. Stored away in a place where she is generally unseen, except famously during intercourse with Red, she has been removed from visibility, which metaphorically keeps her tied to Pap's blindness.

But it is not only because of his deeply psychological presence at and centrality to Temple's disabling experience that I place the old man as the central figure of the novel but also because in his disability his presence informs the character of another disabled character in the novel—Popeye. One of the eeriest revelations in a novel full of them is that Popeye, the seemingly invincible villain who rapes and corrupts Temple Drake, is in fact impotent. Eerie, this revelation, because our first intimation of it comes when Temple screams at him "You're not even a man! [. . .] You, a man, a bold man, when you cant even—When you had to bring a real man in to—And you hanging over the bed, moaning and slobbering like a—" (339). This followed by her telling him "Dont you wish you were Red? Dont you? Dont you wish you could do what he can do? Dont you wish he was the one watching us instead of you?" (340). We later hear from Miss Reba the specific mechanics of what Temple is saying: "Yes, sir, Minnie said the two of them would be nekkid as two snakes, and Popeye hanging over the foot of the bed without even his hat took off, making a kind of whinnying sound" (358). Later still, at the trial, we get the final piece of information that in fact Popeye used a corncob to rape Temple back in the barn at the house-of-horrors in the country.

Popeye's using the corncob to rape Temple speaks to the failure of prosthetics to do anything positive in this novel. At one point during the wake for Red, Miss Myrtle muses that maybe "he went off and got fixed up with one of these glands, these monkey glands, and it quit on him" (357). When recounting her experiences at the house in the country, Temple tells Horace that she imagined herself wearing a chastity belt, a prosthetic that should empower her, reversing the disabling fact of femininity. "I was thinking if I just had that French thing. I was thinking maybe it would have long sharp spikes on it and he wouldn't know it until too late and I'd jab it into him. I'd jab it all the way through him and I'd think about the blood running on me and how I'd say I guess that'll teach you! I guess you'll let me alone now!" (329), she exclaims, all of this imaging being of no final help to her, though. As another of Faulkner's "idiots"—like Benjy and Ike he too walks "with a shambling, bear-like gait" (186)—Tommy seems the best candidate for prosthetic disabled character along the lines of what Mitchell and Snyder argue for, but he ultimately fails both Temple as someone to depend on and the reader in fulfilling a narrative role if for no other reason than that he dies before he can, like Darl in *As I Lay Dying,* narrate Temple's catastrophe. Fittingly enough, the scene must be narrated with the vision of Pap present, but where he provides us a narrative in for the rape scene, he fails as a figure upon whom Temple can depend. The corncob, ironically, provides the reader with the answer to how the impotent Popeye could have raped Temple to the extent of her bleeding so much, but that bodily substitute has devastated Temple's life. Furthermore, the revelation of the corncob as prosthetic (if I may be allowed to read the corncob as a kind of prosthetic) does not open up but rather closes the range of interpretive possibilities in the text regarding Temple's rape. Where Benjy, Darl, and Ike inculcate the text with mystery by their narrativizing or even mere presence, Popeye and his corncob seal off mystery despite this novel's participating much more explicitly in the detective/mystery genre tradition.

The matter of Popeye's impotence extends into material and metaphorical levels beyond just the corncob, however. Again, when Temple recounts her time at the Frenchman's house to Horace, she comments: "Then I thought about being a man, and as soon as I thought it, it happened. It made a kind of plopping sound, like blowing a little rubber tube wrong-side outward. It felt cold, like the inside of your mouth when you hold it open. I could feel it, and I lay right still to keep from laughing about how surprised he was going to be. I could feel the jerking going on inside my knickers ahead of his hand and me lying there trying not to laugh about how surprised and mad he was going to be in about a minute" (331). These comments are made through the lens of Temple's current knowledge about Popeye, which is to say that how accurate they are intended to be about what she was actually thinking at the moment is not as significant as how her experience frames the telling of that narrative. Temple's transforming into a man with a flaccid member is "funny" not just because its presence would surprise Popeye but also because it would condemn him, reflecting back to him his own disability and, in the logic of Temple's comments, reversing her own disablement.

The material of rubber brings us back to Popeye's eyes, which are repeatedly referred to as appearing to be made of black rubber. Besides the fact that describing his eyes so casts them as signifiers of his lack of sexual virility, the focus on his eyes also reveals his connections to the old man Pap. Where Pap's eyes are unseeing yellowish clay marbles/clots of phlegm, Popeye's are knobs of rubber that may convey his impotence but nevertheless are in working order for the business of seeing. Yet Popeye's vision is not so stable as it may seem, and his association with and experience of disability extend beyond his impotence. In the backstory of Popeye's life Faulkner provides at the end of the novel we learn that when Popeye was born "[a]t first they thought he was blind. Then they found that he was not blind, though he did not learn to walk and talk until he was about four years old" (389). Moreover, we find that he "had no hair at all until he was five years old, by which time he was already a kind of day pupil at an institution: an undersized, weak child with a stomach so delicate that the slightest deviation from a strict regimen fixed for him by the doctor would throw him into convulsions" (392). The doctor says of the child Popeye that "he will never be a man, properly speaking. With care, he will live some time longer. But he will never be any older than he is now" (392) and that "[a]lcohol would kill him like strychnine" (392).

The question of why Faulkner felt the need to tack this biography of Popeye onto the end of the novel is a persistent one. In showing the horrific conditions of his childhood, it offers an avenue toward finding a way to sympathize with this villain. At least it offers some kind of explanation beyond simply pure inherent evil for Popeye's actions. The fact of his being hairless for the first five years of his life might even be read as adding a certain poignancy to his final moment, which I quote here for dramatic effect.

> They came for him at six. The minister went with him, his hand under Popeye's elbow, and he stood beneath the scaffold praying, while they adjusted the rope, dragging it over Popeye's sleek, oiled head, breaking his hair loose. His hands were tied, so he began to jerk his head, flipping his hair back each time it fell forward again, while the minister prayed, the others motionless at their posts with bowed heads.
>
> Popeye began to jerk his neck forward in little jerks. "Psssst!" he said, the sound cutting sharp into the drone of the minister's voice; "pssssst!" The sheriff looked at him; he quit jerking his neck and stood rigid, as though he had an egg balanced on his head. "Fix my hair, Jack," he said.
>
> "Sure," the sheriff said. "I'll fix it for you"; springing the trap. (397–98)

Popeye's obsession with his hair is striking in the context of the concept of prosthesis. If we can think about a prosthesis enabling and moving a body toward an ideal of normality, then perhaps Popeye's Ed Pinaud hair tonic can be seen as a prosthesis that "fixes" his hair so that he can conform to a certain appearance, to create the illusion that he is a normate, or at least that he is able to conform to the image he has of what he wants to look like.

We might even go a step further and think of Faulkner providing us with a story of "triumphing" over disability, albeit a triumph that leads not to a happy ending but one of mayhem not unlike that of Arturo that Katherine Dunn later fashions in her novel *Geek Love.* Mitchell and Snyder's discussion of a prostheticizing narrative seems particularly pertinent in relation to such a line of thought. They write that

> a narrative issues to resolve or correct—to "prostheticize" in David Wills's sense of the term—a deviance marked as improper to a social context. A simple schematic of narrative structure might run thus: first, a deviance or marked difference is exposed to a reader; second, a narrative consolidates the need for its own existence by calling for an explanation of the devia-

> tion's origins and formative consequences; third, the deviance is brought from the periphery of concerns to the center of the story to come; and fourth, the remainder of the story rehabilitates or fixes the deviance in some manner. This fourth step of the repair of deviance may involve an obliteration of the difference through a "cure," the rescue of the despised object from social censure, the extermination of the deviant as a purification of the social body, of the revaluation of an alternative mode of being. Since what we now call disability has been historically narrated as that which characterizes a body as deviant from shared norms of bodily appearance and ability, disability has functioned throughout history as one of the most marked and remarked upon differences that originates the act of storytelling. Narrative turns signs of cultural deviance into textually marked bodies. (*Narrative Prosthesis* 53–54)

In the end, Popeye's attempt to remove his deviance fails, for his reshaping his image ultimately marks him as more evil in a novel in which disability invariably signifies threat. In offering a kind of negative and, as it were, partial story of overcoming disability, Faulkner seems to tease the reader with the possibility of rehabilitating the novel's most evil force.

In addition to these things, I believe Faulkner added this material to the end precisely because it serves to highlight the centrality of Pap and his blindness to the novel. This material was not in Faulkner's original version of the novel. As important as voyeurism is in both versions, it is not the relentless force in the so-called "Ur-Sanctuary" as it is in the published version. Many scholars have appropriately noted that Faulkner's revision removes Horace Benbow from the center of the novel, Lurie well pointing out that the revision moves vision to the thematic center. What has not been noted is that the result of this revision also moves Pap to the center. My guess is that as Faulkner worked through the changes in the book he realized that Pap's presence in Temple's mind at the rape moment loomed larger than ever with Horace and his fretting largely removed from the text. Realizing this, he perhaps saw the need to rework Popeye as a disabled figure and relate him directly to Pap. Just as he had already linked Tommy with Temple through disablement, Faulkner in his revision linked the two people whose names start with P in their shared disability, the explicit connection of blindness. Popeye is Pap-with-eye, Pap+Eye.

And when he watches Temple and Red having sex it is as if Pap is still watching, only this time the eyes can see. Conversely, Pap's two phlegm-clots above Temple can be seen as the abled testicles Popeye lacks, Pap's eyes thus serving a prosthetic function for the villain, in ironic contrast to their failing of the victim. Pap, Faulkner seems surely to have realized, is the common denominator.

The common denominator in a novel concerned with absent and/or inadequate fathers. Powerful as he may be politically, Temple's father is conspicuously absent as a real character or force in the novel. Again, in the Memphis brothel she calls Popeye "Daddy," suggesting that he has replaced Pap in the business of watching her in a moment of sexual intercourse. Popeye himself seems to use Red as merely another prosthetic where, for Temple, Red has moved into a role Popeye could not adequately perform himself and Popeye moves into the disabled role, even if Popeye *is* far more dangerous than Pap. In a very different sense, it is as though the "disabled" Temple embraces Pap as a kind of protective prosthetic "father," and then is forced to move on to claiming Popeye as such. Such an assertion, I realize, carries the disturbing implication that Temple needs a father and his protection for completion—and yet such seems to be Faulkner's point. It is her father's name that endows her with any status beyond a cheap flirt back at the university. It is the status of being his daughter that empowers her as the belle of the campus just as much if not more than her looks. Her movement into and throughout a world in which the structures of her ablement are thus marked by different "fathers"—this is a world beyond the reach of her true father, where the denizens are unimpressed with her father being Judge Drake of Jackson. When at the trial that signals her reentry back into the world in which she is abled, she is told by the district attorney, "Let these good men, these fathers and husbands, hear what you have to say" (377), and she returns to her real father, who with her brothers retrieves her and carries her back home and later to Paris and Luxembourg Garden. In the final scene of the novel, she sits with her father in Luxembourg, he in the same passive stance she imagines him to be in when she was living her nightmare at the Frenchman's house when she thinks of him "sitting on the porch at home, his feet on the rail, watching a negro mow the lawn" (213).

Where Temple at least reunites with her father, other characters are not as lucky. Popeye's true father has left his mother before he is even born (he comes into the world the day his mother receives the last communication she will ever get from him), and her second husband leaves when Popeye is a child, likely still an infant. The lynching of Lee Goodwin leaves an infant fatherless, an infant that Faulkner spends much time focusing on throughout the novel. Then there is Little Belle, her mother divorced from her father, and Horace in the role of, not father exactly, as Temple and Belle become one in his mind and he battles the attraction he has to both. Horace's situation is in fact not unlike Faulkner's own, or at least it is not surprising that the issues of divorce and becoming a guardian of children should be on his mind. During the months between January and May 1929 when Faulkner was writing the original version of the novel in which Horace figures so largely, Estelle was getting a divorce from her husband. She and Faulkner married in June, and he found himself with both a wife and two children, one of whom it was rumored he had fathered. It is commonplace to point out that Horace may be voicing Faulkner's own thoughts when he says, "When you marry your own wife, you start off from scratch . . . maybe scratching. When you marry somebody else's wife, you start off maybe ten years behind, from somebody else's scratch and scratching" (190). Perhaps not only the things distasteful to him about marrying a divorced woman (even if it was—or perhaps more-so because it was—his childhood sweetheart) weighed on his mind but also the problems of being a parent and the children's being away from their real father. Certainly the weakness of his own father as compared to his powerful grandfather and legendary great-grandfather had been marked in the missing generation of Sartoris men in *Flags in the Dust.* No wonder that Faulkner should describe the summer after Temple's trial as "gray" (398).

To carry this biographical thread further, just as fathers fail to make the grade, the mothers, somewhat like Faulkner's own mother, can be competent and even heroic figures. Ruby keeps her baby with her at all times and cares for the baby whatever the living conditions of the moment may be. The final vision we get of her is with her holding her baby: "The child made a fretful sound, whimpering. 'Hush,' the woman said.

'Shhhhhhhh'" (380). However absent his father is, Popeye's mother has deep devotion which he arguably reciprocates to some degree, visiting her all the way in Pensacola once a year and protecting her from knowing the realities of his lifestyle. The socialite women do not seem to have the same power and prowess—neither Temple nor Belle is memorable for her motherly tendencies—but these lower-class women, lacking other things, are lauded in the novel's logic for the skills and tendencies of motherhood.

What is especially striking is that both mothers are marked by an experience of an association with disability. Popeye's mother is referred to as being "an invalid" and seems to have been so from an early age, apparently at the time during which he has been at "a home for incorrigible children" (393). The text says of his mother that the "woman who had tried to befriend the child supported her, letting her do needlework and such" (393). It is an interesting detail, the charitable means of support, for its blatant purpose of infusing her and consequently Popeye's life with pathos. It betrays a borrowing from the sentimental novel that further heightens the uncomfortable effect of casting the murderous Popeye in a sympathetic light. Just as the genre/style-borrowing in Faulkner's depiction of Ike's love affair with the cow may leave a reader uneasy at what could be read as a cheap exploitation of disability, so this function of disability may seem a disappointing shorthand incorporation of disability for sentimental effect for a character thoroughly undeserving of such. On the other hand, Popeye's mother is disabled in the very different sense of being so ill-treated by men in a novelistic setting that requires women's dependence on men; this disablement may even be read as contributing to her invalidism.

Ruby, meanwhile, lives in the house with the cognitively disabled Tommy and the blind and deaf Pap. When Popeye brings Horace to the house and commands Ruby to cook for him she replies, "Yes [. . .]. I cook. I cook for crimps and spungs and feebs" (185). Popeye retorts, "You can quit. I'll take you back to Memphis Sunday. You can go to hustling again. [. . .] You're getting fat here. Laying off in the country. I wont tell them on Manuel Street" (185). At that point, Tommy makes his entrance and then leaves again, prompting Popeye to remark, "I wont tell them on Manuel street that Ruby Lamar is cooking for a dummy and a feeb too" (186). Like Popeye's own mother, the dependency on men leads to a setting characterized by disability. Dim options: women treated cheaply by men without the aid of high society that women such as Temple and Belle have are rendered finally invalid, whether *in*valid as Popeye's mother or in*va*lid as Ruby, a woman who performs a function that would seem to make her integral—providing food, for heaven's sake—but in fact only makes her dispensable. At any moment, she can be sent back to Memphis to be pimped out or perhaps even banished forever and immediately replaced by another. In this light, her comment to Temple that, if a "real man" goes so far as "to call you a whore, you'll say Yes Yes and you'll crawl naked in the dirt and mire for him to call you that" (219) becomes disturbing for yet another reason in addition to those that feminist readings have long provided.

Which brings us back to Pap, who again, as I see it, occupies the center of all this disability. Back to the scene of his mastication. He chews the food that Ruby cuts up for him, and when he finishes he spits it back out, then is led away as the patriarch. The food he gums seems in the context of the novel a metaphor for women and their treatment by the patriarchal structures that use them and expunge them. However innocuous Pap the character may be as a disabled person, his being a disabled *man* makes him a representative of an empowered masculine cruelty that finds most concentrated manifestation in Popeye. Discovering the full extent of Popeye's disability, especially the fact that he was at first thought to be blind warrants and even demands reading back over and revising any reading of Pap that sees him as only helpless. Where Faulkner's revealing Popeye's disability modifies the latter's villainy to whatever extent, Popeye's villainy may be read as modifying Pap's status as a figure of horror, not just in his presence in the house but as a man. Pap may in a sense be read as a critique of the idea of the masculine line of descent as dynasty embodied in Jim Bond in *Absalom, Absalom!* the ironic end of Thomas Sutpen's relentless attempt to establish everlasting power in the begetting of a disabled person. Such is the reverse of what Pap represents, which is that the well is poisoned, as it were, from the start—the very fountain of a masculine dynasty is disabled, and we might wonder if we are to read Faulkner's description of Ruby and Lee's child's "lead-colored eyelids show[ing] a thin line of eyeball" (216) as an indication that this child is disabled too, either blind or in some other way.

The matter of degenerative line of descent—perhaps "feeblemindedness" resulting from a recessive gene causing disabledness ("feeb" short for feeblemindedness)—ultimately sends my mind to the rural horror genre and its roots in *Sanctuary* and other Faulkner novels. In the *Preacher* comic-book series by Garth Ennis and Steve Dillon, the final descendent of the protected line of Christ is a disabled teenager; that series revels in disability in the backwoods of the South, as the preacher Jesse's family is from the swamps of southeastern Texas, which are depicted as being full of disabled inbred people. Such a notion obviously does not come just from Faulkner: James Agee and Walker Percy's *Let Us Now Praise Famous Men* and Erskine Caldwell's novels and stories among others provide plenty of fodder for that (Ashley Craig Lancaster's essay on feeblemindedness in *God's Little Acre* and *Tobacco Road* is particularly enlightening regarding these matters). Of course a current reader may recall James Dickey's *Deliverance* and the film version of it. But the motif of the rural house of horrors inhabited by disabled people finds a significant precedent in the Frenchman's house presided over by blind Pap.

In the end, *Sanctuary* is an X-rated novel. I say this not so much because of the content (the term would not have existed when the novel was published), but because of the chiasmic contours of the book. Temple and Tommy seem the most opposite of extremes on the scale of normality and abnormality, yet Temple crosses back over him, as it were, in her change into social abnormal. With the revelation of his biography, Popeye's character reverses over itself. Haunting about Horace, from his days in *Flags in the Dust,* is his obsession with the Keatsian urn, a poem that contains one of the most famous statements of chiasmus ever, "Beauty is Truth, Truth beauty, that is all ye know on earth and all you need to know." Even the composition of the novel may be viewed in such a light, with Faulkner writing one kind of novel and then changing his mind, crossing back and crossing out much of the text to make it something very different, something brimming with disability.

I mention this chiasmus business not as some mere academic exercise (I am sparing you my combing of the text for references to and images of crosses) but rather because highlighting Faulkner's recursive positioning and repositioning of characters shows what someone interested in disability can glean from Faulkner. It is a curious fact about *Sanctuary* that it tends to elicit totalizing appraisals, especially regarding its composition/reason for composition. Faulkner's famous comment that the novel was a cheap idea conceived to make money was taken at face value by many readers for years; such readers adopted the comment as a value judgment of the novel, and dismissed it accordingly. Over the past twenty or so years more and more scholars have seen Faulkner's comment as a marketing pose and have discounted it entirely as being neither true to Faulkner's actual appraisal of the novel nor helpful as a value judgment. It strikes me that neither stance is exactly true to the spirit of Faulkner's statement, to the chiasmic nature of the text's creation, because they both totalize. I do not think Faulkner meant the statement as a totalizing one, although he surely knew it would be taken as such and that the comment could indeed lead to greater interest, which has succeeded presumably in helping sales and has certainly added to its intrigue among scholars. But his essay, however baiting it is in its hyperbole, nevertheless carries truths—Faulkner *did* need money, he *did* write a sensational novel.

And the reality is that from a standpoint sensitized to disability the novel *is* a cheap idea. Compared to the subtlety of Benjy and the large questions Faulkner allows to loom regarding the line between sanity and insanity in regard to Darl, in *Sanctuary* Faulkner hitches his disabled characters to a plow and tells them to go to, unabashedly using them as representatives of horror and/or evil. At the same time, though, the sympathy that he does impart to Tommy, hints at with Popeye's biography, and makes at least discernable in Temple's plight cuts back across that very cheapness. In any of these cases, the reader makes a mistake if he or she approaches the text with a totalizing mentality. Neither the unique history nor the structure nor the strategies of characterization in the novel warrant such totalizing.

Which helps us to understand what the novel has to offer disability studies in a larger sense. On one hand, it does not seem to offer much: in making disabled people the carriers of horror it panders to normate prejudices and reifies harmful stereotypes. Where Benjy might provoke a reader to think about cognitive disability in complex and sensitive ways, the characters in *Sanctuary* are finally easy to dismiss as stock figures revelatory of normate fears. But if we take into account the novel's refusal to totalize, then we can move through its elements of disability to witness something very significant—the strategies people with bodies and minds that *do* not because they *can*not conform to an imagined norm use to lay claim to normality. Scholars have repeatedly noted that Faulkner foregrounds the role of discursivity in constructing and constituting history; *Absalom, Absalom!* with its recursive movements, its relentless retelling, is a much-lauded example of what is seen as an integral Faulkner technique. The same technique may be applied to *Sanctuary,* only the retelling serves not just to modify, clarify, and/or revise history (create history) but to do the same in regard to one's status as normal or abnormal, abled or disabled. Just as *Absalom, Absalom!* lifts historical fiction into a nuanced foregrounding of the act of telling itself, so *Sanctuary* complicates the "cheap" genre of hard-boiled detective fiction. In this sense, the novel can be seen as performing a generic prosthetic role, showing how disable characters and themes can liberate and expand works operating within the narrow confines of popular genre fiction.

Sanctuary is a book that demonstrates the central tenant of disability studies that, as Ann Shearer puts it, "the difference between what people define as 'disabled' live with every day and the everyday experience of us all is not one of kind, but only one of degree" (5). The novel strains, like most of Faulkner's writings, to produce even one unquestionably "normal" character. What it more accurately does is show how characters slide across the spectrum of normality-abnormality either constantly revising or constantly having their identities revised in ways that move them to different places in that spectrum. In Popeye we can witness a man who is himself disabled distance himself from other disabled people and even to involve himself with and meet head-on the very activities from which and symbols of which his disability deprives him. He can neither drink nor have sex, so he makes his living in bootlegging and prostitution. He can overcome the weakness and sickliness of his childhood by means of the power of the prosthetic of a gun, which ultimately provides him with both a literal and rhetorical hyper-ableism. If he had overcome a different disability to become a "legitimate" businessman—say he overcame blindness to become a writer—he might be praised, as I have mentioned before, as triumphing over his disability. As it is, we see a man whose own disability he not only tries to hide but which also does not cause him to be sympathetic to other people with disabilities. Dummies and feebs, he calls others, echoing Ruby in the latter but adding his own vicious appellation in the former, as if were perfectly fitted to the ideal of the normal. Such is the very motivation behind his comment and his behavior in general. Everybody else is weird and sick, see? Popeye is noimal, see? He'll plug ya, see?

In fact almost all the novel's characters position themselves or are positioned in relation to normality. Poor Virgil and Fonzo might be full-grown normal adults back in the Mississippi small-town setting, but in the city whorehouse they are as children. Gowan Stephens is a regular Joe about town, only when he gets drunk his impairment disables him to the extent that he falls far short of the gallant beau ideal chivalric protector of feminine chastity that his lofty name, derived from "Sir Gawain," promises. And Horace, who might seem to stand in for normality in the same manner that Gavin Stephens does in Faulkner's later works, swings into elaborate monologues during his visit to the Frenchman's house that prompt Ruby to say, frankly, "He's crazy" (189). Normality is elusive, unstable, something to say at, to protest, to define and redefine. Meanwhile disability and abnormality foster solipsism—many disability theorists have observed that disabled people do not easily form a coherent group, not seeing themselves as necessarily having much in common with other people with disabilities as, for example, African Americans may see common experiences with other African Americans or people in the African diaspora. People born without arms in many cases see little common ground between themselves and a former athlete now in a wheelchair because of an injury. This very disparateness we can see clearly at work in Popeye's attitudes toward other people with disabilities. We can also see it at work in the ways other characters are isolated in various ways by not conforming to constructs of normality. The novel itself seems to have further heightened Faulkner's own status as disabled, as by many accounts it was the novel he was for many years most asked about at dinner parties and the one that of course garnered him the nickname of "Corn Cob Man."

I close by saying that there is one final thing I would like to mention regarding *Sanctuary* and disability. And that is . . .

GOOBLE-GOBBLE

They Ain't Human Like Us

deformation. In tacking Popeye's biography onto the end of the novel, Faulkner arguably unbalances the narrative in that doing so creates a deformation of conventional narrative form. Such deforming did not begin in Faulkner's career with *Sanctuary. The Sound and the Fury* is no less unusual, and Faulkner would repeat the tacked-on story-at-the-end technique in *Light in August.* In a 1931 essay on Faulkner, Granville Hicks actually linked disability, deformity, and Faulkner's style, observing that Faulkner's writing is marked by "distorted form," perhaps made so after an initially straightforward telling, and that it "echoes with the hideous trampling march of lust and "disease" (17–24). In *Sanctuary* the form itself can disable the reader, further centering Pap not just on a metaphorical level but also a structural one.

To speak of variations in form is a bit like describing abnormal snowflakes, which ideally would be the same as discussing human bodies generally. Ostensibly no norm exists for the structure and form of novels. Yet even now readers often see Faulkner's fictional structures as radical deformations of expected novelistic form, which is to say the kind of linear narrative that has for at least a couple of centuries signified standard structural approach. Indeed, where formal variation has practically always characterized poetry, the novel and short-story tradition, despite its many experiments, has maintained an uneasy, tacitly accepted imagined expected form, especially in popular genre writing, which Faulkner attempted to produce even early in his career (recall how he deforms even as he employs the detective genre in Benjy's section of *The Sound and the Fury*).

If Lennard Davis is to be believed, normality and abnormality are intimately connected to novelistic plot and form. In his essay "Who Put the *the* in the Novel? Identity Politics and Disability in Novel Studies," Davis takes on plot in the context of his assertion that the rise of the novel coincided with and actually encoded the development of "realism" as a mode that codified constructs of normality. He writes provocatively that plot "in the novel, then, is really a device to turn what is perceived as the average, ordinary milieu into an abnormal one" (97). An intriguing assertion: Davis elaborates: "Plot functions in the novel, especially during the eighteenth and nineteenth centuries, by temporarily deforming or disabling the fantasy of nation, social class, and gender behaviors that are constructed as norms. The *telos* of the plot aims to return the protagonists to this norm by the end of the novel. The end of the novel represents a cure, a repair of disability, a nostalgic return to a normal time. In this sense, the identity of the novel, if we can see the novel as having an identity, revolves around a simple plot. A normal situation becomes abnormal and, by the end of the novel, normality or some variant on it is restored" (97–98). In Davis's thinking, then, the novel's ontological roots clutch within the foundational soil of the ideology of ability, and I think his comments are best taken to describe not only the origins of the novel-as-ontology but also the novel as an item for bourgeois readership and consumption in its various historical incarnations.

Meanwhile, the reality of actual novels' identities are hardly so neat (Davis ironically replicates the normal-abnormal relation/divide in his argument). Faulkner was hardly the only experimenter of his time, much less in the history of the novel. Significantly, though, his formal experiments represent a deforming of normality that, at least on one occasion, coincided with human disability. When answering a question about his favorite novel of those he had written, he said to a West Point cadet,

> I think that no writer is ever quite satisfied with the work he has done, which is why he writes another one. If he ever wrote one which suited him completely, nothing remains but to cut the throat and quit. And in

> my own case, the one that is closest to me would be the one that failed the most, that gave me the most trouble. So no writer can judge what he thinks is the best. It's like the mother with the child who is an idiot or born crippled—that that child has a place in the heart which the hale, strong child never has. That may be true of any writer, that the one that's closest to him is the one he worked the hardest at—the failure which was the most painful failure. So I'd have to answer that question in the—which is the one that cost me the most anguish and that I still don't like the most, which is one called *The Sound and the Fury*. (*Faulkner at West Point* 47)

This restatement of the familiar Faulkner line about failure uttered in the context of disability might well express the quintessence of Faulkner as writer of disability. His very conception of writing is anti-ableist, with success defined not as the achievement of normality and health but rather as the celebration of "imperfection," figured here in the context of human bodies, minds, and emotions. However problematic it may be to attempt to identify a stable identity of novelistic form, Faulkner's efforts do deform on formal and thematic levels. And these techniques—the same names assigned to different characters, the unqualified or vaguely anteceded pronouns, long complex convoluted sentences, omissions of major and even climactic events and moments—deliberately disable the reader.

Faulkner's adding the long back-story of Popeye to the end of *Sanctuary* not only unbalances the book's structure, it can also be seen to disable any hope of a neat moral division of good and evil, a maneuver that shows how bodies, whether real or fictional, can shape and then reshape perception. A strong naturalistic streak runs through the novel as environment mangles and molds characters; alongside this aspect, bodies and their changes and limitations affect "character." Faulkner wants the reader to feel the ways a body and its condition dictate experience; he insists that the body of the text, like one's physical body, defines the limits and horizons of the individual and that the individual is bound by his or her body and its peculiar abilities and disabilities. By removing, obscuring, or overloading "parts" of texts, he approximates absent, enlarged, or misshapen human body parts. It might be said that Faulkner creates freakish texts marked by deformity.

Upon first glance, Faulkner's body of work seems surprisingly bereft of deformed character bodies. For all of his concern with disability and abnormality, there are very few characters with missing or deformed limbs or disfigured faces. Obviously Pap's eyes are not normal and Popeye is an odd-looking fellow, but neither's body is marked by extreme variation. Even Ab Snopes, with his limp, is not "unusually" formed, his disability being from a wound that impairs but does not disfigure. Otis in *The Reivers* is a dwarf, but even taking account of the tenuous reading of a little person's body as deformed, the fact of his dwarfism is made clear only once his age is revealed. As I hinted earlier, Otis's being a littler person registers the threat of a freak, but that threat emerges only after he has posed a different kind of threat when perceived as a hyper-abled dangerous child. Faulkner's own small stature might be significant here, including accounts of his being teased in a Memphis whorehouse for being "little" (Blotner 101). On a different note, Faulkner's developing a disfigurement in the form of his humped back as he grew older suggests a personal experience of physical deformation. Still, few of Faulkner's characters are memorable for the disfigurement of their physical bodies, however mentally, emotionally, or spiritually disfigured they may be.

One notably deformed character who appears in Faulkner is not an active person in his fictional world but rather the subject of a tall tale. When Fairchild brings up the name "Al Jackson" in *Mosquitoes* he explains that this "direct descendant of Old Hickory [. . .] Wont let anyone see him barefoot. A family deformity you see" (308). Fairchild's joke is that Al Jackson and his illustrious ancestor both have webbed feet, which is why Andrew Jackson was able to defeat the British in the swamps in New Orleans (this he says to Major Ayers, who is from England). As has often happened in historical perceptions of human deformity, Fairchild imagines Andrew and Al Jackson as being part animal. He further imagines such interspecies hybridity when he refers to the animals Jackson allegedly employed in the Battle of New Orleans, explaining, "some of these horses strayed off into the swamps and in some way the breed got crossed with alligators. And so, when Old Hickory found he was going to have to fight his battle down there in those Chalmette swamps he sent over to his Florida place and had 'em round up as many of those half horse-half alligators as they could, and he mounted some of his infantry on 'em and the British couldn't stop 'em at all" (309). The tenuous line between species within single bodies serves as humorous material for Fairchild, but this early text sets the stage for Faulkner's future writing about deformed, freakish hybridity in serious as well as humorous ways.

In fact, arguably the most memorable deformed body in the Faulknerian canon is an animal—Old Ben the bear of "The Bear." In the original, shorter magazine version of the story, the bear's deformity is presented outright, in the very first paragraph: "[Ike] had already inherited them, without ever having seen it, the tremendous bear with one trap-ruined foot which, in an area almost a hundred miles deep had earned for itself a name, a definite designation like a living man" (*Uncollected Stories* 281). The bear is twice-marked—it is "tremendous" and "disabled," two designations that seem ostensibly to cancel each other out. He is also designated by another pair of markers: his age, and his having a name. And not just any name, as the longer version of the story makes clear: "Old Ben, the two-toed bear in a land where bears with trap-ruined feet had been called Two-Toe or Three-Toe or Cripple-Foot for fifty years, only Old Ben was an extra bear (the head bear, General Compson called him) and so had earned a name such as a human could have worn and not been sorry" (*Go Down, Moses* 169–70). Faulkner's anthropomorphizing the bear is crucial to his constructing him as a character in the logic of the men who hunt him, or at least the logic Sam Fathers instills in the young Ike McCaslin. The logic of deep spiritual connection between the hunter and the hunted, that is. The kind of logic that sees a white man's trap as being far from a noble way to hunt, capable rather of a maiming that on the one hand lessens the bear while on the other it increases his nobility as a grand figure in the tradition of Captain Ahab. Indeed, that naming casts the bear as being in human company, if the bear is not exactly itself human.

Ironically, where such a deforming mark earns the bear a "human" identity, deformity often consigns humans to the status of "animal." In her discovery of the Francis Terry Leak diary, Sally Wolff has suggested that the diary contains names suggestive of characters in several of Faulkner's novels besides *Go Down, Moses.* Particularly interesting is that Faulkner might have assigned the names of slaves to white characters, an act that can be seen as an attempt on Faulkner's part to resurrect those names and their owners and recast them in more empowered positions or, at the very least, to let the names live again in fiction as well as their stories, some of which Faulkner seems to have reworked in his writing, and Wolff finds in the diary precedent for the character of Benjy, right down to the name "Ben." What I think is a much more remarkable link with this necessarily even name that Faulkner would not have needed an antique ledger to think of but that connects *Go Down, Moses* and *The Sound and the Fury* also is that he should assign the name to two central disabled figures. I have already mentioned the connection through disability between the disabled bear named Ben and an earlier created character referred to by the third-person narrator in the fourth section of *The Sound and the Fury* as Ben and described for the first time from such a perspective thusly: "She heard the feet cross the diningroom, then the swing door opened and Luster entered, followed by a big man who appeared to have been shaped of some substance whose particles would not or did not cohere to one another or to the frame which supported it. His skin was dead looking and hairless, dropsical too, he moved with a shambling gait like a trained bear" (1088).

Did Faulkner mean for his readers to remember the "older" Ben created years before the Old Ben in "The Bear"? Placed side by side they present mirror images, being the reverse of one another. Maury's being referred to by the name of "Benjy" represents different things to different characters; one of its signals for the reader is that the person originally named Maury does not turn out to be an adequate bearer (no pun intended, really) of that august name. "Maury" is a drunken but sophisticated uncle. "Maury" is the name of a baby born into an aristocratic family. "Benjy" is a person with a cognitive disability. "Benjy" is seen by many characters as less human. "Ben," as the narrator calls this person, is bear-like. "Ben" in "The Bear" is a sure enough bear, but that name signals that entity's being humanized, which at the same time creates a gendering, in this case rather predictably as male, where Benjy's disability feminizes him. Ben the bear's deformity makes him more noble, more heroic. Where Benjy is passive, Ben is active, a rapacious thief and killer. It does not seem to disable him at all but rather does the opposite.

In being so welcomed into human company, the bear Ben accrues a narrative prosthetic significance. This role is complicated. It is tempting to see the narrative of which the bear is a part—the narrative of the development of a young hunter—as being as anthropocentric as the bear's naming. But in Sam Fathers's view, the center of meaning is shifted so that humans, bear, deer, and so on are all part of a common interdependent existence. Beyond this narrative (or perhaps this one is more accurately beyond the other) the bear's deformity signifies his presence and function in what is very much an anthropocentric and ultimately masculinist narrative—that of men proving their mettle by pursuing and killing the largest, most legendary bear of all. These conflicting narratives congeal around the famous paw print, the calling card that lets hunters know they have just missed the ghostly elusive game of their dreams. That print is the means of tracking the bear and would seem in that endeavor a disabling thing for the bear. But for Ike it is an admonition and invitation: he can recognize the bear not just by the injured paw but by the others as well. It is Ike who finds the "crooked print" so fresh in the mud that "it continued to fill with water until it was level full and the water began to overflow and the sides of the print began to dissolve away" (*Go Down, Moses* 153). At which point he, having no gun and learning that the interaction of creatures is about far more than killing, is hardly about the kill at all, sees the bear. Both narratives—the hunters' and Sam and Ike's—depend on the bear.

Deformity is integral to "The Bear" on several levels. The story has often drawn comparisons to *Moby-Dick,* and they are indeed similar in featuring entities marked by physical variation; they also feature a similar deformation of conventional notions of plot and structure, at least in the case of the longer version of the bear, which, like Melville's novel, interrupts the plot for a lengthy digression on matters related to but not properly part of the plot. On another level, the story features the disabling and deformation of the big woods, their disappearance before the march of an environment-changing technology that renders the likes of Sam Fathers obsolete, extraneous, nonfunctioning, and marginal. The bear's paw symbolizes this disabling technology, and the bear too has no place in this new environment. Faulkner makes the deforming, disabling effects of these changes clear in the story's final scene, when Ike sees "Boon, sitting, his back against the trunk, his head bent, hammering furiously at something on his lap. What he hammered with was the barrel of his dismembered gun, what he hammered at was the breech of it. The rest of the gun lay scattered about him in a half-dozen pieces while he bent over the piece on his lap his scarlet and streaming walnut face, hammering the disjointed barrel against the gun-breech with the frantic abandonment of a madman" (*Go Down, Moses* 246). The big woods have all but vanished, the gun is deformed and disabled, and in this new world the heroic Boon is nothing more than a crazy man as quaint and obsolete as Daniel Boone and his woodsman era have themselves become—a type of figure and environment soon to be living only in the Disneyfied performance of the likes of Fess Parker.

Where the bear is the most famous of Faulkner's deformed animals, there is another vivid if less-known case to be found in *Flags in the Dust* when young Bayard visits the MacCallums. One of the MacCallum sons, Jackson, has decided to try an experiment in eugenics, an effort to create the perfect creature for hunting foxes by mating the fox Ethel with the hound General. "In the shadowy corner" of the house, we read, "a number of small, living creatures moiled silently" (318). Faulkner describes them thusly:

> No two of them looked alike, and none of them looked like anything else. Neither fox nor hound; partaking of both, yet neither; and despite their soft infancy, there was about them something monstrous and contradictory and obscene. Here a fox's keen, cruel muzzle between the melting, sad eyes of a hound and its mild ears; there a limp ear tried valiantly to stand erect and failed ignobly in flapping points; shoebutton eyes in meek puppy faces, and limp brief tails brushed over with a faint golden fuzz like the inside of a chestnut burr. As regards color, they ranged from

> pure reddish brown through an indiscriminate brindle to pure ticked beneath a faint dun cast; and one of them had, feature for feature, old General's face in comical miniature, even to his expression of sad and dignified disillusion. (828)

While not in all cases strictly deformed, as a group these offspring are monstrosities. There follows a demonstration of their collective hunting abilities. As Mr. McCallum states, they "Cant smell, cant bark, and damn ef I believe they kin see" (828) is grotesquely proven as they whirl and stumble about when discovering there is meat to pursue, which they learn only when Jackson forces pieces of it into their mouths.

Why does Faulkner include these creatures in this novel beyond their being another of a number of disabled background elements? Jay Watson sees a eugenics "recessive gene" discourse at work here, divining in these creatures "the anxiety and confusion surrounding questions of purity and hybridity in *Flags,* even when displaced onto nonhuman contexts and forms" (33). There is not much sympathy on Faulkner's part for these puppies unless one reads a stark pity for them inherent in their very repulsiveness and inability to recognize and chase meat. Also, one can detect a commentary on functionality to be read here in that Jackson sees these animals only in terms of their potential functioning, and this kind of informal backwoods mad-scientist activity naturally creates, as it were, monsters. Whether Faulkner meant this scene as more than a joke—as a broader statement on the ethics of such activity—is difficult to tell: Watson offers the justifiably puzzled admission that the "point of all this remains unclear" (33). Perhaps the name Jackson could be read as obliquely referring to Andrew Jackson, whom Faulkner had already imagined in terms of freakish hybridity and whose policy of Indian Removal manifests the same kind of philosophical machinery that derives from eugenics, but in fact the MacCallum sons are named after Confederate generals, presumably Stonewall instead of Andrew Jackson in this case (thinking back over the family claim that it was Colonel Falkner instead of Thomas Jackson who should have been named "Stonewall" it might be of interest to imagine deforming an application of a sobriquet that the Falkners already saw as a deforming). Hideous as the scene is, it is a minor one that does not seem to carry larger implications beyond its comments on the misguided and comically unintelligent ingenuity of a bumpkin, a scene of mild horror forecasting the horrors in *Sanctuary* but not the deeper if still problematic depiction of Ben. "The Bear" exhibits a much more complex pondering of human desires in regard to animals, and this is a depth of thought and engagement that develops in the ten-plus years that separate the two works.

Right in the middle of those ten years appeared another text about freaks.

To move toward speaking of this text, we can consider freakery more specifically. Joke or not, Faulkner's description of this litter—the very language he uses—conforms to the classic definition of a freak as advanced by Leslie Fiedler. As mentioned earlier, according to Fiedler, freaks fascinate normates because the latter recognize them as being part of the same family of humanity but at the same time alienatingly different. As Fiedler puts it, the freak "stirs both supernatural terror and natural sympathy, since, unlike the fabulous monsters, he is one of us, the human child of human parents, however altered by forces we do not quite understand into something mythic and mysterious" (24). Fiedler's work has spawned an entire subdiscipline of freak studies, all of which in one way or another, explicitly or implicitly, relates back to his originary definition. But his own definition depends on a precedent too, as he uses the phrase "one of us" very deliberately, consciously evoking the exact same phrase from the very controversial 1932 film *Freaks.* The film depicts life in a circus sideshow and includes a number of famous freaks of that time. The basic plot is that a normate—a beautiful but cruel young woman—marries a little person for his money. After the wedding ceremony, the freaks initiate her into their group by having her carry out the symbolic act of drinking from the same cup as they. She refuses to do so, which does not bode well for her, as this act and her blatant insulting of her husband and attempt to poison him later lead to the freaks' great wrath and act of vengeance, which is surgically to turn her into a freak, half-human and half-chicken. Before her duplicity is found out and her freakification is made literal, the ceremony of her symbolic freakifying is driven by a chant in which the freaks sing "we accept her, one of us, one of us, gooble-gabble one of us."

The director of this film was Tod Browning. Browning is perhaps more widely remembered for another famous film he directed, the 1931 *Dracula,* starring the inimitable Bella Lugosi. Originally censored not only for what was considered offensive visual material but also for its too thinly veiled sexual innuendoes, *Freaks* has never enjoyed as much mainstream attention, although it has endured censorship to become a cult classic. Controversy about its questionable ethics has haunted the film from its first release. Browning wanted to depict a vanishing mode of entertainment and a misunderstood group of people, and his putting true freaks on screen speaking for themselves and actually winning the day as the victorious sympathetic characters have been seen as a noteworthy step in empowering disabled people. At the same time, the film has been seen as exploitative, a charge that some of the actors themselves raised against Browning. In any event, Browning and his film are now firmly fixed as important in disability studies.

What is not generally talked about among scholars of disability studies *nor* often remembered among Faulknerians is that Browning and Faulkner knew one another. In 1933, the year after the release of *Freaks,* Faulkner was assigned to work with Browning on a film to be entitled *Louisiana Lou* (it would actually be released after work on it by nine other writers as *Lazy River*). Browning was in New Orleans and Faulkner, whose daughter was about to be born, was hesitating to make the trip to the Crescent City and so delayed, taking an airplane from Memphis rather than a train. His stay in New Orleans was famously short, and quite a tale arose regarding his dismissal from the project. The story (apparently partly perpetuated by Faulkner himself) is that no progress was being made on the script. He and Browning went to the set day after day, but Faulkner was prevented from working on the script because "the continuity writer refused to let him see his story line until he showed the writer some dialogue" (Blotner 317). According to the story, two telegrams came over the wire: the "first, Faulkner said, read, FAULKNER IS FIRED. MGM STUDIO. After Browning assured Faulkner that he would obtain his reinstatement and an apology, the second arrived: BROWNING IS FIRED. MGM STUDIO" (317). In reality, the problem was that MGM was tired of Faulkner's absenting himself from California (he had been working in Oxford) and so terminated his contract until such time as he should be in California again. Meanwhile, when asked about why the script had not moved along satisfactorily, Browning had written of Faulkner: "PARTY REFERRED TO . . . BRILLIANT CAPABLE MAN BUT HAD UNFORTUNATE START" (317).

Those few words in the telegram roll out of the dead wire-hum with tantalizing secrecy. I find myself wanting to try and imagine the two men on the set in New Orleans, sitting in cloth-back chairs, Faulkner's legs crossed, the rich rye smell of whiskey and pipe smoke emanating from him, Browning at ease, waiting. It makes sense that they could have hit it off. They were both southerners—Browning was from Louisville, Kentucky (for the moment we will set aside the fact that not a few Mississippians are unsure as to whether Kentucky is part of the South). They were also drawn to the aberrant, the disabled body. In presenting some of the material to follow a few years back, I made the comment that there was not evidence that Faulkner had heard of, much less seen, Browning's film. After running across the above-related anecdote in Joseph Blotner's biography I have changed my mind. I still do not know if Faulkner saw the film, but I suspect he at least knew about it and that he and Browning on some level compared notes, even if not openly at least by awareness of each other's work. Tod Browning, maker of *Dracula* and *Freaks.* William Faulkner, maker of *The Sound and the Fury* and *Sanctuary.* Was ever there a better match (other than maybe Faulkner and Ed Wood)? It fairly breaks my heart that the two did not see the film through to completion together or that they did not undertake some other project—what a bizarre and fascinating piece of film mongery could have come from such a union.

Whether the fact that these two men knew each other interests readers in itself, the time and place of their meeting I believe carries immense implications for the novel I now want to discuss that appeared in the years between *Flags in the Dust* and *Go Down, Moses.* That novel is *Pylon.* Faulkner would write this book set in New Orleans only a year after his meeting with Browning in that city as well as a second visit there, and this much-maligned text is one that takes on especial importance in terms of disability and disability studies because it grapples with freakery even as it envisions a world in which human variation is the order of the day. *Pylon*'s very existence is an aberration in Faulkner's canon in that it is a novel that never takes on Mississippi in any significant way. Even *A Fable* cannot help but evoke Faulkner's home at critical points. But *Pylon* is about the Midwest and New Orleans, and Yoknapatawpha plays no explicit role in it. Pointing out its being a "freak" among Faulkner's books is merely the beginning of discussing the novel's grappling with abnormality and normality, a pointing to the cover that conveys the volume's contents.

It is perhaps the case that New Orleans seemed different to Faulkner upon his return to it as a middle-aged man. Maybe the romance his youthful mind saw in the city now was replaced with a recognition of the ways that romance had come to be marketed or had been so all along. Certainly the barnstorming scene he took in during the particular trip to the city out of which this novel grew represented a different kind of engagement from the bohemian life he had led in the French Quarter as a youth. It strikes me that on an organizational level, the novel revises, by which I mean reforms, by which I further mean *de*forms that very romanticism. Macbeth's soliloquy from which Faulkner took the title for his fourth novel reappears here in the chapter divisions of "Tomorrow" and "And Tomorrow," but where that poignant moment in Shakespeare's play is meant, despite all its irony, still to evoke hubris, waste, and ultimately tragedy, Faulkner evokes it in *Pylon* more to stress the "petty pace" that characterizes life, especially the reporter's accustomed existence. Then there is the chapter title "The Love Song of J. Alfred Prufrock," a resurrection of one of the poems whose influence is clear in Faulkner's poetic efforts, especially *The Green Bough.* This evocation of T. S. Eliot's poem seems a more "grown-up" one—the reporter is Prufrockian, but Faulkner's presentation of him seems harsher than that of, say, Taliafero in *Mosquitoes.* Not to play up Faulkner's early romanticism too much, as his sharp irony was in place from the beginning of his career, but *Pylon* I believe is light years from the early New

Orleans treatments in that it reads like an experience of a real modern metropolis rather than as a kind of florid Old World–like city.

The evocation of Eliot's poem is also significant from a disability standpoint because one of its most famous images is that of the patient etherized upon a table. Faulkner casts the passed-out drunken reporter as being the representative of such a body (788), and like Prufrock he certainly lacks the ability to find love, to court Laverne, or even to fulfill the "normal" expectations of a reporter as per the definition of its editor. The implied presence of a sick body might also apply to New Orleans itself. Faulkner had described the city as a "a faintly tarnished and languorous courtesan" in the past. But this New Orleans, renamed as New Valois no less, seems morphed into something else—a city of hard rather than soft edges. Note the clinical presentation of the shop Jiggs (jagged?) visits at the beginning of the novel: "He entered the store, his rubber soles falling in quick hissing thuds on pavement and iron sill and then upon the tile floor of that museum of glass cases lighted by an unearthly daycolored substance in which the hats and ties and shirts, the beltbuckles and cufflinks and handkerchiefs, the pipes shaped like golfclubs and the drinking tools shaped like boots and barnyard fowls and the minute impedimenta for wear on ties and vestchains shaped like bits and spurs, resembled biological specimens put into the inviolate preservative before they had ever been breathed into" (779). Quite a description—a vision of a special room in a hospital where are kept not just the unborn but the monstrous. Such a collection of "specimens" is a more scientific version of the curiosity cabinet that so fascinated people during the Enlightenment and beyond. Such a collection could easily be found in a freak show even in Faulkner's time. Here, at the very opening of the novel, we are presented with an intense focus on bodies ensconced in the larger body of the city and which serve as a gloss for that metropolitan body. It is a body of hard edges strewn with spent materials of carnival. Even though there are people in it, even crowds at times, it feels strangely empty, dead.

Indeed, as I have noted in various contexts, environment can determine normality and abnormality, and included in environment are built spaces the structuring of which is inseparable from the defining and functioning of bodies in the novel as it is in real life. That structures of culture are by turns both defined by and constitutive of constructions of normality and abnormality is a point that disability studies theorists have continually stressed. I cite, by way of example, Garland-Thomson:

> Stairs [. . .] create a functional "impairment" for wheelchair users that ramps do not. Printed information accommodates the sighted but "limits" blind persons. Deafness is not a disabling condition in a community that communicates by signing as well as speaking. People who cannot lift three hundred pounds are "able-bodied," whereas those who cannot lift fifty pounds are "disabled." Moreover, such culturally generated and perpetuated standards as "beauty," "independence," "fitness," "competence," and "normalcy" exclude and disable many human bodies while validating and affirming others. [. . .] Thus, the ways that bodies interact with the socially engineered environment and conform to social expectations determine the varying degrees of disability or able-bodiedness, of extra-ordinariness or ordinariness. (*Extraordinary Bodies* 6–7)

Garland-Thomson's comments concatenate in interesting ways with Yi-Fu Tuan's exploration of experiences as dictating the laying out of spatial grids. He writes that "[h]uman spaces reflect the quality of the human sense and mentality. The mind frequently extrapolates beyond sensory evidence" (16) and goes on to explain that in "the Western world systems of geometry—that is, highly abstract spaces—have been created out of primal spatial experiences. Human beings not only discern geometric patterns in nature and create abstract spaces in the mind, they also try to embody their feelings, images, and thoughts in tangible material. The result is sculptural and architectural space, and on a large scale, the planned city. Progress here is from inchoate feelings for space and fleeting discernments of it in nature to their public and material reification" (17).

"Biology conditions our perceptual world," Tuan asserts, tracing the development of perception during the progression of childhood: he notes that, when an infant begins to become mobile, moving "the body along a more or less straight line is essential to the experiential construction of space into the basic coordinates of ahead, behind, and sideways" (20). The particular physiological capabilities of a given moment of development determine the spatial constructs of that moment, so that because "the first few weeks of life the infant's eyes cannot focus properly" only so much surrounding space can be negotiated (20). Tuan introduces a Marxist slant to his discussion, observing that, while a "child's biological equipment" limits his or her constructionist abilities, the "inability, for most people, to recapture the mood of their own childhood world suggests how far the adult's schemata, geared primarily to life's practical demands, differ from those of a child" (19–20). In fact, the adult's market-driven perspective dictates his or her experiences of space, as Tuan points out that "the human body is the measure of direction, location, and distance" and that spatial "prepositions are necessarily anthropocentric, whether they are nouns derived from parts of the human body or not" (44–45). In this regard, he offers the observation that a book is *on* a desk "because [that preposition] immediately helps us to locate the book by directing our attention to the large desk. It is hard to imagine a real-life circumstance in which the [statement] 'the desk is *under* the book' is appropriate. We say an object is on, in, above, or under another object in reply to practical and even pressing concerns" (45).

Disability studies shows that, however provocative Tuan's observations are, however true they are to the majority of spatial constructions, they mystify and naturalize a normative perspective. As Garland-Thomson writes, although constructs of space "are partly founded on physiological facts about typical humans [. . .] their sociopolitical meanings and consequences are entirely culturally determined" (*Extraordinary Bodies* 6). What I find telling in placing Tuan's and Garland-Thomson's works side by side are their respective ways of claiming the term "human." In Tuan, the term covertly achieves an exclusion: experience for Tuan is basic, unproblematized, and intimately tied to a normal adulthood that begs the question. An infant's eyes cannot see "properly." Garland-Thomson's comments acknowledge the same thing about constructions of space by normates, but in her hands "human"—especially when read against Tuan—is a more inclusive and complicated appellation. Where Tuan's writing carries a hint of nostalgia for a child's experience, Garland-Thomson's shows awareness of the perniciousness of the exclusionary and relegating nature of so-called typical adult normates' constructs and how that nostalgia does not extend to grown-ups who for reasons of disability do not develop those "typical" spatial experiences. We might think back to Benjy's "experiences" of things coming or going away according to his different—in Tuan's terms "childlike"—spatial sense.

As you will also recall, Fiedler too uses the term "human" in noting that freaks are "one of us," which, again, is a quote from Tod Browning's film, which leads us back to Faulkner. While there is no way to know conclusively if Faulkner saw Browning's controversial film or discussed it with him, there appears in *Pylon* a suspicious phrase that distills these matters of humanity, freakishness, and socially engineered structures. At one point, when the reporter is attempting to describe the barnstormers he is so obsessed with, he tells his editor "they aint human like us; they couldn't turn those pylons like they do if they had human blood and senses and they wouldn't want to or dare to if they just had human brains. Burn them like this one tonight and they don't even holler in the fire; crash one and it aint even blood when you haul him out: it's cylinder oil the same as in the crankcase" (804). The phrase "they aint human like us" evokes the famous phrase from Browning's film, but Faulkner gives us something different from Browning's "one of us" and Fiedler's gloss on it. For where freaks may not *look* human externally they nevertheless are, where the fliers *look* human but actually are not when dissected. As the reporter later observes about the child Jack, "Yair; cut him and it's cylinder oil; dissect him and it aint bones: it's little rockerarms and connecting rods" (933–34). These folk are not humans, they are robots in human clothing.

They may even be a type of alien. Jeffrey A. Weinstock observes that, "[a]lthough never 'human,' the extraterrestrial can fall anywhere on the continuum between human and monster" and that when the "freak show" vanished in the 1930s it gave way by the 1940s to the "Golden Age of Science Fiction" in which "freaks" were repackaged as aliens who "fall somewhere between monster and human: into the freak zone" (328). With their amazing reflexes, perhaps the fliers are of a race from outer space. Their "station," the Feinman Airport, Faulkner describes in terms that evoke comic-strip science fiction:

> the shell road ran ribbonblanched toward something low and dead ahead of it—something low, unnatural: a chimaera quality which for the moment prevented one from comprehending that it had been built by a man and for a purpose. The thick heavy air was full now of a smell thicker, heavier, though there was yet no water in sight; there was only the soft pale sharp chimerashape above which pennons floated against a further drowsy immensity which the mind knew must be water, apparently separated from the flat earth by a mirageline so that, taking shape now as a doublewinged building, it seemed to float lightly like the apocryphal turreted and battlemented cities in the colored Sunday sections, where beneath sill-less and floorless arches people with yellow and blue flesh pass and repass: myriad, purposeless, and free from gravity. (785–86)

In referring to the "colored Sunday sections," Faulkner likely was thinking of *Buck Rogers,* which had been running in the Sunday strips since 1930 and would have featured such images. I find it provocative to think of Faulkner's anticipating the creation of Superman, who already existed in the minds of his creators but would not appear in print until 1938. Provocative because the fliers, like Superman, look human at skin-level but are not.

I am not sure it is unfair to see *Pylon* as a type of science-fiction novel, but freakishness extends beyond bodily make-up. The reporter assigns the barnstormers to nonhuman status not simply because of what he imagines their insides to be but also because they outrage normate spatial affiliation. He repeats to the editor, they "aint human, you see," because they have no

> ties; no place where you were born and have to go back to it now and then even if it's just only to hate the damn place good and comfortable for a day or two. From coast to coast and Canada in the summer and Mexico in winter, with one suitcase and the same canopener because three can live on one canopener as easy as one or twelve—wherever they can find enough folks in one place to advance them enough money to get there and pay for the gasoline afterward. Because they don't need money; it aint money they are after anymore than it's glory because the glory cant only last until the next race and so maybe it aint even until tomorrow. And they dont need money except only now and then when they come in

> contact with the human race like in a hotel to sleep or eat now and then or maybe to buy a pair of pants or a skirt to keep the police off them. (805–6)

The reporter's comments present an intersection of bodies and space and economy that relates strongly to concerns among disability studies theorists regarding capitalism and bodies. In a capitalistic system that, as Lukacs and others have argued, posits the producer as a product as much as the product that person produces, quality control—with its imagined normate—demands a workable working body that performs within provided efficiency-minded built spaces. Work space is as socially engineered as any other and can just as readily inhibit a body that cannot function within its confines.

Faulkner actually ponders the problematic of the market, labor, space, and bodies as products. Consider, for example, the description of the reporter's quest for breakfast after awaking, "like so many people who, living always on the outside of the mechanical regimentation of hours, seem able to need to coincide with a given moment with a sort of unflagging instinctive facility" (918). As the reporter rushes through the city streets, he passes the street lamps which are set to go out at a certain time of the day, eventually stopping at "one of ten thousand narrow tunnels furnished with a counter, a row of buttockpolished backless stools, a coffeeurn and a Greek proprietor resembling a retired wrestler adjacent to ten thousand newspapers dubbed by ten thousand variations about the land" (919). The lights might go out at a certain time and the coffee-houses may be one of a thousand all designed to fit into the regimented clocks of the city's systems of labor, but those backless stools, you better believe, are buttockpolished. And then what of the Other—the Greek man with the extraordinary body of the wrestler? The Greek man is, of course, a product as well, for he is as myriad and interchangeable in this particular architecture as are "the immemorial grapefruit halves which apparently each morning at the same moment at which the street lamps went out would be set, age- and timeproved for intactness and imperviousness" (919). Meanwhile, the night in this machine-world is the non-working time, as it were, when "the ill and the weary were supposed to be prone to die" (918).

Despite the reporter's claims to the contrary, the fliers need money too; but it *is* true that they resist the kinds of established spaces that confine the regular workers of the world, including the reporter himself. And this freedom from such structures seems ironically enough to preserve their external normalcy where the bodies of characters confined to earth are finally disfigured by those structures. Indeed, the reporter's body much more evidently approaches freakishness than the internally alien fliers; Faulkner writes that the reporter is "a creature which, erect, would be better than six feet tall and which would weigh about ninetyfive pounds, in a suit of no age nor color [. . .] which ballooned light and impedimentless about a skeleton frame as though suit and wearer both hung from a flapping clothesline;—a creature with the leashed, eager loosejointed air of a halfgrown highbred setter puppy [. . .]" (788).

The reporter looks like a "scarecrow" and has a "cadaver face" and at one point "collapsed upon the chair with a loose dry scarecrowlike clatter as though of his own skeleton and the wooden chair's in contact" (803), as if he were an insect-man, with an exoskeleton. Such bodily freakishness also appears in the form of Jiggs, who although a part of the flier crowd does not actually leave the earth. Jiggs has a "short thick musclebound body like the photographs of the one who two years before was lightmiddleweight champion of the army or Marine Corps or navy," and he wears "cheap britches overcut to begin with and now skintight like both they and their wearer had been recently and hopelessly rained on and enclosing a pair of short stocky thick fast legs like a polo pony's, which descended into the tops of a pair of boots footless now and secured by two rivetted straps beneath the insteps of [. . .] tennis shoes" (780). Perhaps endowed with some robotic qualities resulting from his connections with the fliers, he walks with a "fast stiff hard gait like a mechanical toy that has but one speed" (782). Jiggs the man-pony and the reporter the insect-man (or bat-man, as he is also described) are ultimately hybrids, representing both self and an at least partially nonhuman other in a way that conforms to Fiedler's definition of freaks. These animal evocations in cases of deformity also correlate with those in *Flags in the Dust* and "The Bear."

The Body of the Text: Gooble-Gobble

In *Pylon* Faulkner achieves his grandest vision of what can be seen as a positive abnormality in the form of freakishness-alienness, and this "positive abnormality" takes the form of a potential cultural deformation. While it is difficult to pin a writer like Faulkner down when it comes to authorial sympathies, I do not think it daft to assert that the fliers can be seen as the heroes of the novel and that in their freedom, however problematic it can be because of infighting, Faulkner presents a model of disrupting and escaping normate space that can be a good one. I have argued in the past that Faulkner takes a grim view of attempts to colonize the air—to transfer the cruel history of imperialism of land to the space of air. But these barnstormers in their ability to leave the earth behind may well represent a freedom that Faulkner favors and also mourns when it is "grounded" by Roger Shumann's death.

It strikes me that in the novel Faulkner continually tries to find a new order, whether in his radical play with language, his sharp departure from the content of his past novels, or his very different way of imagining space as more urbane, less specific, pastless, and therefore malleable. In a way *Pylon* could be seen as Faulkner's most overtly "modern" work in the vein of Wallace Stevens, Djuna Barnes, James Joyce, and of course Eliot from whom Faulkner so heavily borrows. The novel reads much more like their works than Faulkner's other novels in its presentation of a recognizably modernist wasteland presented in a language that goes over the top in making things strange. One stance on this aspect of the novel is to see it as a more derivative project far from Faulkner's unique rooted home turf, his peculiar envisioning of modernism through the lens of his home. The readers who find this novel less impressive for this and other reasons are perhaps more numerous than those who would defend it. Although I happen to love the novel—perhaps vainly because one of its characters has my own name—I am not so much interested at the moment in criticizing or defending its channeling of modernism as I am in stressing that the novel is very much about modernism and that in its considering aberrant bodies in the context of modernism it relates to an especially intriguing treatment of modernity and its offspring/successor postmodernity in the context of disability.

In what is in my opinion one of if not the most provocative essays yet produced by disability studies, Lennard Davis envisions a cultural-historical period I mentioned early in this book that he labels "dismodernism." The essay is entitled "The End of Identity Politics and the Beginning of Dismodernism: On Disability as an Unstable Category," and in it Davis makes the rather bold assertion that identity politics should best be framed according to an imagined "dismodernism" moment. Davis pits what he calls dismodernism against postmodernism because the latter fails to dismantle the privileging of abledness. Dismodernism, on the other hand, posits dependency itself as "normal," thus exploding the inherently untenable concept of the noncontingent individual and replacing it with the realization that disability is the uber-identity of humanity. Because of its broad claims and implications, I should like to linger with the essay, for its precepts seem to me of a piece with what Faulkner seems to be working out not only in *Pylon*'s channeling—and perhaps pressuring—of modernism but also the bodily-spatial issues at work in "The Bear" and in the case of the monstrous offspring in *Flags in the Dust.*

Davis begins his essay by actually criticizing postmodernism's great sacred cow, identity politics. He dismisses even so central a tenet as "strategic essentialism" as being a cop-out, writing, "For all the hype of postmodern and deconstructive theory, these intellectual attempts made little or no impression on identity politics. Rather, those who pushed identity had strong Enlightenment notions of the universal and the individual. The universal subject of postmodernism may be pierced and narrative-resistant but that subject was still whole, independent, unified, self-making, and capable" (26). The lone-ranger mentality is then, according to Davis, untouched, a hold-out ideal. It is the inability to achieve an Emersonian self-reliance that inhibits the social progress of marginalized groups; the ideal of the self-reliant individual meanwhile remains unchalleneged.

This notion of a noncontingent individual is thus the true enemy that neither modernism *nor* postmodernism deconstructs. The "dismodern era" is needed for this task. Davis writes, the "dismodern era ushers in the concept that difference is what all of us have in common. That identity is not fixed but malleable. That technology is not separate but part of the body. That dependence, not individual independence, is the rule" (26). A dismodern world has no center of normality enslaved to a bodily ideal; the machinery of center-periphery as a social configuration ceases to exist when interdependency becomes the fundamental practice of social interaction, dispersing the former energy of the center throughout a leveled field. The idea is almost heartbreakingly utopic, especially when Davis proclaims that "[w]hat dismodernism signals is a new kind of universalism and cosmopolitanism that is reacting to the localization of identity. It reflects a global view of the world" (27). Identity is localized because individual traits enter into a universalized catalog bound by variation. Is this American *e pluribus unum* channeled through new utopic lines?

Davis does provide "practical" guidance for realizing the dismodern era. He explains that to "accomplish a dismodernist view of the body, we need to consider a new ethics of the body. We may take Kierkegaard's by-now naïve belief in the universal and transform it, knowing that this new universalism cannot be a return to Enlightenment values. Rather it must be a corrective to the myths not only of the Enlightenment but of postmodernism as well" (27). Davis roots his utopic idea in the body, a move that seems to carry the implication that material makes real. He outlines three areas of this "new ethics of the dismodernist body" (27) in a distinctly Lincolnesque tone: care *of* the body, care *for* the body, and care *about* the body (each time he uses these phrases, he italicizes them as shown here). Regarding the first, he makes the provocative statement that

> care *of* the body is now a requirement for existence in consumer society. We are encouraged and beseeched to engage in this care; indeed, it is seen as a requirement of citizenship. This care of the body involves the purchase of a vast number of products for personal care and grooming, products necessary to having a body in our society. Although we are seen as self-completing, the contemporary body can only be completed by means of consumption. This is the official stance: that the contemporary human body is incomplete without deodorant, hair gel, sanitary products, lotions, perfumes, shaving creams, toothpastes, and so on. In addition, the

> body is increasingly becoming a module onto which various technological additions can be attached. The by-now routine glasses, contact lenses, and hearing aids are supplemented by birth-control implants, breast implants, penile implants, pacemakers, insulin regulators, monitors, and the like. Further work will also intimately link us to more sophisticated cybertechnology. All this contributes to what Zygmund Bauman calls "the privatization of the body," which he sees as the "primal scene of postmodern ambivalence." The aim and goal, above all, is to make this industrial-modeled, consumer-designed body appear "normal." And even people with disabilities have to subscribe to this model and join the ranks of consumers. (27)

These comments immediately start me thinking of *Pylon,* with its robotic bodies, its envisioning a new "race." Interestingly, Davis acknowledges this bodily-completion ethic as already in place in a capitalist-conditioned consumer society, a rather too gleeful mixing of ideals, it seems to me. Likewise, in his thinking, care *for* the body "also links the economy with the body" (27) and includes the entire health-care profession as part of dismodernism. Meanwhile, care *about* the body means discussing the kinds of issues raised in disability studies. As Davis writes, "This area begins with attention paid to human rights and civil rights that have to be achieved to bring people with disabilities to the awareness of other identity groups. Here we must discuss the oppression of so-called abnormal bodies, and the treatment of the poor with disabilities. Class again becomes an issue in identity" (28). Davis further notes that "caring *about* the body subsumes and analyzes care *of* and care *for* the body. The latter two produce oppressive subjection, while the former gives us an ethic of liberation. And the former always involves the use of culture and symbolic production in either furthering the liberation or the oppression of people with disabilities" (29).

The latter anti-capitalist safeguard of sensitive intellectualism and activism provides the superego in this trinity. Davis finds himself faced with the conundrum of disability studies—that even though everyone is touched by disability, there are people who are truly marginalized and severely hampered by and in society because of their disabilities, and the very attempt to show disability studies' universal relevance threatens to drain the field's very specificity and, perhaps, usefulness. Aware of this, again, strikingly U.S. democracy-esque paradoxical situation, Davis charges on. Disability must be key, as he points out that race, gender, and sexual orientation have at times historically been seen as disabled conditions. Building on this dubious universalizing of disability, Davis writes, "Disability studies can provide a critique of an identity politics to discuss how all groups, based on physical traits or markings, are selected for disablement by a larger system of regulation and signification. So it is paradoxically the most marginalized group—people with disabilities—who can provide the broadest way of understanding contemporary systems of oppression" (29). Thus privileging disability as a predominant marginal position that is in fact the center of marginality (a move that looks suspiciously like a reinscription of center-margin structures), Davis works out his vision of a new order with disability as centered. I quote at length:

> Politics have been directed toward making all identities equal under a model of the rights of the dominant, often white, male, "normal" subject. In a dismodernist mode, the ideal is not a hypostatization of the normal (that is, dominant) subject, but aims to create a new category based on the partial, incomplete subject whose realization is not autonomy and independence but dependency and interdependence. This is a very different notion from subjectivity organized around wounded identities; rather, *all* humans are seen as wounded. Wounds are not the result of oppression, but rather the other way around. Protections are not inherent, endowed by the creator, but created by society at large and administered to all. The idea of a protected class in law now becomes less necessary since the protections offered to that class are offered to all. [. . .] The dismodernist subject is in fact disabled, only completed by technology and by interventions. Rather than the idea of the complete, independent subject, endowed with rights (which are in actuality conferred by privilege), the dismodernist subject sees that metanarratives are only "socially created" and accepts them as that, gaining help and relying on legislation, law, and technology. It acknowledges the social and technological to arrive at functionality. [. . .] The fracturing of identities based

> on somatic markers will eventually be seen as a device to distract us from the unity of new ways of regarding humans and their bodies to further social justice and freedom. (30)

What Davis is calling for is a very delicate thing: an honest, pure-hearted rethinking of power and its administration—and it has the problems of any such utopic vision. How does one remove the desire for power completely from humans? Breed it out?

Davis's program might seem underwhelming, if touching: "Clearly, what I am describing is the beginning of a long process. It began with the efforts of various identities to escape oppression based on their category of oppression. That struggle is not over and must continue. While there is no race, there is still racism. But dismodernism argues for a commonality of bodies within the notion of difference. It is too easy to say, 'We're all disabled.' But it is possible to say that we are all disabled by injustice and oppression of various kinds. We are nonstandard, and it is under that standard that we should be able to found the dismodernist ethic" (31–32). In short, we need to return to a "grown-up" universalism that is aware of all the pitfalls and abuses of power and is marked by decency and common concern for one another as all being on the same side as dependents. A pessimist might point out that such a mentality plays right into the hands of power mongers and that more truly practical recommendations might be made for moving this "long process" along. How, exactly, does one neutralize the power-hungry, oppression-minded forces while these fundamental changes in thinking and policy take root and grow?

Many things in Davis's essay lead back to *Pylon*. The fliers depend on one another—that canopener again—even as they in their rootlessness exemplify a cosmopolitanism "reacting to the localization of identity." The reporter imagines their bodies to be completed by technology. Little Jack's identity resists fixedness: he might be the son of either big Jack or Roger, or when he fights he might be Jack Dempsey. Moreover, the identity issues connected with paternity or race do not apply to him any more than spatial-cultural-political boundaries. Little Jack can hit the road whenever he likes, and he is the way of the future. To state what

I am obviously driving at, the fliers can be seen as constituting a group resembling what a dismodern culture might look like, marked both by uniqueness and group interdependency.

The subtle and riveting implication of Davis's essay is that it calls for a deforming of society itself, and here can be found especial resonance in *Pylon.* Constantly in the novel Faulkner struggles for a new rhetoric that comprehends the mash-up of people and mediated realities and objects. New Valois is a new New Orleans, which for Faulkner is a futuristic reach and vision of something he both imagines and sees signs of already in existence. New Orleans had been the site of his own rebirth as a writer of prose, and now it was the location in which he could imagine a new kind of fiction to go with a new kind of future. This future is deformed in a broad sense, so that the fliers represent a coming new order that Faulkner tries to make sense of. I find illumination, in fact, in the comment of another minor character who, like Pap in *Sanctuary,* provides arresting commentary. The character is the elevator man the reporter encounters after first visiting Hagood the editor; the man says to the reporter about barnstorming generally, "I think they are all crazy [. . .]. Them that do it and them that pay money to see it" (810). Such a resonant comment in light of the freak-show contexts swirling all around the novel. "Craziness," used as an uneasy hyperbolization of literal cognitive and emotional disability, applies to a broad cultural phenomenon. Dismodernism *is* crazy: you'd have to be crazy to change ideals, laws, the very ideology of ability itself.

A very real theoretical question emerges in such deforming of culture very much along the lines of "craziness," especially if that word is taken in its sense of referring to disarray and lack of order. Does dismodernism propose to replace the ideology of ability with an ideology of disability? And would that replacement, or if not that then the alteration of the ideology of ability, mean jettisoning the drives toward success and achievement that seem so entrenched in such ideology? Keeping Faulkner in dialogue with Davis and (implicitly now Siebers), *Pylon* can be seen as pressuring that very question in its closing scene featuring the reporter's two different write-ups of Shumann's death. Both pieces might be read as deformations of ideals of journalistic style. The one that actually reaches Hagood's desk gives the details but does so in a lifeless manner, treating an event that the editor likely would not even consider news. The discarded piece the copyboy finds is equally problematic, though.

Although earlier the editor upbraids the reporter for trying to be one of the "Lewises or Hemingways or even Tchekovs" (808), the fact is that the discarded essay reads not so much like these writers but actually a lot like Faulkner. A very specific version of Faulkner, in fact. I quote it and then a text from none other than *Flags in the Dust:*

> On Thursday Roger Shumann flew a race against four competitors and won. On Saturday he flew against but one competitor. But that competitor was Death, and Roger Shumann lost. And so today a lone aeroplane flew out over the lake on the wings of dawn and circled the spot where Roger Shumann got the Last Checkered Flag, and vanished back into the dawn from whence it came. (*Pylon* 991).

> The music went on in the dusk softly; the dusk was peopled with ghosts of glamorous and old disastrous things. And if they were just glamorous enough, there was sure to be a Sartoris in them, and then they were sure to be disastrous. Pawns. But he Player and the game He plays. . . . He must have a name for His pawns, though, but perhaps Sartoris is the game itself—a game outmoded and played with pawns shaped too late and to an old dead pattern, and of which the Player Himself is a little wearied. (*Flags in the Dust* 875)

The parallelisms of these two quotes are to me very revealing, especially in light of the latter's coming also after a character's death in a plane crash. It is not without irony that Faulkner notes that the high-school-age copyboy believes the reporter's piece "to be not only news but the beginning of literature" (991). There is an implied parallel here: just as *Flags in the Dust* stands as a germ that really begins Faulkner's Yoknapatawpha apocrypha on the strength of the death of the Sartorises, so *Pylon* seems to pack in its hull a germ of something altogether different—crazy—based on a self-parodying killing off of Faulkner's own prose style and attempt at a different one. Yet just as Shumann's death would seem to signal death for the little progressive dismodernist community of fliers, so both of the reporter's pieces fail to succeed even as they deform, and he is left drunk and without "jack," seemingly referring both to money and the future in the form of the now landed little Jack, dashing the hopes of a future deformed the way the reporter imagines. Of course, everyone is still crazy.

It might be objected that I am taxing *Pylon*'s cultural reach by considering its premises in so big and sweeping a concept as dismondernism, but as I alluded to in part one of this body of text I would argue that this same anti-ableism and vision of a new order appears on an equally microscopic scale of macroscopic implications in *A Fable.* In that novel we get what Davis does not offer, an example of an active effort to change things. By the example of the mysterious Christ-like corporal, the enemy soldiers lay down their arms, vacate the trenches, and meet each other halfway in peace. It is a fine attempt to realize the kind of dismodernist mentality Davis presents, a practical, radical case to follow, even if an imagined one. The corporal seems to have no nationality; it is not even possible to pin down a single name to call him. He represents, like Christ, a world where the meek and poor in spirit can seize control and bring warfare's grim and inexorable engines to a halt. Such a move carries a belief in a utopia that looks a great deal like the one Davis outlines. Yet where Davis's optimism is boundless, sweeping, and only vaguely systematic, Faulkner's is measured at best. In providing a concrete example in *A Fable* of something *to do* toward bringing about a dismodernist order, Faulkner goes farther than Davis. But the soldiers' actions also bring down the wrath of the powers that actually run the war, for the dissenters are shot down by planes ordered to quash this subversive act. Significantly, it is the very attempt to realize a new peaceful universalism that creates a physically disabled and deformed character, when the corporal's chief disciple is severely wounded and reappears at the end of the novel as a disruptive disabled person.

Faulkner's mind is clearly on matters of global significance in *A Fable;* on perhaps a less grand scale the shadow of general failure lies over "The Bear" as well. Contexts of dependency surround the latter text. Old Ben and Sam Fathers represent a cultural past that already had this grand leveling interdependency business figured out. Then there is the very intriguing subtext connected with "The Bear" of Faulkner's evident part-dependence on the Leak diary: not so much the independent artist working alone, he (perhaps in this case and clearly in many others) relied on others' writing, which he then continued to riff on, turning it into art. I would add as an integral aside that I think it an appropriate thing that just a few years before Wolff's discovery of the diary Noel Polk and Richard Godden cowrote an essay on the ledgers, a move that had already evoked the MacCaslin brothers' own joint work and that carries on the dependency exemplified by that text. But however enabling these aspects of dependency, there is a failure of deforming, and Faulkner is rarely one to celebrate anything that deforms nature, as happens in "The Bear." Indeed, despite his own interest in certain kinds of technology, Faulkner well raises the question, since when has technology been a friend to humanity? Davis seems to want to forge an alliance between humanism and technology in a general ethics of dependency, but technology's track record has arguably not always been so good. Certainly its potential for good is limited in Faulkner's writing—witness the apocalyptic vision of the old general in *A Fable,* the fliers in *Pylon,* and the rapacity of the railroad as the machine in the garden symbolized by Old Ben's wounded paw in "The Bear." And who really believes Jackson in *Flags in the Dust* will keep those puppies around once he fully realizes they will not be able to fulfill the market hopes they were "created" for?

At the same time, these seeming recursive failures of new orders or new styles or new voice in *Pylon, Flags in the Dust,* "The Bear," and *A Fable* can be seen as major elements of revision that seem consonant with what dismodernism may well be understood to necessitate. Faulknerian "failure" is of course a kind of success. It is a crazy notion of success, and one would probably have to be crazy to embrace it. The Faulkner canon can be read as deeply dismodern throughout, and viewed from such an angle *Pylon* becomes a lynchpin in it. The question might be raised that, if *Pylon* represents a germ in the same way *Flags in the Dust* does, then what grew out of it? My answer would be the novel that appears after a period of novelistic silence titled with striking symmetry to the first "germ" novel *Intruder in the Dust,* in which the interdependency of race becomes so significant and which sets up Gavins Stevens as a normal character dealing with a crazy world, a Snopes world that produces at its apex a character in Linda Snopes Kohl who may be as unable to "speak" as the unspeaking scions of the old order Benjy Compson and Jim Bond, but who is no "idiot." Rather, she relies on an interdependency with others, including Gavin as a hybrid new-old order figure. The crazy world these characters inhabit is one in which V. K. Ratliff has transformed from an insignificant man who gives young Bayard whiskey to incapacitate him when he is wounded to a man with a Russian name who can buy a crazy tie in Greenwich Village.

I have worked to bring these texts, especially *Pylon* and Davis's essay into dialogue here at the end of this body of text to try and model yet another way it seems to me Faulkner participates in the disability discussion. That such a dialogue might be seen as deforming Faulkner's moment or work does not bother me very much, since such deforming would presumably follow in a shift to something dismodernism could look like. But his attempt to dismantle the ideology of ability in his fiction and the way he consciously or unconsciously defied that ideology in his life might be seen as providing ideas as to how to forge effective art that does not necessarily have to enslave itself to an ableist-defined "success." What I hope can be seen is that Faulkner belongs in the conversation and defining of this process alongside Davis, Fiedler, and Garland-Thomson as well as writers such as Helen Keller, Katherine Dunn, or Eli Clare. One of the things that Wolff's discovery of Faulkner's awareness of the Leak diary offers is that it gives him greater factual street-cred as it shows a link between "fictional" prose and "factual" documentation, not that the distinction between the two is ever very stable or great. As he deformed and reformed literary style, contemporary understandings of perspective and disability, actual diaries, and whatever else, Faulkner gave us examples of how current forms can be deformed, broken apart, and transformed into something else, hopefully something better.

Faulkner, for all of his realistic understanding of power and its devastating effects, was able to turn deformity and disablement into positive agents of change. This hopefulness, measured as it is, I think especially recommends Faulkner as a useful writer within the discussions and goals of disability theorists. The Faulknerian ethic is one of intelligent engagement with the constantly changing present and the past that present changes. This engagement meets form and its deformations according to its own deforming methodology, privileging failure as success and maintaining a razor-sharp focus on constructedness and its border patrol. The increasingly disabled Faulkner did not shed his realistic understanding of humanity's problems when he offered hope and the promise of change in his Nobel Prize speech or in his later writing. In the end maybe it is the promise of change measured with realism that is the most useful gift of Faulkner, writer of disability.

A NOTE PERTAINING TO THE CONTENTS OF THE BODY OF THE TEXT

I want to begin this note by addressing certain terms and dynamics in disability studies. The field is a broad interdisciplinary one that includes medical and sociological inquiry along with that of humanities. Developing out of the civil rights movements of the 1960s, it seeks to see how disabled people are marginalized in the same way (other) minority groups are. As Siebers writes,

> the emerging field of disability studies defines disability not as an individual defect but as the product of social injustice, one that requires not the cure or elimination of the defective person but significant changes in the social and built environment. Disability studies does not treat disease or disability, hoping to cure or avoid them; it studies the social meanings, symbols, and stigmas attached to disability identity and asks how they relate to enforced systems of exclusion and oppression, attacking the widespread belief that having an able body and mind determines whether one is a quality human being. More specifically, disability studies names the states of social oppression unique to people with disabilities, while asserting at the same time the positive values that they may contribute to society." (3–4)

There are problems unique to seeing disabled people as a homogenous group, though, for where, say, African Americans might identify a tacitly agreed-upon cluster of racial signifiers long compacted historically as a common bond from which to articulate specific experiences of oppression, disabled people often have varying disabilities and hence unique experiences of marginalization. At its heart, disability studies as a field in the humanities wants to understand how disability is constructed, and in so doing it pays close attention to the ways it is constructed against and in the context of ability. These two constructs are locked in a kind of dualistic battle. And this dualism is articulated in a series of binary terms, concepts, relationships: ableism versus disableism, normal versus abnormal, etc. Ultimately disability studies wants to claim that the construct of normality is not possible for any body to conform to (even the wonders of plastic surgery must continually chase the ideal without final success because in fact that construct is a fluid one). This observation leads to the fundamental tenet that disability is a universal, even something that one personally evolves and matures into if one lives long enough, as Garland-Thomson has noted in various settings. This assertion of universality however is paradoxical, for the very claim of universality threatens to obliterate the real marginalization that people marked as disabled suffer and that people who may not be ideal but who still fall in the somewhat elastic zone of the normal do not.

I address Lennard J. Davis's way of reconciling this paradox in the section preceding this note, but I would here mention another thing that haunts about the pages of this book and that I would take a moment to elaborate on. Specifically, I am talking about terminology, which is no small matter, as terms are often contested at some length in this field. In the pages of this body of this text I use a variety of words according to the nuances of the context of a given point. I tend to use "normal," "abled," "abnormal," and "disabled" often with an effort to bring into light their relevance in a particular utterance and/or the ironies and constructedness of their use. I also use such terms as "not normal" or "normate": the latter term was coin by Garland-Thomson as a "neologism that names the veiled subject position of cultural self, the figure outlined by the array of deviant others whose marked bodies shore up the normate's boundaries" (*Extraordinary Bodies* 8). Finally, there is the term "impaired," which is used in opposition to "disabled," and it is in the opposition of these terms that the universal-specific paradox has been most often worked out. The term "impaired" is employed in two ways. One is to signal a general social category as against a personal one, with "disability" referring to a large social category and "impaired" referring to an individual's case (see Tom

Shakespeare's discussion of this matter in *Disability Rights and Wrongs*). The second use of the term refers to "impairment" as a bodily condition that hampers performance but is not totalizing where "disability" is a condition that dominates a person's identity (see Michael Oliver's *The Politics of Disablement: A Sociological Approach* on this topic). It may be noticed that this impairment-disability debate lies at the heart of the second section of this book regarding wounding, fraud, and totalizing of disability. I opted not to insert a discussion of this term there because I found it more productive in that case to show the various players in the Fa(u)lkner family and in Faulkner's writings struggling to define themselves, each other, and their spaces and place in the context of totalizing identities of which wounded veteran is chief. Suffice it here to say that impairment as a useful term might have helped clear up certain difficulties of definition, and then again it might not have. Either way, I found it more appropriate to allow the tensions of the various interactions detailed therein to allow the large attempts to categorize to shine through, as they do in Chick Mallison's frantic attempts to put Linda Snopes Kohl in her place, a place, any place.

Throughout the book I acknowledge intersections of constructs of animality and disability. At the time of this writing, animal studies scholars seem to write more about these intersections than do disability theorists, perhaps because equations of animality with disabled humans is too problematic for a field so concerned with expanding inclusion as a feature of the human community. My thinking on these intersections is especially indebted to Cary Wolfe's *Animal Rites* and Jacques Derrida's *The Animal That Therefore I Am*. Thank you also to Tiffany Frost, an MA student at Florida Atlantic University, for her provocative theorizing on the intersections of these fields.

As a final general comment on the contours of the field of disability studies before tending to other specifics in the book, I would simply note that certain scholars' names appear repeatedly while others of much importance in the shaping of this book seldom do or not at all. Davis, Garland-Thomson, Mitchell and Snyder, and Siebers are in the first category, as I mention their names and their ideas often. No less important or provocative, though, are Gary L. Albrecht, Michael Berube, Mairion Corker, Tom Shakespeare, Sara E. Hosey, Michelle Jarman, Simi Linton,

Michael Oliver, Robert McRuer, Ato Quayson, Ellen Samuels, Ann Shearer, and Henri-Jacques Stiker. I have included a selection of their works in the bibliography along with additional ones by Davis and Mitchell and Snyder that have been influential to me and that find their ways into the principles set forth in this book. Of course any body-sensitive analysis is indebted to the work of Michel Foucault, especially *Discipline and Punish*.

Turning now to the other parts of the body of the text, the first one cites or evokes most of the issues and some of the names listed above. I address the matter of disabled characters' ontology in various ways throughout the book, but I would offer an additional comment here on the problems of a pragmatic material approach to bodies in literary texts, which disabilities studies must to some extent be. One of the more provocative philosophers of body and "somaesthetics" is Richard Shusterman, and his notions of inner-outer complementarity in conversation and in his work (including the less body and more aesthetically turned *Surface and Depth*) have been very illuminating for me, especially in my discussion of Darl Bundren. Yet the ontological problems of bodies in literature are so thorny as to make his and many other pragmatic theories of body difficult to apply. Such theories find greater traction in specific cases, where characters' disability markers receive myopic focus, such as in the case of Pap in *Sanctuary*. But, again, disabled bodies not only face the troping paradoxes Mitchell and Snyder note but also the general ontological waverings that, as I see it, plague a sustained presence of such bodies or minds. I implicitly consider these ontological matters throughout the book; I believe it a theoretical problem worthy of many volumes dealing with it on the most abstract and theoretical levels.

Another point I would add more about is obesity and black women's bodies. Dilsey is not the only one of Faulkner's black woman characters whose bodies do not conform to the stereotypical black woman's body: on the whole, Faulkner's black women tend to be little. Consider Mollie Beauchamp in the titular story of *Go Down, Moses*. Faulkner writes that "by appearance she would have owned in [a] breeze no more of weight and solidity than the intact ash of a scrap of burned paper—a little old negro woman with a shrunken, incredibly old face beneath a white headcloth and a black straw hat which would have fitted a child" (271). Then there is the description of her in *Intruder in the Dust* "—a tiny old almost doll-sized woman much darker than [Lucas], in a shawl and an apron, her head bound in an immaculate white cloth on top of which sat a printed straw hat bearing some kind of ornament" (290). My thinking about such bodies is informed by a number of works in fat studies, which borrows much of its machinery from disability studies in examining how fat bodies are marginalized and even abused behind what fat studies theorists see as the smoke screens of the health industry. Such scholars include Paul Campos, Laura Fraser, Sander Gilman, Hillel Schwartz, Peter N. Stearns, and the essays in *Bodies Out of Bounds: Fatness and Transgression* (edited by Jana Evans Braziel and Kathleen LeBesco), *Cultures of the Abdomen: Diet, Digestion, and Fat in the Modern World* (edited by Christopher E. Forth and Ana Carden-Coyne), and *The Fat Studies Reader* (edited by Esther Rothblum and Sondra Solovay). It should be noted that fat studies scholars tend to want to distance themselves from disability studies despite the similarities between the two fields.

I mention the South's alterity in the first part of the body of the text, and I would point the reader not only to Woodward, Duck, and others mentioned in the text, but also to the essays in *South to a New Place* (edited by Suzanne Jones and Sharon Montieth), *Look Away!* (edited by Jon Smith, Debra Cohn, and Donald Pease), and Scott Romine's fascinating examination of the continuing constructions of southernness in *The Real South*.

For another reading of *A Fable* and a different take on the Nobel Prize speech that focuses especially on scars, see Alice Hall's *Disability and Modern Fiction: Faulkner, Morrison, Coetzee, and the Nobel Prize for Literature*.

I would expand slightly on the second part of the book, offering some material that would have interrupted the narrative flow but that is worthwhile in my opinion. First, I mention Malcolm Cowley's strained exchange with Faulkner regarding the latter's military experience, and you can read this for yourself in *The Faulkner-Cowley File* (edited by Cowley) on pages 74–85.

I would add to the paradoxes involved in disability and employment Lennard Davis's article "Bending Over Backwards: Narcissism, the ADA, and the Courts." In it, he argues that court cases dealing with disability, especially since the passing of the Americans with Disabilities Act, tend to have judges drawing the line at the point where employers are seen as "bending over backwards" to accommodate employees with disabilities. Citing the concept of the equality of pain (a notion of justice that dictates that one party's pain or discomfort be in some way deemed similar to that of another's), Davis points out that if employers build ramps to doors and appropriate toilet facilities for employers but fail to adjust the height of restroom sinks to accommodate disabled employees resulting in these employee's complaints, then courts tend to argue that employers have met the pain equation while employees continue to make further demands ultimately deemed unreasonable. In other words, after employers have been reasonable by bending over backwards for the employees, the employees are being unreasonable by asking for "too much" accommodation—so much, in fact, that providing such a degree of accommodation ultimately hurts businesses. Indeed, people who advocate such "extreme" accommodation (extreme from a normate viewpoint) are sometimes even seen as attempting to strike a blow at capitalism itself. In making these points, Davis notes that nondisabled people see certain complaints of disabled people as being "trivial."

In addition to the treatments of *Soldiers' Pay* mentioned and for discussion of it in relation to *A Fable*, see Hall, *Disability and Modern Fiction*.

I discuss Ab Snopes in terms of trauma, and I should mention that trauma theory has been no stranger to Faulkner scholarship. In *Children of the Dark House*, Noel Polk writes on the power of psychic trauma in the life of Joe Christmas in *Light in August*, explaining that the scene in Christmas's youth when he hides in the closet and steals and eats toothpaste while the dietician has sex with a young doctor is a primal scene that goes on to affect the rest of his life, culminating in his castration and death at the hands of Percy Grimm. Lisa Hinrichsen explores the devastating irrecoverability of the event that precipitates trauma in Faulkner's depiction of Temple Drake's rape in *Sanctuary*. And Caroline Garnier applies Cathy Caruth's theories of trauma to explore witnessing and women's narratives in a number of Faulkner's novels.

Finally, I would add a few insightful and relevant quotes regarding Linda Snopes Kohl and disabled women characters in general. I mention Keith Louise Fulton: to allow him to speak for himself, he suggests that Faulkner finds in Linda a way to resolve problems he had with white southern aristocratic patriarchal society that his "own identity as white, privileged, and male prevented him from resolving" (426). Fulton also offers the following distinctly Faulknerian sentence: "Whereas Linda's singular existence dramatizes the power of the patriarchy to isolate women from their mothers, from each other, and even from their mates, and while her bomb-deafened ears and quacking voice evidence the dehumanizing, desexualizing, and silencing assault she has survived, her strength and vision are the powers that Faulkner imagines will not only outlast the letter-of-the-law rapacity of the titular fathers and the respectable although self-serving guardianship of the timid uncles but will destroy and transcend them" (435).

Like Fulton, Claire Crabtree, whom I also cite in the text, sees Linda as being more radical, more independent, but also argues that this independence brings punishment to her: "In Linda, Faulkner creates a woman who 'speaks' in the sense of taking a stand and exercising moral choice, fighting as a Communist in the Spanish Civil War and resisting marriage to her companion Barton Kohl. But Faulkner literally silences her—even before the novel opens—so that Linda's punishment for speaking undercuts her speech itself. The explosion which kills Kohl leaves its physical scar in Linda's deafness, a mark of her bereavement, which also inhibits her power of speech" (528).

Beyond these two, Deborah Kent offers some particularly salient observations on literary representations of disabled women in the context of sexuality and sexual attraction. Looking to such characters as Laura Wingfield in Tennessee Williams's *The Glass Menagerie* and Gertie McDowell in James Joyce's *Ulysses*, Kent stresses that physical disability stands as a barrier to and relegates sexual attractiveness and either prevents or severely hampers the ability for such women to find sexual mates at all. As Kent notes, "many nondisabled men in these works feel pity and revulsion at their initial meeting with the disabled women" (53). Kent also goes on to note, however, that "revulsion and avoidance are not the total picture. Perversely, the same men who are repelled by a disabled woman are at times attracted by the disability as well" (53). Such is the case with Leopold Bloom and Gertie McDowell, as Kent notes, and one may think of Manley Pointer's fascination with Hulga's prosthetic leg in Flannery O'Connor's "Good Country People," although Kent does not mention that case. Kent writes,

> Nearly all of the relationships I have described turn upon the woman's disability. If she is an isolate, deemed unqualified by men, it is because she is disabled. Potential mates doubt her competence to tend to a family. Frequently the man feels he will be diminished in the eyes of others if he can only acquire a substandard partner. If on the other hand a man finds the disabled woman attractive, it is because her disability draws him to her, making her mysterious, heroic, or appealingly vulnerable. In either case, disability looms as an overwhelming issue for the men in most of these works. They may be repelled or attracted to the disabled woman, or struggle with both feelings at once. But the woman's disability is nearly always seen as her first and most salient attribute. (56–57)

Kent points out that in many cases of representations of disabled women (as is the case with the depiction of disabled people generally), "the disabled woman is little more than a metaphor through which the writer hopes to address some broader theme. Her disability may stand for helplessness, innocence, or blighted opportunities" (60). Ending on a hopeful note, Kent observes that "some writers have managed to create books and plays which show disabled women as total persons, capable of love and hatred, joy and anguish, the full range of human experience and emotion. Perhaps these works can open the way for an understanding of disabled women based upon awareness and respect" (63).

Paul K. Longmore's discussion of images of disabled people in film is helpful in thinking about Faulkner's treatment of Linda (the differences between filmic and literary bodies noted), especially the formula of what Longmore calls the narrative of "adjustment." He writes:

> The most prevalent image in film and especially television during the past several decades has been the maladjusted disabled person. These stories involve characters with physical or sensory, rather than mental, handicaps. The plots follow a consistent pattern: the disabled central characters are bitter and self-pitying because, however long they have been disabled, they have never adjusted to their handicaps, and have never accepted themselves as they are. Consequently, they treat nondisabled family and friends angrily and manipulatively. At first, the nondisabled characters, feeling sorry for them, coddle them, but eventually they realize that in order to help the disabled individuals adjust and cope they must "get tough." The stories

> climax in a confrontation scene in which a nondisabled character gives the disabled individual an emotional "slap in the face" and tells him or her to stop feeling sorry for themselves. Accepting the rebuke, the disabled character quits complaining and becomes a well-adjusted adult. (70)

As Longmore notes, these "portrayals suggest that disability is a problem of psychological self-acceptance, of emotional adjustment" (70). He also asserts that the "drama of adjustment seems to have developed in the aftermath of World War II, probably in response to the large numbers of disabled veterans returning from that conflict" (71). Longmore cites such examples as the 1947 film *The Best Years of Our Lives* and the 1950 film *The Men*.

Regarding the third part of the body of the text, I want first to thank Géraldine Blattner for checking and refining my translation of Spill. I would repeat that much has been written on Benjy Compson and his disability. I would urge the reader to see treatments of Benjy by Ineke Bockting, L. Moffitt Cecil, Carvel Collins, Arthur F. Kinney, Robert Dale Parker, Stephen M. Ross, and Seiji Sasamoto. Early on I present Maria Truchan-Tataryn's criticism of Faulkner and Faulkner scholarship for their depiction and treatment of Benjy. She is not alone in her stance. Mitchell and Snyder point out that "nearly all of the criticism of the novel 'promotes' Benjy to the status of a symbolic representative of human tragedy" despite the fact that "on closer reading the chapter provides an important sustained reading of the social circumstances surrounding the reception of cognitive disability" (*Narrative Prosthesis* 167). Noting that "[a]ll of the Compson family members are explicitly judged in relation to their ability to imagine Benjy's humanity" (167), Mitchell and Snyder conclude their brief treatment of the novel by asserting that "[a]lthough it has gone critically unrecognized that the novel provides a scathing critique of this dehumanizing environment within which disabled people function, the novel holds out Benjy's experience not as a sign of wider cultural collapse but as the barometer for just how far the social fabric has unraveled around him" (168).

Jay Watson's excavation of the historical circumstances of the novel's moment attest to Faulkner's awareness of this social fabric unraveling, as he writes that the landmark eugenics sterilization case of *Buck v. Bell* "was followed by a resurgence of eugenic sterilization legislation in the U.S., especially in the South. Mississippi's bill, which according to historian

Steven Noll followed the Virginia statute 'word for word' (*Feeble-Minded* 71), was approved by the state house of representatives on Tuesday, April 10, 1928 (Larson 117–18)—only two days, that is, after a severely retarded man who has undergone a crude and historically before-the-fact version of compulsory sterilization sits howling in a horse-drawn buggy on a Mississippi town square, in the closing section of Faulkner's fourth novel" (25).

Most recently, Alice Hall reads Benjy in this historical sense along with Ike and the war-wounded characters in *A Fable* and *Soldiers' Pay*. Beyond these things I would add that I believe the soundness, the interior narrative solidity, of Benjy's text finds confirmation in the existence of the hypertext version of *The Sound and the Fury*. John Collins, producer of an off-Broadway performance of the Benjy section in the spring of 2008 confirms this as well in his using that edition of the novel to unravel the text and discern its chronological flow. Toward the end of my discussion of Benjy, I note that the consensus has been that Benjy is unconsciously complex: a notable exception is Ted Roggenbuck, who argues that "[a]s a child Benjy demonstrates greater intellectual ability than most critics give him credit for" (581). Roggenbuck cites such scholars as Kinney and Brooks as seeing ways that Benjy does have will, but they locate that will in Benjy's unconscious—certainly they do not see him as a conscious and skillful forger of narrative. Ultimately, even Roggenbuck modifies his claim for Benjy's intellectual ability, writing that "by 1928 [Benjy] has so withdrawn both mentally and emotionally from the world and the people around him that he no longer possesses enough emotional investment in it to attempt to interpret much of what transpires" (581).

Eagleton's description of Empson's style as "lemon-squeezing" appears in *Literary Theory* (44).

I would add to the material on Ike Snopes an essay by William J. Mistichelli exploring the similarities in perspective and authorial/narratorial manipulation of it in the Benjy and Ike sections of *The Sound and the Fury* and *The Hamlet* respectively.

Concerning the fourth part, I realize my presenting Pap as the lynchpin of *Sanctuary* may leave me open to a reasonable charge of over-reaching out of zealousness to prove my point regarding disability's centrality to Faulkner's writing. I well know that Pap is a minor character; however,

I do believe that when the novel is turned so that its prismic facets illuminate with the beam of a disability perspective the importance of this character's wide-reaching structural and metaphorical functions becomes glaring. Just as a change in environment can transform a disabled person into a more- or most-abled person (again, a blind person in the dark can be more abled than those accustomed to orienting themselves by means of their vision) so changing the critical "environment" can show how a minor character can take on great significance just as I assert that many less-valued works emerge as integral to Faulkner' oeuvre.

There is a sizeable body of work on blindness—indeed, a blindness studies. Some of the sources I would reference are Georgina Kleege's *Sight Unseen*, which also utilizes an intriguing essayist style, and C. Edwin Vaughan's *Social and Cultural Perspectives on Blindness*. Blindness is of course an old literary disability—Oedipus was both lame and blind, both of which are used to great metaphorical effect. I have attempted to pay attention to both physical and metaphorical implications of blindness in *Sanctuary*. In addition to the sources already cited, I would include Gaman Wong's essay on voyeurism in the novel.

Additionally, I want to thank the anonymous reader for Louisiana State University Press for the provocative observation that the urban legends about Popeye's skill with the gun lend him a level of hyper-ableism. It was also this reader who observed the possibilities of thinking about *Sanctuary* as performing a prosthetic role in the detective-fiction genre.

I do not have much to add to the fifth part of the book. Regarding freak studies, I would direct the reader not just to Fiedler's book but also the work of Rachel Adams, Nancy Bombaci, and the essays in *Freakery: Cultural Spectacles of the Extraordinary Body*, edited by Garland-Thomson. Browning's *Freaks* is a film to see if the reader has not already, and there is a biography of Browning by David J. Skal and Elias Savada. Throughout the book, I have touched on issues of disability in connection with nonhumans, this section most particularly, and in addition to work on freaks and aliens, I would also cite Cary Wolfe's work on nonhuman animals, agency, and the politics of representation.

I have already thanked certain people in specific contexts in this note; I will now add fuller acknowledgments. This book began when I attended a plenary lecture at the 2005 South Atlantic Modern Language Association Convention delivered by Rosemarie Garland-Thomson. Her provocative discussion of human variation and the political, economic, structural, and cultural forces that intersect with and dictate its functions affected me powerfully. Although I have never met her, I want to thank her for her influential work.

The bulk of this book was drafted during the time I was on a Fulbright in Munich, and I want to thank the Fulbright Commission for granting me this wonderful opportunity and the Amerika Institut at Ludwig-Maximilians-Universität München for hosting me and for being so very, very kind and good, making me feel a part of that excellent program.

I am always grateful to the Faulkner scholarly community for its support and encouragement. Rather than risk leaving out names, let me thank as a group from the fledgling to the most advanced these wonderful scholars and people who have been so important to me in my career. Concerning this project specifically, Deborah Clarke and Barbara Ladd have been especially encouraging. Also, because I dedicate this book to them I want to say that I speak for so many when I acknowledge the late Noel Polk as someone who constantly supported young colleagues, and Joseph R. Urgo has played a crucial role in my career and has been a great friend to me.

My gratitude is deep also to the students in the many settings in which I have been able to discuss disability. These include graduate seminars dedicated specifically to disability studies and a multitude of moments in undergraduate courses in which I could raise the many questions the field poses. I have especially benefited from the questions raised by Simone Puleo and Julia König.

As always, certain people have been so very helpful in so many ways that have nothing to do with Faulkner and disability and everything to do with support, friendship, and a thousand other things. These include colleagues at Florida Atlantic University who have been so good to me. I particularly want to thank Andrew Furman, whom I have been privileged to know and work with as colleague, friend, and department chair; Wenying Xu, for professional support and friendship; Ayse Papatya Bucak, for insightful comments and support; and Mary Faraci as always. My colleagues and friends at Ludwig-Maximilians-Universität I also thank, especially Klaus

Benesch for all of his support then and since; Thea Diesner for wise guidance; Anna Flügge for being a great friend and asker of questions; Sascha Pöhlman for tremendous help and patient thought; and Kerstin Schmidt for her wonderful energy and confidence. Because it would take far too much space to list all the ways they have been important to me and this project, I want to list a group of friends whose support has been invaluable, the less said being designed to signify their great importance, too voluminous to detail: these include Eric Gary Anderson, Chris Bundrick, Ashley Craig Lancaster, Randy Jasmine, Scott Henkle, Warren Kelley, John Lowe, Travis Montgomery, Suzanne Penuel, Sika Dagbovie Mullins, David Ramm, Daniel Cross Turner, and Nicole Zehr. Thank you as always to Laura Cade. And to David Noble. And Marsha Dutton. I remain grateful to the recently departed Howard Wisch.

To my family, thank you again and again and again and again.

My second time working with Louisiana State University Press has been just as wonderful as the first. Margaret Lovecraft patiently stayed with me through the revisions of this book. I was incredibly fortunate in the anonymous peer reviewer—thank you whoever you are. Thank you to Scott Romine for including this book in the Southern Literary Studies series. Stan Ivester's skillful copyediting and intuitive understanding of this book's nature were wonderful. And thank you to everyone at the press who has been involved in the production and marketing of this volume.

Parts of this text have appeared in print before. The material on Benjy Compson in part three originally appeared as "The Secret Machinery of Textuality, Or, What Is Benjy Compson Really Thinking?" in *Faulkner and Formalism: Returns of the Text,* edited by Annette Trefzer and Ann J. Abadie, published by the University Press of Mississippi, 2012. I have developed my thoughts on Lennard J. Davis's concept of "dismodernism" and Mitchell and Snyder's ideas about narrative prosthesis through two previous essays: "Disability Studies and American Literature," *Literature Compass* 7.6 (2010): 387–96 (which also includes material on other aspects of disability theory) and "Disability, Reactionary Appropriation, and Strategies of Manipulation in Simms's *Woodcraft,*" from *The Southern Literary Journal* 45, copyright 2013 by the Department of English and Comparative Literature of the University of North Carolina at Chapel Hill; published by the University of North Carolina Press; used by permission of the publisher; www.unc press.unc.edu). Thank you to these respective presses and journals for permission to reprint. Thank you also to the many conference organizers for the opportunities to present parts of this book in settings that provided tremendous feedback.

I want to close by pointing out that this book is obviously not meant to be exhaustive. Disability studies itself is still largely in its youth, and I feel sure that as the field advances other scholars will visit disability in Faulkner's life and writing in ways I have not dreamt of in my philosophy. I have not attempted to provide the great compendium of disability in Faulkner but rather to promote a discussion that I hope others will continue with more advanced information and greater ability.

BIBLIOGRAPHY

Adams, Rachel. "An American Tail: Freaks, Gender, and the Incorporation of History in Katherine Dunn's *Geek Love*." *Freakery: Cultural Spectacles of the Extraordinary Body*. Ed. Rosemarie Garland-Thomson. New York: New York University Press, 1996. 277–90.

———, ed. *Sideshow U.S.A.: Freaks and the American Cultural Imagination*. Chicago: U of Chicago P, 2001.

Albrecht, Gary. *The Disability Business*. Newbury Park: Sage, 1994.

Albrecht, Gary L., Katherine D. Seelman, and Michael Bury, eds. *Handbook of Disability Studies*. Thousand Oaks, CA: Sage, 2001.

Alexander, Jeffrey C. "Towards a Theory of Cultural Trauma." *Cultural Trauma and Collective Identity*. Ed. Jeffrey C. Alexander, Ron Eyerman, Bernhard Giesen, Neil J. Smelser, Piotr Sztompka. Berkeley: U of California P, 2004. 1–30.

Anderson, Sherwood. "A Meeting South." *The Portable Sherwood Anderson*. Ed. Horace Gregory. New York: Viking P, 1949. 518–32.

Baker, Houston, A., Jr. *I Don't Hate the South: Reflections on Faulkner, Family, and the South*. Oxford, UK: Oxford UP, 2007.

Barasch, Moshe. *Blindness: The History of a Mental Image in Western Thought*. New York: Routledge, 2001.

Berube, Michael. "Disability and Narrative." *PMLA* 120 (2005): 568–76.

———. *Life As We Know It: A Father, a Family, and an Exceptional Child*. New York: Pantheon, 1996.

Biklen, Douglas. "Framed: Print Journalism's Treatment of Disability Issues." Gartner and Joe 79–95.

Blotner, Joseph. *Faulkner: A Biography*. New York: Random House, 1984.

Bockting, Ineke. "Mind Style as an Interdisciplinary Approach to Characterisation in Faulkner." *Language and Literature* 3 (1994): 157–74.

Bombaci, Nancy. *Freaks in Late Modernist American Culture: Nathanael West, Djuna Barnes, Tod Browning, and Carson McCullers.* New York: Peter Lang, 2006.

Braziel, Jana Evans, and Kathleen LeBesco, eds. *Bodies Out of Bounds: Fatness and Transgression.* Berkeley: U of California P, 2001.

Brooks, Cleanth. *William Faulkner: The Yoknapatawpha Country.* Baton Rouge: Louisiana State UP, 1990.

Brown, Wendy. *States of Injury: Power and Freedom in Late Modernity.* Princeton: Princeton UP, 1995.

Byerman, Keith. "Black Voices, White Stories: An Intertextual Analysis of Thomas Nelson Page and Charles Waddell Chestnutt." *North Carolina Literary Review* 8 (1999): 98–105.

Caldwell, Erskine. *God's Little Acre.* New York: Modern Library, 1934.

Campos, Paul. *The Obesity Myth: Why America's Obsession with Weight Is Hazardous to Your Health.* New York: Gotham Books, 2004.

Carothers, James. *William Faulkner's Short Stories.* Ann Arbor: UMI Research P, 1985.

Caruth, Cathy. *Unclaimed Experience: Trauma, Narrative, and History.* Baltimore: Johns Hopkins UP, 1996.

Cecil, L. Moffitt. "A Rhetoric for Benjy." *Southern Literary Journal* 3 (1970): 32–46.

Clare, Eli. *Exile and Pride: Disability, Queerness, and Liberation.* Cambridge, MA: South End P, 1999.

Collins, Carvel. "The Interior Monologues of *The Sound and the Fury.*" *English Institute Essays, 1952.* Ed. Alan S. Downer. New York: Columbia UP, 1954. 29–56.

Corker, Mairian, and Tom Shakespeare, eds. *Disability/Postmodernity: Embodying Disability Theory.* London: Continuum, 2002.

Cowley, Malcolm. *The Faulkner-Cowley File: Letters and Memories, 1944–1962.* New York: Viking, 1966.

Crabtree, Claire. "Plots of Punishment and Faulkner's Injured Women: Charlotte Rittenmeyer and Linda Snopes." *Michigan Academician* 24 (1992): 527–39.

Davis, Lennard J. *Bending Over Backwards: Disability, Dismodernism, and Other Difficult Positions.* New York: New York UP, 2002.

———. "Bending Over Backwards: Narcissism, the ADA, and the Courts." *Bending Over Backwards* 119–44.

———. "Crips Strike Back: The Rise of Disability Studies." *Bending Over Backwards* 33–46.

———. "Dr. Johnson, Amelia, and the Discourse of Disability." *Bending Over Backwards* 47–66.

———. "The End of Identity Politics and the Beginning of Postmodernism: On Disability as an Unstable Category." *Bending Over Backwards* 9–32.

———. *Enforcing Normalcy: Disability, Deafness, and the Body.* New York: Verso, 1995.

———. “The Rules of Normalcy: Politics and Disability in the U.S.A. [United States of Ability].” *Bending Over Backwards* 102–18.

———. “Who Put the *the* in the Novel? Identity Politics and Disability in Novel Studies.” *Bending Over Backwards* 79–101.

———, ed. *The Disability Studies Reader.* 2nd ed. New York: Routledge, 2006.

Derrida, Jacques. *The Animal That Therefore I Am.* Trans. David Wills. New York: Fordham UP, 2008.

Dickey, James. *Deliverance.* Boston: Houghton Mifflin, 1970.

Duck, Leigh Anne. *The Nation's Region: Southern Modernism, Segregation, and U.S. Nationalism.* Athens: U of Georgia P, 2006.

Duclos, Donald Philip. *Son of Sorrow: The Life, Works, and Influence of Colonel William C. Falkner, 1825–1889.* San Francisco: International Scholars Publications, 1998.

Dunn, Katherine. *Geek Love.* New York: Warner Books, 1989.

Eagleton, Terry. *Literary Theory: An Introduction.* 2nd ed. Minneapolis: U of Minnesota P, 1996.

Eliot, T. S. *The Complete Poems and Plays, 1909–1950.* New York: Harcourt, Brace, and World, 1971.

Ennis, Garth, and Steve Dillon. *Preacher.* 9 vols. New York: Vertigo, 1995–2000.

Eyerman, Ron. *Cultural Trauma: Slavery and the Formation of African American Identity.* New York: Cambridge UP, 2001.

Fant, Gene C., Jr. “The Blind Man, the Idiot, and the Prig: Faulkner's Distain for the Reader.” *Literature and the Writer.* Ed. Michael J. Meyer. Amsterdam: Rodopi, 2004. 155–74.

———. “Faulkner's *The Sound and the Fury.*” *Explicator* 52.2 (1994): 104–6.

Faulkner, John. *My Brother Bill: An Affectionate Reminiscence.* New York: Pocket Books, 1964.

Faulkner, William. *Absalom, Absalom!* 1936. *The Corrected Text.* New York: Vintage International, 1990.

———. “Afternoon of a Cow.” *Uncollected Stories of William Faulkner.* New York: Vintage, 1997. 424–34.

———. *As I Lay Dying.* 1930. *The Corrected Text.* New York: Vintage International, 1990.

———. *Collected Stories.* New York: Vintage, 1977.

———. *A Fable.* 1954. *William Faulkner: Novels 1942–1954.* New York: Library of America, 1994. 665–1072.

———. *Faulkner at West Point.* Ed. Joseph L. Fant and Robert Ashley. Jackson: UP of Mississippi, 2002.

———. *Flags in the Dust. William Faulkner: Novels 1926–1929.* New York: Library of America, 2006. 541–875.

———. *Go Down, Moses and Other Stories. William Faulkner: Novels 1942–1954.* New York: Library of America, 1994. 1–281.

———. *The Hamlet.* 1940. *William Faulkner: Novels 1936–1940.* New York: Library of America, 1990. 727–1075.

———. *The Mansion.* 1959. *William Faulkner: Novels 1957–1962.* New York: Library of America, 1999. 327–721.

———. *The Marble Faun* and *A Green Bough.* New York: Random, 1965.

———. *Mosquitoes.* 1927. *William Faulkner: Novels 1926–1929.* New York: Library of America, 2006. 257–540.

———. *New Orleans Sketches.* 1958. Jackson: UP of Mississippi, 2002.

———. *The Portable Faulkner.* Ed. Malcolm Cowley. New York: Penguin, 1977.

———. *Pylon.* 1935. *William Faulkner: Novels 1930–1935.* New York: Library of America, 1985. 775–992.

———. *The Reivers.* 1962. *William Faulkner: Novels 1957–1962.* New York: Library of America, 1999. 723–971.

———. *Sanctuary: The Original Text.* Ed. Noel Polk. New York: Random House, 1981.

———. *Sanctuary.* 1931. *The Corrected Text. William Faulkner: Novels 1930–1935.* New York: Library of America, 1985. 179–398.

———. *Selected Letters of William Faulkner.* Ed. Joseph Blotner. New York: Random, 1977.

———. *Soldiers' Pay. William Faulkner: Novels 1926–1929.* New York: Library of America, 2006. 1–256.

———. *The Sound and the Fury.* 1929. *The Corrected Text. William Faulkner: Novels 1926–1929.* New York: Library of America, 2006. 877–1141.

———. The Sound and the Fury: *A Hypertext Edition.* Ed. R. P. Stoicheff, Joel Deshaye, et al. Updated July 2004. U of Saskatchewan. Accessed 8 Sept. 2008. www.usask.ca/english/faulkner.

———. *The Town.* 1957. *William Faulkner: Novels 1957–1962.* New York: Library of America, 1999. 1–326.

———. *Uncollected Stories of William Faulkner.* Ed. Joseph Blotner. New York: Vintage, 1997.

Fiedler, Leslie. *Freaks: Myths and Images of the Secret Self.* New York: Touchstone, 1978.

Forth, Christopher E., and Ana Carden-Coyne, eds. *Cultures of the Abdomen: Diet, Digestion, and Fat in the Modern World.* New York: Palgrave Macmillan, 2005.

Foucault, Michel. *Discipline and Punish: The Birth of the Prison.* Trans. Alan Sheridan. New York: Vintage, 1995.

Fraser, Laura. *Losing It: America's Obsession with Weight and the Industry That Feeds on It.* New York: Dutton, 1997.

Fulton, Keith Louise. "Linda Snopes Kohl: Faulkner's Radical Woman." *Modern Fiction Studies* 34 (1988): 425–36.

Funk, Robert. "Disability Rights: From Caste to Class in the Context of Civil Rights." Gartner and Alan 7–30.

Garland-Thomson, Rosemarie. *Extraordinary Bodies: Figuring Physical Disability in American Culture and Literature.* New York: Columbia UP, 1997.

———. *Staring: How We Look.* Oxford, UK: Oxford UP, 2009.

———, ed. *Freakery: Cultural Spectacles of the Extraordinary Body.* New York: New York University Press, 1996.

Garnier, Caroline. "Temple Drake's Rape and the Myth of the Willing Victim." *Faulkner's Sexualities: Faulkner and Yoknapatawpha, 2007.* Eds. Annette Trefzer and Ann J. Abadie. Jackson: UP of Mississippi, 2010. 164–83.

Gartner, Alan, and Tom Joe, eds. *Images of the Disabled, Disabling Images.* New York: Praeger, 1987.

Giesen, Bernhard. "The Trauma of Perpetrators: The Holocaust as the Traumatic Reference of German National Identity." *Cultural Trauma and Collective Identity.* Ed. Jeffrey C. Alexander, Ron Eyerman, Bernhard Giesen, Neil J. Smelser, Piotr Sztompka. Berkeley: U of California P, 2004. 112–54.

Gilman, Sander. *Fat: A Cultural History of Obesity.* Cambridge, UK: Polity, 2008.

———. *Fat Boys: A Slim Book.* Lincoln: U of Nebraska P, 2004.

Goffman, Erving. *Stigma: Notes on the Management of Spoiled Identity.* Englewood Cliffs, NJ: Prentice-Hall, 1963.

Gold, Joseph. "The 'Normality' of Snopesism: Universal Themes in Faulkner's *The Hamlet.*" *Wisconsin Studies in Contemporary Literature* 3.1 (1962): 25–34.

Hagood, Taylor. *Faulkner's Imperialism: Space, Place, and the Materiality of Myth.* Baton Rouge: Louisiana State UP, 2008.

———. "Prodjickin', or mekin' a present to yo' fam'ly: Rereading Empowerment in Thomas Nelson Page's Frame Narratives." *Mississippi Quarterly: The Journal of Southern Cultures* 57 (2004): 423–40.

Hale, Dorothy J. "'*As I Lay Dying*'s' Heterogeneous Discourse." NOVEL: *A Forum on Fiction* 23.1 (1989): 5–23.

Hall, Alice. *Disability and Modern Fiction: Faulkner, Morrison, Coetzee, and the Nobel Prize for Literature.* New York: Palgrave Macmillan, 2012.

Hamblin, Robert W. "The Leg." *A William Faulkner Encyclopedia.* Eds. Robert W. Hamblin and Charles A. Peek. Westport: Greenwood P, 1999. 225.

Hearne, Vicki. *Adam's Task: Calling Animals by Name.* New York: Random House, 1987.

Hicks, Granville. "The Past and Future of William Faulkner." *Bookman* 74 (1931): 17–24.

Hinrichsen, Lisa. "A History That Has No Place: Trauma and Temple Drake in *Sanctuary.*" *Miscegenation, Race, and the Real in Faulkner's Fiction.* Eds. Michael Zeitlin, André Bleikasten, and Nicole Moulinoux. Rennes: PU de Rennes, 2004. 127–40.

Hosey, Sara E. *Curious Persons: Disability and Representation in American Literature and Culture.* Diss. U of Wisconsin–Madison, 2007.

———. "One of Us: Identity and Community in Contemporary Fiction." *Journal of Literary and Cultural Disability Studies* 3.1 (2009): 35–50.

Hühn, Peter. "The Politics of Secrecy and Publicity: The Functions of Hidden Stories in Some Recent British Mystery Fiction." *Theory and Practice of Classic Detective Fiction.* Ed. Jerome H. Delamater and Ruth Prigozy. Westport, CT: Greenwood P, 1997. 39–50.

Irigiraray, Luce. *This Sex Which Is Not One.* Trans. Catherine Porter and Carolyn Burke. Ithaca, NY: Cornell UP, 1985.

Irwin, John T. *Doubling and Incest/Repetition and Revenge: A Speculative Reading of Faulkner.* Expanded edition. Baltimore: Johns Hopkins UP, 1996.

Jarman, Michelle. *Eugenic Anatomies: Disability Disruption in Modernist American Literature.* Diss. U of Illinois at Chicago, 2006.

Jones, Suzanne W., and Sharon Monteith, eds. *South to a New Place: Region, Literature, Culture.* Baton Rouge: Louisiana State UP, 2002.

Joyce, James. *Portrait of the Artist as a Young Man.* New York: Viking, 1982.

Karem, Jeff. *The Romance of Authenticity: The Cultural Politics of Regional and Ethnic Literatures.* Charlottesville: U of Virginia P, 2004.

Kartiganer, Donald. *The Fragile Thread: The Meaning of Form in Faulkner's Novels.* Amherst: U of Massachusetts P, 1979.

Keely, Karen A. "Marriage Plots and National Reunion: The Trope of Romantic Reconciliation in Postbellum Literature." *Mississippi Quarterly: The Journal of Southern Culture* 51 (1998): 621–48.

Kent, Deborah. "Disabled Women: Portraits in Fiction and Drama." Gartner and Joe 47–63.

Kinney, Arthur F. *Faulkner's Narrative Poetics: Style as Vision.* Amherst: U of Massachusetts P, 1978.

Kleege, Georgina. *Sight Unseen.* New Haven, CT: Yale UP, 1999.

Kreyling, Michael. *Inventing Southern Literature.* Jackson: UP of Mississippi, 1998.

Kriegel, Leonard. "The Cripple in Literature." Gartner and Joe 31–46.

Lancaster, Ashley Craig. "Weeding Out the Recessive Gene: Representations of the Evolving Eugenics Movement in Erskine Caldwell's *God's Little Acre.*" *Southern Literary Journal* 39.2 (2007): 78–99.

Larson, Edward J. *Sex, Race, and Science: Eugenics in the Deep South.* Baltimore: Johns Hopkins UP, 1995.

Linton, Simi. *Claiming Disability: Knowledge and Identity.* New York: New York UP, 1998.

London, Jack. *White Fang.* 1906. New York: Viking, 1999.

Longmore, Paul K. "Screening Stereotypes: Images of Disabled People in Television and Motion Pictures." Gartner and Joe 65–78.

Lukács, Georg. *History and Class Consciousness: Studies in Marxist Dialectics.* Trans. Rodney Livingstone. Cambridge, MA: MIT P, 1971.

Lurie, Peter. *Vision's Immanence: Faulkner, Film, and the Popular Imagination.* Baltimore: Johns Hopkins UP, 2004.

McRuer, Robert. *Crip Theory: Cultural Signs of Queerness and Disability.* New York: New York UP, 2006.

Mistichelli, William J. "Perception Is a Sacred Cow: The Narrator and Ike Snopes in William Faulkner's *The Hamlet.*" *Faulkner Journal* 5.2 (1990): 15–33.

Mitchell, David T., and Sharon L. Snyder. *Cultural Locations of Disability.* Chicago: U of Chicago P, 2006.

———. *Narrative Prosthesis: Disability and the Dependencies of Discourse.* Ann Arbor: U of Michigan P, 2000.

———, eds. *The Body and Physical Difference: Discourses of Disability.* Ann Arbor: U of Michigan P, 1997.

Moak, Franklin E. "On the Roots of the Sartoris Family." *Critical Essays on William Faulkner: The Sartoris Family.* Ed. Arthur F. Kinney. Boston: G. K. Hall, 1985. 264–66.

Noll, Steven. *Feeble-Minded in Our Midst: Institutions for the Mentally Retarded in the South, 1900–1940.* Chapel Hill: U of North Carolina P, 1995.

O'Donnell, Patrick. "Between the Family and the State: Nomadism and Authority in *As I Lay Dying.*" *Faulkner Journal* 7.1–2 (1991–1992): 83–94.

Oliver, Michael. *The Politics of Disablement: A Sociological Approach.* New York: St. Martin's P, 1990.

Paddock, Lisa. *Contrapuntal in Integration: A Study of Three Faulkner Short Volumes.* Lanham, MD: International Scholars Publications, 2000.

Page, Thomas Nelson. *In Ole Virginia, Or, Marse Chan and Other Stories.* Nashville: J. S. Sanders, 1991.

Parker, Robert Dale. "'Through the Fence, between the Curling Flower Spaces': Teaching the First Section of *The Sound and the Fury.*" *Approaches to Teaching Faulkner's* The Sound and the Fury. Ed. Stephen Hahn and Arthur F. Kinney. New York: MLA of America, 1996. 27–37.

Polk, Noel. *Children of the Dark House: Text and Context in Faulkner.* Jackson: UP of Mississippi, 1996.

———. *Faulkner and Welty and the Southern Literary Tradition.* Jackson: UP of Mississippi, 2008.

———. "Testing Masculinity in the Snopes Trilogy." *Faulkner and Welty and the Southern Literary Tradition.* Jackson: UP of Mississippi, 2008. 44–67.

———, and Richard Godden. "Reading the Ledgers." *Mississippi Quarterly: The Journal of Southern Cultures* 55 (2002): 301–59.

Puleo, Simone Maria. "'Fat as You Is': Jason Compson's Bullied Body in *The Sound and the Fury.*" *Critical Insights:* The Sound and the Fury. Ed. Taylor Hagood. Ipswich, MA: Salem P, 2014. 212–26.

Quayson, Ato. *Aesthetic Nervousness: Disability and the Crisis of Representation.* New York: Columbia UP, 2007.

Rafter, Nicole Hahn. *Creating Born Criminals.* Urbana: U of Illinois P, 1997.

———, ed. *White Trash: The Eugenic Family Studies, 1877–1919.* Boston: Northeastern UP, 1988.

Roberts, Diane. "Eula, Linda, and the Death of Nature." *Faulkner and the Natural World: Faulkner and Yoknapatawpha, 1996.* Ed. Donald M. Kartiganer and Ann J. Abadie. Jackson: UP of Mississippi, 1999. 159–78.

Rogers, Cheryl. "The Employment Dilemma for Disabled Persons." Gartner and Joe 117–27.

Roggenbuck, Ted. "'The way he looked said Hush': Benjy's Mental Atrophy in *The Sound and the Fury.*" *Mississippi Quarterly: The Journal of Southern Cultures* 58 (2005): 581–93.

Romine, Scott. *The Real South: Southern Narrative in the Age of Cultural Reproduction.* Baton Rouge: Louisiana State UP, 2008.

Ross, Stephen M. *Fiction's Inexhuastible Voice: Speech and Writing in Faulkner.* Athens: U of Georgia P, 1989.

Rothblum, Esther, and Sondra Solovay, eds. *The Fat Studies Reader.* New York: New York UP, 2009.

Samuels, Ellen. "'Complications of Complaints': Untangling Disability, Race, and Gender in William and Ellen Craft's *Running a Thousand Miles for Freedom.*" *MELUS: The Journal for the Society for the Study of the Multi-Ethnic Culture of the United States* 31.3 (2006): 15–47.

———. "Critical Divides: Judith Butler's Body Theory and the Question of Disability." *NWSA Journal: National Women's Studies Association Journal* 14.2 (2002): 58–76.

———. *Fingerprinting the Nation: Identifying Race and Disability in America.* Diss. U of California, Berkeley, 2006.

———. "From Melville to Eddie Murphy: The Disability Con in American Literature and Film." *Leviathan: A Journal of Melville Studies* 8.1 (2006): 61–82.

———. "My Body, My Closet: Invisible Disability and the Limits of Coming-Out Discourse." *GLQ: A Journal of Lesbian and Gay Studies* 9.1–2 (2003): 233–55.

Sasamoto, Seiji. "The First Section of *The Sound and the Fury*: Benjy and His Expressions." *William Faulkner: Materials, Studies, and Criticism* 4.2 (1982): 19–36.

Schivelbusch, Wolfgang. *The Culture of Defeat: On National Trauma, Mourning, and Recovery*. Trans. Jefferson Chase. New York: Metropolitan Books, 2003.

Schwartz, Hillel. *Never Satisfied: A Cultural History of Diets*. New York: Free P, 1986.

Schwartz, Lawrence. *Creating Faulkner's Reputation: The Politics of Modern Literary Criticism*. Knoxville: U of Tennessee P, 1988.

Seed, David. "The Evidence of Things Seen and Unseen: William Faulkner's *Sanctuary*." *American Horror Fiction: From Brockden Brown to Stephen King*. Ed. Brian Docherty. New York: St. Martin's P, 1990. 73–91.

Sensibar, Judith L. *Faulkner and Love: The Women Who Shaped His Art*. New Haven, CT: Yale UP, 2009.

Shakespeare, Tom. *Disability Rights and Wrongs*. Oxon, UK: Routledge, 2006.

Shaw, Andrea Elizabeth. *The Embodiment of Disobedience: Fat Black Women's Unruly Political Bodies*. Lanham: Lexington Books, 2006.

Shearer, Ann. *Disability: Whose Handicap?* Oxford, UK: Basil Blackwell, 1981.

Shusterman, Richard. *Body Consciousness: A Philosophy of Mindfulness and Somaesthetics*. Cambridge, UK: Cambridge UP, 2008.

———. *Surface and Depth: Dialectics of Criticism and Culture*. Ithaca, NY: Cornell UP, 2002.

Siebers, Tobin. *Disability Theory*. Ann Arbor: U of Michigan P, 2008.

Simon, John K. "What Are You Laughing at, Darl?: Madness and Humor in *As I Lay Dying*." *College English* 25.2 (1963): 104–10.

Skal, David J., and Elias Savada. *Dark Carnival: The Secret World of Tod Browning*. New York: Anchor Books, 1995.

Smith, Jon, Deborah Cohn, and Donald Pease, eds. *Look Away! The U.S. South in New World Studies*. Duke UP, 2004.

Snyder, Sharon L., Brenda Jo Brueggemann, and Rosemarie Garland-Thomson, eds. *Disability Studies: Enabling the Humanities*. New York: MLA of America, 2002.

Spill, Frédérique. *L'idiote dans l'oeuvre de Faulkner*. Paris: Presses Sorbonne Nouvelle, 2009.

Spivak, Gayatri Chakravorty. "Can the Subaltern Speak?" *Colonial Discourse and Post-Colonial Theory: A Reader*. Ed. Patrick Williams and Laura Chrisman. New York: Columbia UP, 1994. 66–111.

Stearns, Peter N. *Fat History: Bodies and Beauty in the Modern West.* New York: New York UP, 2002.

Stiker, Henri-Jacques. *A History of Disability.* (1982) Trans. William Sayers. Ann Arbor: U of Michigan P, 1999.

Truchan-Tataryn, Maria. "Textual Abuse: Faulkner's Benjy." *Journal of Medical Humanities* 26.2–3 (2005): 159–72.

Tuan, Yi-Fu. *Space and Place: The Perspective of Experience.* Minneapolis: U of Minnesota P, 1977.

Vaughan, C. Edwin. *Social and Cultural Perspectives on Blindness.* Springfield, IL: Charles C. Thomas, 1998.

Wann, Marilyn. "Foreword: Fat Studies: An Invitation to Revolution." Rothblum and Solovay xi–xxv.

Watson, James Gray. *William Faulkner: Self-Presentation and Performance.* Austin: U of Texas P, 2000.

Watson, Jay. "Genealogies of Deviance: The Eugenic Family Studies, *Buck v. Bell,* and William Faulkner, 1926–1931." *Faulkner and Whiteness.* Ed. Jay Watson. Jackson: UP of Mississippi, 2011. 19–55.

Weinstein, Philip. *Becoming Faulkner: The Art and Life of William Faulkner.* New York: Oxford UP, 2010.

Weinstock, Jeffrey A. "Freaks in Space: 'Extraterrestrialism' and 'Deep Space Multiculturalism.'" *Freakery: Cultural Spectacles of the Extraordinary Body.* Ed. Rosemarie Garland-Thomson. New York: New York UP, 1996. 327–37.

Wilde, Meta Carpenter, and Orin Borsten. *A Loving Gentleman: The Love Story of William Faulkner and Meta Carpenter.* New York: Simon and Shuster, 1976.

Wills, David. *Prosthesis.* Palo Alto, CA: Stanford UP, 1995.

Wolfe, Cary. *Animal Rites: American Culture, the Discourse of Species, and Posthumanist Thought.* Chicago: U of Chicago P, 2003.

Wolff, Sally. *Ledgers of History: William Faulkner, an Almost Forgotten Friendship, and an Antebellum Plantation Diary.* Baton Rouge: Louisiana State UP, 2010.

Wong, Gayman. "The Prying Eye: Voyeurism in William Faulkner's *Sanctuary.*" *Eros USA: Essays on the Culture and Literature of Desire.* Ed. Cheryl Alexander Malcolm and Jopi Nyman. Gdańsk, Poland: Wydawnictwo Uniwersytety Gdańskiego, 2005. 86–99.

Woodward, C. Vann. *The Burden of Southern History*. Baton Rouge: Louisiana State UP, 1960.

Wulfman, Clifford E. "Sighting/Siting/Citing the Scar: Trauma and Homecoming in *Soldiers' Pay.*" *Studies in American Fiction* 31.1 (2003): 29–43.

INDEX